THE
DEATH
OF
TRAGEDY

THE
DEATH
OF
TRAGEDY

GEORGE STEINER

OXFORD UNIVERSITY PRESS
New York

Library of Congress Cataloging in Publication Data
Steiner, George, 1929—
The death of tragedy.

Reprint, with new foreword, of the ed. published by Knopf, New York.
Includes index.
1. Tragedy. 2. Tragedy—History and criticism.
3. Drama—History and criticism. I. Title.
PN1892.S7 1980 809.2′51 79-21658 ISBN 0-19-502702-7 pbk.

FOR

MY FATHER

Acknowledgments

IN A SHORTER, more schematic version, this book
was first presented at a Gauss Seminar at Princeton
University. Those who have attended these occasions will know how much the speaker owes to the
chairmanship and cross-fire of R. P. Blackmur and
to the erudite vigilance of Professors E. B. E. Bor-
gerhoff and Edward Cone. I wish to add a special
thanks to Roger Sessions, who gave to the seminar
the warmth and authority of his presence.

The expansion of the book into its present form
was made possible by a grant from the Ford Foun-
dation administered through the Council of the
Humanities of Princeton University to foster work
in comparative literature. This grant enabled me to
get on with the job while teaching only part-time.

ACKNOWLEDGMENTS

My warmest thanks go to Professor Whitney Oates and Professor R. Schlatter. I am the more grateful as this book does not represent precisely what its learned sponsors had in mind. But writers tend to be mutineers, even against generosity.

I owe particular thanks to my editor, Mr. Robert Pick, of Alfred A. Knopf, Inc. The counsel he gave and the pleasure he took in the work were both of great value to me.

Principally, however, this essay belongs to my father. The plays I discuss in it are those which he first read to me and took me to see. If I am able to deal with literature in more than one language, it is because my father, from the outset, refused to recognize provincialism in the affairs of the mind. Above all, he taught me by the example of his own life that great art is not reserved to the specialist or the professional scholar, but that it is best known and loved by those who live most intensely.

G. S.

Foreword to the Galaxy Book Edition

IT IS AN AMBIGUOUS PRIVILEGE to be allowed to write a new foreword to a book which is now twenty years old. One is not the same writer as was the author at the time. And one is not the same reader. This is true in two respects. I do not read, I do not try to interpret today the texts cited in *The Death of Tragedy* as I read and interpreted them before 1960. But, this displacement being the more disconcerting, I do not even read myself as I then did. Inevitably, this book has taken on an identity of its own. It stands somewhat outside what I now (inexactly) remember to have been its aim and conduct of persuasion. It has induced a certain secondary literature. Other readers have approved of the argument or rejected it, proposed addenda and corrections, used one or another of its sections for their own purposes. Today, these external readings are bound, in some measure, to interleave with my own.

If I was to rewrite *The Death of Tragedy* (and my favourite critic was the one who lamented the waste of so fine a title on this particular work), I would attempt a change of emphasis at two significant points. Furthermore, I would try to develop a theme which, as I now see it, was implicit in the argument from the outset, but which I did not have the nerve or acuity to make explicit.

The book begins by stressing the utter uniqueness of "high tragedy" as it was performed in fifth-century Athens. Despite suggestive attempts by comparative anthropology to relate Greek tragedy to more archaic and widespread forms of ritual and mimetic practise, the fact remains that the plays of Aeschylus, of Sophocles and of Euripides are unique not only in stature but also in form and technique. No fertility or seasonal rites however expressive, no dance–dramas of south-east Asia however intricate, are at all comparable in inexhaustibility of meaning, economy of means and personal authority of invention with Greek classical tragedy. It has been argued, plausibly, that Greek tragedy, as it has come down to us, was devised by Aeschylus, that it represents one of those very rare instances of the creation of a major aesthetic mode by an individual of genius. But even if this is not the case in any strict sense, and even if Aeschylaean drama stems from a multiple background of epic idiom, public mythology, lyric lament and the ethical-political postulate of compelling civic and personal issues as we find it in Solon, such drama nevertheless constitutes a unique phenomenon. No other Greek *polis*, no other antique culture, produced anything that resembles fifth-century Attic tragic drama. Indeed, the latter embodies so specific a congruence of philosophic and poetic energies, that it flourished during only a very brief period, some seventy-five years or less.

The book is unequivocal on this point. What I ought to have made plainer is the fact that within the corpus of extant Greek tragic plays those which manifest "tragedy" in an absolute form, which give to the word "tragedy" the rigour and weight I aim at throughout the argument, are very few. What I identify as "tragedy" in the radical sense is the dramatic representation or, more precisely, the dramatic testing of a view of reality in which man is taken to be an unwelcome guest in the world. The sources of his estrangement—German *Unheimlichkeit* conveys the actual meaning of "one who is thrust out of doors"—can be various. They can be the literal or metaphorical consequences of a "fall of man" or primal chastisement. They can be located in some fatality of over-reaching or self-mutilation inseparable from man's nature. In the most drastic cases, the human estrangement from or fatal intrusion upon a world hostile to man can be seen as resulting from a malignancy and daemonic negation in the very fabric of things (the enmity of the gods). But absolute tragedy exists only where substantive truth is assigned to the Sophoclean statement that "it is best never to have been born" or where the summation of insight into human fortunes is articulated in Lear's fivefold "never."

The plays which communicate this metaphysic of desperation would include *The Seven Against Thebes*, *King Oedipus*, *Antigone*, the *Hippolytus* and, supremely, the *Bacchae*. They would not include such dramas of positive resolution or heroic compensation as the *Oresteia* and the *Oedipus at Colonus* (though the epilogue makes of the latter an ambivalent case). Absolute tragedy, the image of man as unwanted in life, as one whom the "gods kill for their sport as wanton boys do flies," is almost unendurable to human reason and sensibility. Hence the very few cases in which it has been rigourously professed. My study should have made this classification sharper and should have been more thorough in differentiating between the theological implications of absolute and of "tempered" tragedy.

At the close of *The Death of Tragedy*, I put forward the opinion that the works of Beckett and of the "dramatists of the absurd" will not amend the conclusion that tragedy is dead, that "high tragic drama" is no longer a naturally available genre. I remain convinced that this is so, and that the masters of drama in our century are Claudel, Montherlant and Brecht (Lorca over brief, lyric stretches). But the discussion ought to have been fuller, and I should have tried to show in what ways the minimalist poetics of Beckett belong, for all their express bleakness and even nihilism, to the spheres of irony, of logical and semantic farce rather than to that of tragedy. It is as if the best of Beckett's, of Ionesco's, of Pinter's plays were the satyre-plays to unwritten tragedies, as *Happy Days* is the satiric epilogue to some distant "Prometheus." If there has been a recent tragedian in a genuine sense, it is probably Edward Bond. But both *Bingo* and his variations on *Lear* are literary, almost academic reflections on the nature and eclipse of tragic forms rather than inventions or re-inventions in their own right.

The third point is the major one. Inherent in this book, but insufficiently stated and never pressed home, is the intimation of a radical split between true tragedy and Shakespearean "tragedy." I have said that there are very few writers who have chosen to dramatize a stringently negative, despairing view of man's presence in the world. They include the Greek tragedians, Racine, Büchner and, at certain points, Strindberg. The same vision animates *Lear* and *Timon of Athens*. Shakespeare's other mature tragic plays have in them strong, very nearly decisive, counter-currents of repair, of human radiance, of public and communal restoration. Danemark under Fortinbras, Scotland under Malcolm, will be eminently better realms to live in, an amelioration to which the preceding griefs contribute directly. Though devastating, the catastrophe in *Othello* is, finally, too trivial a thing, its triviality, its purely contingent character being both augmented and subtly undermined by the grandeur of the rhetoric. As Dr. Johnson saw, Shakespeare's bent was not natively a tragic one. Because it is so encompassing, so receptive to the plurality and simultaneity of diverse orders of experience—even in the house of Atreus someone is celebrating a birthday or cracking jokes—the Shakespearean vision is that of tragi-comedy. Only *Lear* and *Timon of Athens*, an eccentric and perhaps truncated text whose intimate links with *Lear* are obvious but difficult to make out, form a real exception.

Thus, to an extent which I failed to grasp clearly when writing this book, the dramas of Shakespeare are not a renascence of or humanistic variant on the absolute tragic model. They are, rather, a rejection of this model in the light of tragi-comic and "realistic" criteria. It is in Racine that the tragic ideal is still instrumental with unqualified force. From this finding there might, perhaps there should, follow certain judgments and preferences more exposed than any I dared formulate twenty years ago.

Can Bérénice remain standing under the hammering of sorrow on Racine's naked stage or will she have to call for a chair, thus bringing on to that stage the whole contingency and compromise of the mundane order of the world? I admit that, today, this question and the executive conventions from which it springs, seem to me to crystallize the truth of absolute tragedy with an integrity, with an economy of means, with a transcendence of theatrical "business" and verbal orchestration beyond that which we find on Shakespeare's loud and prodigal scene. It needs no cosmic storms or peregrine woods to reach the heart of desolation. The absence of a chair will do.

At the last, there is an "adultness," an inescapability in the issues posed by the *Oresteia*, by *Antigone*, by the *Bacchae* (a play which asks explicitly what price man and his city must pay if they venture to inquire, via art, into the existence of man, into the morality of the divine), by *Bérénice* and by *Phèdre*, which Shakespeare's richer but hybrid forms only rarely enforce. If this is so, the enigmatic but unmistakable links between *Lear* and *Oedipus at Colonus* and the antique substance of *Timon of Athens* would not be accidental. It may be that the essential distinction is that drawn by Wittgenstein in a note dated 1950: between the "prodigally thrown forth, disseminated *sketches* of one (Shakespeare) who can, so to speak, allow himself *all*," and that other ideal of art which is containment, abnegation and completion. But there lies another book.

G.S.

Geneva,
1979

THE
DEATH
OF
TRAGEDY

All translations from French, German, and Italian are by the author.

I

WE ARE ENTERING on large, difficult ground. There are landmarks worth noting from the outset.

All men are aware of tragedy in life. But tragedy as a form of drama is not universal. Oriental art knows violence, grief, and the stroke of natural or contrived disaster; the Japanese theatre is full of ferocity and ceremonial death. But that representation of personal suffering and heroism which we call tragic drama is distinctive of the western tradition. It has become so much a part of our sense of the possibilities of human conduct, the *Oresteia*, *Hamlet*, and *Phèdre* are so ingrained in our habits of spirit, that we forget what a strange and complex idea it is to re-enact private anguish on a public stage. This idea and the vision of man which it implies are Greek. And nearly till the moment of their decline, the tragic forms are Hellenic.

3

Tragedy is alien to the Judaic sense of the world. The book of Job is always cited as an instance of tragic vision. But that black fable stands on the outer edge of Judaism, and even here an orthodox hand has asserted the claims of justice against those of tragedy:

So the Lord blessed the latter end of Job more than the beginning: for he had fourteen thousand sheep, and six thousand camels, and a thousand yoke of oxen, and a thousand she-asses.

God has made good the havoc wrought upon His servant; he has compensated Job for his agonies. But where there is compensation, there is justice, not tragedy. This demand for justice is the pride and burden of the Judaic tradition. Jehovah is just, even in His fury. Often the balance of retribution or reward seems fearfully awry, or the proceedings of God appear unendurably slow. But over the sum of time, there can be no doubt that the ways of God to man are just. Not only are they just, they are rational. The Judaic spirit is vehement in its conviction that the order of the universe and of man's estate is accessible to reason. The ways of the Lord are neither wanton nor absurd. We may fully apprehend them if we give to our inquiries the clear-sightedness of obedience. Marxism is characteristically Jewish in its insistence on justice and reason, and Marx repudiated the entire concept of tragedy. "Necessity," he declared, "is blind only in so far as it is not understood."

4

Tragic drama arises out of precisely the contrary assertion: necessity is blind and man's encounter with it shall rob him of his eyes, whether it be in Thebes or in Gaza. The assertion is Greek, and the tragic sense of life built upon it is the foremost contribution of the Greek genius to our legacy. It is impossible to tell precisely where or how the notion of formal tragedy first came to possess the imagination. But the *Iliad* is the primer of tragic art. In it are set forth the motifs and images around which the sense of the tragic has crystallized during nearly three thousand years of western poetry: the shortness of heroic life, the exposure of man to the murderousness and caprice of the inhuman, the fall of the City. Note the crucial distinction: the fall of Jericho or Jerusalem is merely just, whereas the fall of Troy is the first great metaphor of tragedy. Where a city is destroyed because it has defied God, its destruction is a passing instant in the rational design of God's purpose. Its walls shall rise again, on earth or in the kingdom of heaven, when the souls of men are restored to grace. The burning of Troy is final because it is brought about by the fierce sport of human hatreds and the wanton, mysterious choice of destiny.

There are attempts in the *Iliad* to throw the light of reason into the shadow-world which surrounds man. Fate is given a name, and the elements are shown in the frivolous and reassuring mask of the gods. But mythology is only a fable to help us endure. The Homeric warrior knows that he can

5

neither comprehend nor master the workings of destiny. Patroclus is slain, and the wretch Thersites sails safely for home. Call for justice or explanation, and the sea will thunder back with its mute clamour. Men's accounts with the gods do not balance.

The irony deepens. Instead of altering or diminishing their tragic condition, the increase in scientific resource and material power leaves men even more vulnerable. This idea is not yet explicit in Homer, but it is eloquent in another major tragic poet, in Thucydides. Again, we must observe the decisive contrast. The wars recorded in the Old Testament are bloody and grievous, but not tragic. They are just or unjust. The armies of Israel shall carry the day if they have observed God's will and ordinance. They shall be routed if they have broken the divine covenant or if their kings have fallen into idolatry. The Peloponnesian Wars, on the contrary, are tragic. Behind them lie obscure fatalities and misjudgements. Enmeshed in false rhetoric and driven by political compulsions of which they can give no clear account, men go out to destroy one another in a kind of fury without hatred. We are still waging Peloponnesian wars. Our control of the material world and our positive science have grown fantastically. But our very achievements turn against us, making politics more random and wars more bestial.

The Judaic vision sees in disaster a specific moral fault or failure of understanding. The Greek tragic poets assert that the forces which shape or destroy our lives lie outside the governance of reason or justice. Worse than that: there are around us daemonic energies which prey upon the soul and turn it to madness or which poison our will so that we inflict irreparable outrage upon ourselves and those we love. Or to put it in the terms of the tragic design drawn by Thucydides: our fleets shall always sail toward Sicily although everyone is more or less aware that they go to their ruin. Eteocles knows that he will perish at the seventh gate but goes forward nevertheless:

> We are already past the care of gods.
> For them our death is the admirable offering.
> Why then delay, fawning upon our doom?

Antigone is perfectly aware of what will happen to her, and in the wells of his stubborn heart Oedipus knows also. But they stride to their fierce disasters in the grip of truths more intense than knowledge. To the Jew there is a marvellous continuity between knowledge and action; to the Greek an ironic abyss. The legend of Oedipus, in which the Greek sense of tragic unreason is so grimly rendered, served that great Jewish poet Freud as an emblem of rational insight and redemption through healing.

Not that Greek tragedy is wholly without redemption. In the *Eumenides* and in *Oedipus at Colonus*, the tragic action closes on a note of grace. Much has been made of this fact. But we should, I think, interpret it with extreme caution. Both cases are exceptional; there is in them an element of ritual

7

pageant commemorating special aspects of the sanctity of Athens. Moreover, the part of music in Greek tragedy is irrevocably lost to us, and I suspect that the use of music may have given to the endings of these two plays a solemn distinctness, setting the final moments at some distance from the terrors which went before.

I emphasize this because I believe that any realistic notion of tragic drama must start from the fact of catastrophe. Tragedies end badly. The tragic personage is broken by forces which can neither be fully understood nor overcome by rational prudence. This again is crucial. Where the causes of disaster are temporal, where the conflict can be resolved through technical or social means, we may have serious drama, but not tragedy. More pliant divorce laws could not alter the fate of Agamemnon; social psychiatry is no answer to *Oedipus*. But saner economic relations or better plumbing *can* resolve some of the grave crises in the dramas of Ibsen. The distinction should be borne sharply in mind. Tragedy is irreparable. It cannot lead to just and material compensation for past suffering. Job gets back double the number of she-asses; so he should, for God has enacted upon him a parable of justice. Oedipus does not get back his eyes or his sceptre over Thebes.

Tragic drama tells us that the spheres of reason, order, and justice are terribly limited and that no progress in our science or technical resources will enlarge their relevance. Outside and within man is

8

l'autre, the "otherness" of the world. Call it what you will: a hidden or malevolent God, blind fate, the solicitations of hell, or the brute fury of our animal blood. It waits for us in ambush at the crossroads. It mocks us and destroys us. In certain rare instances, it leads us after destruction to some incomprehensible repose.

None of this, I know, is a definition of tragedy. But any neat abstract definition would mean nothing. When we say "tragic drama" we know what we are talking about; not exactly, but well enough to recognize the real thing. In one instance, however, a tragic poet does come very near to giving an explicit summary of the tragic vision of life. Euripides' *Bacchae* stands in some special proximity to the ancient, no longer discernible springs of tragic feeling. At the end of the play, Dionysus condemns Cadmus, his royal house, and the entire city of Thebes to a savage doom. Cadmus protests: the sentence is far too harsh. It is utterly out of proportion with the guilt of those who fail to recognize or have insulted the god. Dionysus evades the question. He repeats petulantly that he has been greatly affronted; then he asserts that the doom of Thebes was predestined. There is no use asking for rational explanation or mercy. Things are as they are, unrelenting and absurd. We are punished far in excess of our guilt.

It is a terrible, stark insight into human life. Yet in the very excess of his suffering lies man's claim to dignity. Powerless and broken, a blind beggar hounded out of the city, he assumes a new grandeur. Man is ennobled by the vengeful spite or injustice of the gods. It does not make him innocent, but it hallows him as if he had passed through flame. Hence there is in the final moments of great tragedy, whether Greek or Shakespearean or neoclassic, a fusion of grief and joy, of lament over the fall of man and of rejoicing in the resurrection of his spirit. No other poetic form achieves this mysterious effect; it makes of *Oedipus*, *King Lear*, and *Phèdre* the noblest yet wrought by the mind.

From antiquity until the age of Shakespeare and Racine, such accomplishment seemed within the reach of talent. Since then the tragic voice in drama is blurred or still. What follows is an attempt to determine why this should be.

II

THE WORD "tragedy" entered the English language in the later years of the fourteenth century. Chaucer gave a definition of it in the Prologue to the *Monk's Tale*:

> Tragedie is to seyn a certeyn storie,
> As olde bookes maken us memorie,
> Of hym that stood in greet prosperitee,
> And is yfallen out of heigh degree
> Into myserie, and endeth wrecchedly.

There is no implication of dramatic form. A tragedy is a narrative recounting the life of some ancient or eminent personage who suffered a decline of fortune toward a disastrous end. That is the characteristic medieval definition. Dante observed, in his letter to Can Grande, that tragedy and comedy move in precisely contrary directions. Because its action is that of the soul ascending from shadow to starlight, from fearful doubt to the joy and certitude of grace, Dante entitled his poem a *commedia*. The motion of tragedy is a constant descent from prosperity to suffering and chaos: *exitu est foetida et horribilis*. In Dante, as in Chaucer, there is no inference that the notion of tragedy is particularly related to drama. A misunderstanding of a passage in Livy led medieval commentators to suppose that the plays of Seneca and Terence had been recited by a single narrator, presumably the poet himself. Two Latin tragedies in imitation of Seneca were actually written by Italian scholars as early as 1315 and *c.* 1387, but neither was intended for performance on a stage. Thus the sense of the tragic remained dissociated from that of the theatre. A remark in Erasmus' *Adagia* suggests that even in the sixteenth century classicists still had doubts as to whether Greek and Roman tragedies had ever been intended for dramatic presentation.

Chaucer's definition derives its force from contemporary awareness of sudden reversals of political and dynastic fortune. To the medieval eye, the heavens of state were filled with portentous stars, dazzling in their ascent but fiery in their decline. The fall of great personages from high place (*casus virorum illustrium*) gave to medieval politics their festive and brutal character. Sweeping over men with cruel frequency, the quarrels of princes implicated the lives and fortunes of the entire community. But the rise and fall of him that stood in high degree was the incarnation of the tragic sense for a much deeper reason: it made explicit the universal drama of the fall of man. Lords and captains perished through exceeding ambition, through the hatred and cunning of their adversaries, or by mischance. But even where the moralist could point to a particular crime or occasion of disaster, a more general law was at work. By virtue of original sin, each man was destined to suffer in his own experience, however private or obscure, some part of the tragedy of death. The Monk's lament "in manere of tragedie" begins with Lucifer and Adam, for the prologue to the tragic condition of man is set in Heaven and in the Garden of Eden. There the arrow of creation started on its downward flight. It is in a garden also that the symmetry of divine intent places the act of fortunate reversal. At Gethsemane the arrow changes its course, and the morality play of history alters from tragedy to *commedia*. Finally, and in precise counterpart to the prologue of disobedience, there is the promise of a celestial epilogue where man will be restored to more than his first glory. Of this great parable of God's design, the recital of the tragic destinies of illustrious men are a gloss and a reminder.

The rise of English drama in the Tudor period and its Elizabethan triumph restored to the notion of tragedy the implications of actual dramatic performance. But the images of the tragic estate devised in medieval literature carried over into the language of the theatre. When Fortune abandoned men in medieval allegory, it was with a swift turn of her emblematic wheel. Marlowe preserved this ancient fancy in *The Tragedie of Edward the second*:

> Base fortune, now I see, that in thy wheele
> There is a point, to which when men aspire,
> They tumble headlong downe: that point I
>   touchte,
> And seeing there was no place to mount up higher.
> Why should I greeue at my declining fall?

Mortimer accepts his doom with grim calm. Only a few moments earlier, he had spoken of himself as "Jove's huge tree, And others are but shrubs compared to me." A proud thought, but also an annunciation of disaster, for in medieval iconography trees were dangerously enmeshed with the image of man. They carried the graft of the apple bough from which Adam plucked, and some minute splinter of the desperate consolation of the cross. And it is when they are blasted at the crown, burnt, or wither at the root, that trees are most illustrative of the human condition. In the early Elizabethan tragedy of *Jocasta*, the wheel and the tree are joined together to convey a vision of fatality:

> When she that rules the rolling wheele of
>   chaunce,
> Doth turne aside hir angrie frowning face,
> On him, who erst she deigned to aduance,
> She never leaues to gaulde him with disgrace,
> To tosse and turne his state in euery place,
> Till at the last she hurle him from on high
> And yeld him subject unto miserie:

14

> And as the braunche that from the roote is reft,
> He never wines like leafe to that he lefte.

As Wagner's *Tannhäuser* reminds us, the withered branch did not lose its grip on the poetic imagination. Drawing on two lines by Thomas Churchyard in that most medieval of Elizabethan poetic narratives, the *Mirror for Magistrates*, Marlowe gave to the image a final splendour. In the epilogue to *The tragicall Historie of Doctor Faustus*, the Chorus matches the tree of Apollo to the burnt vine of the eightieth Psalm:

> Cut is the branch that might have growne full straight,
> And burned is *Apolloes* Laurel bough
> That sometime grew within this learned man.

We are asked to regard "his hellish fall" because it holds up a cautionary mirror to the fate of ordinary men. The tragic personage is nobler and closer to the dark springs of life than the average human being. But he is also typical. Otherwise his fall would not be exemplary. This, too, is a medieval conception which retained its vitality in Elizabethan drama. By examples "trewe and olde," Chaucer's Monk would give us warning of pride or soaring ambition. And it is in this light that the authors of *Jocasta* regarded the myth of Oedipus. They saw in it neither a riddle of innocence unjustly hounded nor an echo of some archaic rite of blood and expiation. The play dealt with a clash of representative characters:

> Creon is King, the type of Tyranny,
> And Oedipus, myrrour of misery.

The glass does not break with the close of the medieval period. We find it still in the mirror which Hamlet bids the players hold up to nature.

Thus the wheel, the branch, and the mirror had their strong life more than two centuries after the tragic fables of Chaucer and Lydgate. Translated into the *coup de théâtre* or the "doctrine of realism," these ancient images still govern our experience of drama. But in the Elizabethan theatre, the idea of tragedy lost its medieval directness. The word itself assumed values at once more universal and more restricted. With the decline of hope which followed on the early renaissance—the darkening of spirit which separates the vision of man in Marlowe from that of Pico della Mirandola— the sense of the tragic broadened. It reached beyond the fall of individual greatness. A tragic rift, an irreducible core of inhumanity, seemed to lie in the mystery of things. The sense of life is itself shadowed by a feeling of tragedy. We see this ir Calvin's account of man's condition no less than in Shakespeare's.

But at the same time, "tragedy" also acquired a special meaning. A poem or prose romance might be called "tragic" by virtue of its theme. Yet it was no longer designated as a "tragedy." The rediscovery of Senecan drama during the 1560's gave to the word clear implications of theatrical form. Henceforth, a "tragedy" is a play dealing with tragic matters. But were all such plays tragedies in the true sense? The conflicts of critical definition appeared nearly from the start. They have never ceased in the history of the western theatre. Already at the very beginning of the seventeenth century there are foreshadowings of the difficulties which preoccupy Racine, Ibsen, and Wagner. Theory had begun to harass the playwright with what Ibsen might have called "the claims of the ideal."

We can date rather precisely the moment at which these claims were first presented. In *Sejanus* (1605), Ben Jonson had written a learned tragedy modelled on Senecan rhetoric and Roman satire. Nevertheless, he found himself compelled to defend certain liberties in the play against the canons of strict neo-classicism:

. . . if it be objected, that what I publish is no true poem, in the strict laws of time, I confess it: as also in the want of a proper chorus; whose habit and mood are such and so difficult, as not any, whom I have seen, since the ancients, no, not they who have most presently affected laws, have yet come in the way of. Nor is it needful, or almost possible in these our times . . . to observe the old state and splendour of dramatic poems, with preservation of any popular delight.

Seven years later, in the preface to *The White Devil*, John Webster made the same apologia. He conceded that he had not produced a "true dramatic poem," meaning by that a play in severe accord with Aristotelian precepts. But he added with confident irony that the fault lay with the public.

The Elizabethan and Jacobean audiences had proved themselves unworthy of "the old state and splendour" of tragedy.

These statements arise from the great division of ideals that shaped the history of the European theatre from the late sixteenth century nearly to the time of Ibsen. The neo-classic conception of tragedy had on its side ancient precedent, the force of the Senecan example, and a powerful critical theory. The popular, romantic ideal of drama drew its strength from the actual performance of the Elizabethan playwrights and from the plain fact of theatrical success. The general public cared more for the gusto and variousness of Shakespearean drama than for the noble form of the "true dramatic poem."

Neo-classicism arose with the scholar-poets and critics of the Italian renaissance. It can be traced back to imperfect understanding of Aristotle and Horace, but was given its current shape by the art of Seneca. The neo-classical view found two expositors of genius, Scaliger and Castelvetro. The latter's interpretation of the *Poetics*, *Poetica d'Aristotele vulgarizata*, proved to be one of the decisive statements in the development of western taste. It set forth precepts and ideals which have engaged the concern of critics and dramatists from the time of Jonson to that of Claudel and T. S. Eliot. Its principal arguments were carried over to England and given memorable expression in Sidney's *Defense of Poesy*. Sidney's style bestows a seductive nobility on the spinsterish discipline of the neo-Aristotelian view. "The stage," he tells us, "should always represent but one place, and the uttermost time presupposed in it should be, both by Aristotle's precept and common reason, but one day." Observe the direction of Sidney's appeal: to authority and to reason. Neo-classicism always insists on both. Unity of time and place, moreover, are but instruments toward the principal design, which is unity of action. That is the vital centre of the classic ideal. The tragic action must proceed with total coherence and economy. There must be no residue of waste emotion, no energy of language or gesture inconsequential to the final effect. Neo-classic drama, where it accomplishes its purpose, is immensely tight-wrought. It is art by privation; an austere, sparse, yet ceremonious structure of language and bearing leading to the solemnities of heroic death. From this principle of unity all other conventions follow. The tragic and the comic sense of life must be kept severely apart; the true poet will not "match hornpipes and funerals." Tragedy, moreover, is Augustinian; few are elected to its perilous grace. Or as Sidney puts it, one must not thrust in "the clown by head and shoulders to play a part in majestical matters."

But even as he wrote, clowns were asserting their rights on the tragic stage. They perform their comic turns on Faustus' way to damnation. They open the gates to vengeance in *Macbeth* and trade wisdom with Hamlet. Through the long funeral of

19

Lear's reason sounds the hornpipe of the Fool. Sidney ridicules the kind of popular drama "where you shall have Asia of the one side, and Africa of the other, and so many other under-kingdoms, that the player, when he cometh in, must ever begin with telling where he is." Yet even before the *Defense of Poesy* had been published, Faustus was soaring through the air

> Being seated in a chariot burning bright,
> Drawn by the strength of yoaked dragons neckes.

And below him lay the licentious geography of the Elizabethan theatre, with its instantaneous transitions from Rome to Egypt, and its seacoasts in Bohemia. Sidney argues that it is absurd that a play, which requires a few brief hours to perform, should claim to imitate events which have taken years to come to pass. Nothing of the kind can be cited in "ancient examples," and the "players in Italy," who were the guardians of the neo-classic style, will not allow it. But Shakespearean characters grow old between the acts, and in *The Winter's Tale* some sixteen years go by between the opening discord and the final music.

The Elizabethan playwrights violated every precept of neo-classicism. They broke with the unities, dispensed with the chorus, and combined tragic and comic plots with indiscriminate power. The playhouse of Shakespeare and his contemporaries was *el gran teatro del mundo*. No variety of feeling, no element from the crucible of experience, was

20

alien to its purpose. The Elizabethan and Jacobean dramatists ransacked Seneca. They took from him his rhetoric, his ghosts, his sententious morality, his flair for horror and blood-vengeance; but not the austere, artificial practices of the neo-classic stage. To the genius of Greek tragedy, or rather to its inferior Latin version, Shakespeare opposed a rival conception of tragic form and a rival magnificence of execution.

Despite massive scholarship, the history of that form remains obscure. There were practical reasons why Marlowe, Kyd, and Shakespeare departed from neo-classic models. A playwright could not make a living by the precepts of Castelvetro. The public resolutely preferred the romance and turmoil of the tragicomedy or the chronicle play. It delighted in clowns, in comic interludes, and in the acrobatics and brutality of physical action. The Elizabethan spectator had strong nerves and demanded that they be played upon. There was hotness of blood in the world around him and he called for it on the stage. "Learned" poets, such as Ben Jonson and Chapman, sought in vain to educate their public to more lofty pleasures. But even if we discount the realities of the popular theatre, it would seem that Shakespeare's genius led him toward "open" rather than "closed" forms of stagecraft. Whereas Dante's vision bends all light rays toward a controlling centre, Shakespeare's sense of the world appears to move outward. He used dramatic forms with marvellous pragmatism, shaping them as the

need arose. The real and the fantastic, the tragic
and the comic, the noble and the vile, were equally
present in his apprehension of life. Thus he required a theatre more irregular and provisional
than that of classic tragedy.

But the shape of such plays as *Doctor Faustus*,
Richard II, *King Lear*, or *Measure for Measure*,
represents more than the personal bias of the Elizabethan dramatists. They are a result of the concurrence of ancient and complex energies. Beneath the
fact of the development of dramatic blank verse,
beneath the Senecan spirit of majestic violence, lay
a great inheritance of medieval and popular forms.
This is the live undergrowth from which the late sixteenth century draws much of its strength. In
Shakespeare's sovereign contempt for limitations of
space and time, we recognize the spirit of the mystery cycles which took the world of heaven, earth,
and hell for their setting, and the history of man
for their temporal scale. The clowns, the wise fools,
and the witches of Elizabethan drama carry with
them a medieval resonance. Behind the Senecan funerals come the hornpipes of the Morris dancers.
And one cannot understand Shakespeare's history
plays or his late, dark comedies, without discerning
in them a legacy of ritual and symbolic proceeding
which goes back to the imaginative wealth of the
Middle Ages. How this legacy was transmitted, and
how it conjoined with the nervous freedom of the
Elizabethan temper, is as yet unclear. But we feel
its shaping presence even as late as Jacobean drama.

When the new world picture of reason usurped the place of the old tradition in the course of the seventeenth century, the English theatre entered its long decline.

In retrospect, the contrast between the actual work done by the Elizabethan playwrights and the claims put forward by neo-classic critics is overwhelming. The plays of Marlowe, Shakespeare, Middleton, Tourneur, Webster, and Ford are clearly superior to anything produced in the neoclassic vein. But this disparity is, in part, a matter of focus. Our own experience of the dramatic is so largely conditioned by the open, Shakespearean form, that it is difficult for us even to imagine the validity of an alternative tradition. The Elizabethan classicists were no fools. Their arguments were founded on more than the authority of Italian grammarians and the rather tawdry example of Latin tragedy. The neo-classic view expresses a growing perception of the miracle of Greek drama. This perception was fragmentary. There were few translations of Aeschylus, and the plays of Euripides were known mainly in the versions of Seneca. Renaissance scholars failed to realize, moreover, that Aristotle was a practical critic whose judgements are relevant to Sophocles rather than to the whole of Greek drama (there is no unity of time, for instance, in the *Eumenides*). Nevertheless, the ideals of Sidney and the ambitions of Ben Jonson convey insight into the fact that the tragic imagination owes to the Greek precedent a debt of recognition. Time and again, this insight has mastered the sensibility of western poets. Much of poetic drama, from Milton to Goethe, from Hölderlin to Cocteau, is an attempt to revive the Greek ideal. It is a great and mysterious stroke of fortune that Shakespeare escaped the fascination of the Hellenic. His apparent innocence with respect to more formal classic attainments may account for his majestic ease. It is difficult to imagine what *Hamlet* might have been like had Shakespeare first read the *Oresteia*, and one can only be grateful that the close of *King Lear* shows no conscious awareness of how matters were ordered at Colonus.

The English classicists were not the earliest in the field. Neo-Aristotelian precepts and the Senecan example had already inspired a considerable body of Italian and French drama. Today, only the specialist in theatrical history reads the plays of Trissino and Giraldo Cintio, or Tasso's *Torrismondo*. This neglect extends to Jodelle and Garnier. In the light of Racine, French sixteenth-century tragedy seems an archaic prelude. But this view also is largely one of modern perspective. There is in both these French tragedians a strong music which we shall not hear again, even in the high moments of the classic style. Consider the invocation to death in Jodelle's *Cléopâtre captive* (1552):

> Ha Mort, ô douce mort, mort seule guerison
> Des esprits oppressés d'une estrange prison,
> Pourquoy souffres tu tant à tes droits faire tort?

24

T'avons nous fait offense, ô douce & douce mort?
Pourquoy n'approches tu, ô Parque trop tardive?
Pourquoy veux tu souffrir ceste bande captive,
Qui n'aura pas plustot le don de liberté,
Que cest esprit ne soit par ton dard écarté? [1]

The voice rises in ornate grief above the lament of
the chorus. The lines fall like brocade, but beneath
their stiffness we hear the loosening inrush of
death: *ô douce & douce mort.* The *Parque trop
tardive* is like an allegoric figure arrested in mid-
flight; it is hard to believe that Valéry's eye did not
chance on her.

In Garnier's *Marc-Antoine,* a somewhat later
play, the same moment is dramatized. Refusing
Charmian's advice that she plead with her conquerors, Cleopatra prepares for the ceremonies of
death:

Quel blasme me seroit-ce? hé Dieux! quelle in-
    famie,
D'avoir esté d'Antoine et son bonh-heur amie,
Et le survivre mort, contente d'honorer
Un tombeau solitaire, et dessur luy pleurer?
Les races à venir justement pourroyent dire
Que je l'aurois aimé seulement pour l'Empire,
Pour sa seule grandeur, et qu'en adversité

[1] Ah death, O gentle death, sole remedy
   For spirits pinioned in captivity,
   Why let your rights be flouted thus?
   Did we offend thee, gentle, gentle death?
   Why not draw near, O tardy Fate?
   Why condescend to our captive state,
   Who can no sooner from our bondage part
   Than when our souls are stricken with your dart?

Je l'aurois mechamment pour un autre quitté.
Semblable à ces oiseaux, qui d'ailes passageres
Arrivent au Printemps des terres estrangeres,
Et vivent avec nous tandis que les chaleurs
Et leur pasture y sont, puis s'envolent ailleurs.[2]

The words persuade us by an absence of rhetoric.
Cleopatra refers to herself as Anthony's *amie*. In the
sixteenth century the erotic connotations of the
term were stronger than they are now; but in this
quiet, cruel hour the force of friendship is as vital
as that of love. Her simile lacks all pretension; she
will not be flighty as are the birds. But at the same
time, the quickening of pace and the cadence of
ailes passageres directs our imagination to the
deathward flight of the soul. The royal hawk on
Egypt's crown will open his wings. The values here
are not the same as in Corneille or Racine. The
characters are shown in a manner which marks a
transition from allegory to drama. They tend to live
at the surface of language, and the action is one of
successive ornamentations rather than direct progress. But there is in these tragedies a commitment

[2] How infamous, ye gods! how much to blame,
Had I loved Anthony and his bright fame
And would survive his death, merely content
To shed a tear by his lone monument.
How justly, then, could future races say
I doted only on his sceptre's sway
And on his might, but when his star sank down
Had stolen off to find some other man.
Then were I flighty as the birds of spring
Who come from foreign lands on transient wing
To pasture with us during summer's noon,
But at first winter fly elsewhere again.

of emotion at once more naïve and more humane than in mature neo-classicism.

Four years after Sidney's death, the Countess of Pembroke translated *Marc-Antoine*. Garnier was the model for Samuel Daniel's *Cleopatra* and Thomas Kyd translated his *Cornélie*, a tragedy dealing with the fall of Pompey. These were closet-dramas written for the enjoyment of a coterie. But they initiated a tradition of formal tragedy which extends into the romantic period. Fulke Greville destroyed one of his political tragedies at the time of the Essex rebellion. The two that survive, *Mustapha* and *Alaham*, have the kind of ornate and intricate solemnity which marks the architecture of the high baroque. They foreshadow the Moorish plays of Dryden and the works of a far more talented aristocrat—Byron's Venetian tragedies and his *Sardanapalus*.

The neo-classic view, moreover, found at least partial expression in the Elizabethan and Jacobean theatre. Chapman and Ben Jonson sought to combine the rival conceptions of learned and popular drama. They were at the same time scholars and men of the living stage. Of all the Elizabethans, Chapman is nearest to Seneca. His vision of human affairs was stoic, and his style had a natural darkness and complication. He entirely accepted the neo-Aristotelian belief in the moral purpose of drama. Authentic tragedy must convey "material instruction, elegant and sententious excitation to virtue, and deflection from her contrary." He

shared the feeling of the later Roman historians
that high matters of state are rooted in private lust
and private ambition. *Bussy d'Ambois* and *The
Tragedy of Chabot, Admiral of France* are among
the few major political dramas in English literature. In Chapman's conviction that violence breeds
violence and that evil will not be mocked, there is
something of the lucid grief of Tacitus. Yet simultaneously, Chapman was striving for success on the
popular stage. Hence he gave to the audience its
due ration of physical brutality, witchcraft, and amorous intrigue. His ghosts are as bloody as any in
the Elizabethan theatre, his murders as frequent.
But the stress of conflicting ideals proved too great.
There is no unity of design in Chapman's plays.
Amid the thickets of rhetoric there are sudden
clearings where the grimness of his political vision
carries all before it. But no proportion is sustained,
as if a severe Palladian threshold gave sudden access to a baroque interior.

Chapman's Latinity is that of the Roman decline. The classicism of Ben Jonson belongs to the
high noon of Rome. He is the truest classic in English letters. Other writers have taken from the surface of Latin poetry; Jonson went to the heart. His
powers of close, ironic observation, his salty realism, the urbanity and energy of his statement, show
how strongly his turn of mind was related to that of
Horace. Had Jonson brought to his tragedies the
virtues of *Volpone* and *The Silent Woman*, he
would have left a body of work classic in spirit yet

of a force to rival Shakespeare's. Instead, he resolved to affirm his claims to classic learning and social status. *Sejanus* and *Catiline's Conspiracy* were intended to show that Jonson could use with mastery the erudition and formal conventions of the neo-classic style. Both plays exhibit a sure grasp of the murderous tenor of Roman politics, and there are in each, passages whose excellence resists analysis precisely because Jonson's control was so unobtrusive. One must look to *Coriolanus* to find anything that surpasses the nervous intelligence and contained pressure of the dialogue between Caesar and Catiline:

CAESAR: Come, there was never any great thing
  yet
Aspired, but by violence or fraud:
And he that sticks for folly of a conscience
To reach it—

CATILINE: Is a good religious fool.

CAESAR: A superstitious slave, and will die beast.
Good night. You know what Crassus
  thinks, and I,
By this. Prepare your wings as large as
  sails,
To cut through air, and leave no print
  behind you.
A serpent, ere he comes to be a dragon,
Does eat a bat; and so must you a consul,
That watches. What you do, do
  quickly, Sergius.

But Jonson's tragedies, like Chapman's, suffer from their divided purpose. They grow unwieldy under the attempt to reconcile neo-classic conventions to the very different conventions of Elizabethan historical drama. *Volpone* is far more "classical" than either of the Roman tragedies. It has the cruel tooth of Roman satire and a perfect discipline of proportion. The edges of feeling are hard-cut, and the characters are seen in the kind of direct, somewhat flattening light which is found also in Roman comedy. No other Elizabethan play is more distant from Shakespeare. It belongs with the lyrics of Matthew Prior and Robert Graves in that small corner of English literature which is genuinely Latin.

Neither Chapman nor Jonson fulfilled Sidney's ideal of the "true dramatic poem." Does this mean that there is no English tragedy in a classic mode to set against the world of Shakespeare? Only one, perhaps. Its preface is a rigorous statement of the neo-classic view:

Tragedy, as it was antiently compos'd, hath been ever held the gravest, moralest, and most profitable of all other Poems: therefore said by *Aristotle* to be of power by raising pity and fear, or terror, to purge the mind of those and such like passions. . . . This is mention'd to vindicate Tragedy from the small esteem, or rather infamy, which in the account of many it undergoes at this day with other common Interludes; hap'ning through the Poets error of intermixing Comic stuff with Tragic sadness and gravity; or introducing trivial and vulgar persons . . . brought in without discretion, corruptly to gratifie the people. . . . they only will best judge who are not unacquainted with *Aeschulus*, *Sophocles*, and *Euripides*, the three Tragic Poets un-equall'd yet by any, and the best rule to all who en-deavour to write Tragedy.

"Unequalled yet by any"—the words were written sixty-three years after the publication of *King Lear*. The judgement they convey and the tragedy which they introduce are the great counterstatement in English literature to Shakespeare and to all "open" forms of tragic drama.

Samson Agonistes is difficult to get into focus, exactly because it comes so near to making good its presumptions. The work is a special case by virtue of its power and of its intent. English drama has produced nothing else with which it may justly be compared. The organization of the play is nearly static, in the manner of the Aeschylean *Prome-theus*; yet there moves through it a great progress toward resolution. Like all Christian tragedy, a notion in itself paradoxical, *Samson Agonistes* is in part a *commedia*. The reality of Samson's death is drastic and irrefutable; but it does not carry the major or the final meaning of the play. As in *Oedipus at Colonus*, the work ends on a note of solemn transfiguration, even of joy. The action proceeds from night-blindness of eye and of spirit to a blind-ness caused by exceeding light.

In *Samson Agonistes*, Milton accepted the claims of the neo-classic ideal and met them fully. He wrote a tragedy in a modern tongue; he did not even draw on Greek mythology; he strictly observed the unities and used a chorus. But at the same time, he created magnificent theatre. This assertion should be a commonplace. Performance holds one spellbound, and the merest intelligent reading conveys the formidable excitement of the play. Only an ear deaf to drama could fail to experience, sharp as a whiplash, the hurt and tension of the successive assaults on Samson's bruised integrity. And there is little before Strindberg to match the naked sexual antagonism which flares between Samson and Dalila, "a manifest Serpent by her sting discover'd."

It is through *Samson Agonistes*, more readily perhaps than through archaeology and classical scholarship, that we glimpse the lost totality of Greek drama. Milton's language seems to draw after it the attendant powers of music and the dance. In certain passages the fusion is as complete as it must have been in the choral lyrics of Aeschylus:

But who is this, what thing of Sea or Land?
Female of sex it seems,
That so bedeckt, ornate, and gay,
Comes this way sailing
Like a stately Ship
Of *Tarsus*, bound for th' Isles
Of *Javan* or *Gadier*
With all her bravery on, and tackle trim,
Sails fill'd, and streamers waving,
Courted by all the winds that hold them play. . . .

No theatre since that of Dionysus had heard like music.

The preface to *Samson Agonistes* drew lines of battle which cut across the history of western drama. After the seventeenth century the writer of tragedy faces a persistent conflict of ideals. Should he adopt the conventions which neo-classicism derived from Aeschylus, Sophocles, and Euripides, or should he turn to the Shakespearean tradition of open drama? This problem of rival modes was in itself a difficult one; but there lay beneath it an even more crucial dilemma. Was it possible for a modern writer to create tragic drama which would not be hopelessly overshadowed by the achievements of the Greek and the Elizabethan theatre? Could a man write the word "tragedy" across a blank page without hearing at his back the immense presence of the *Oresteia*, of *Oedipus*, of *Hamlet*, and of *King Lear*?

One may argue, as Lessing and the romantics did, that the rigid distinction between the Sophoclean and the Shakespearean vision of tragedy is false. One may assert that the living should not bend under the weight of the dead. But the facts are undeniable. Until the time of Ibsen, Chekhov, and Strindberg, the problem of tragedy is shaped by the divided heritage of the classic and Elizabethan past. The eyes of later poets were riveted to these summits, and their own ambitions were arrested by the mere fact of comparison. Ibsen was to be the first in whom there were fulfilled ideals of tragic form which derived neither from the antique nor the Shakespearean example. And before this could happen, the centre of expressive language had to shift from verse to prose. These great problems of past magnificence and present failure were first posed in the late seventeenth century. With it must begin any inquiry into the condition of modern drama.

It was a period notable for the sharpness of its critical perceptions. Even prior to *Samson Agonistes*, critics saw that drama was riven by contrary ideals. Richard Flecknoe, in his *Short Discourse of the English Stage*, drew the line between Shakespeare and Ben Jonson. Compare them and "you shall see the difference betwixt Nature and Art." This statement is a Pandora's box from which confusion swarmed. "Nature" and "art" trace a maddening pattern across the weave of criticism. At times, art is equated with classical conventions and nature with the open, mixed forms of Shakespearean drama. More often, rival critics proclaim that their own conception of the theatre achieves the freedom of natural fantasy by means of concealed art. No school will wholly relinquish either term.

The subtlest mind brought to bear on these matters was that of Thomas Rymer. He was a critic whose power lay in a deliberate narrowness of taste. He saw deeply, and the questions he asked were those which two centuries of European drama sought to resolve. Even his critique of Shakespeare,

34

which shows Rymer at his greyest, has a certain memorable honesty. By comparison, Voltaire's attack is disingenuous. In his examination of *The Tragedies of the Last Age,* Rymer tries to show that the conventions of classical drama are not artificial limitations, but rather expressions of the natural modes of reason. The forms of Greek tragedy codify the truth of experience and common understanding. The wildness of incident in *King Lear* or the alternance of grief and buffoonery in *Macbeth* are reprehensible not because they violate the precepts of Aristotle, but because they contradict the natural shape of human behaviour. It was the genius and good fortune of Aeschylus, Sophocles, and Euripides to have inherited and moulded a kind of drama whose conventions were at once satisfying in their proportionate formality and concordant with common sense.

Though clearly argued, Rymer's theory is, in fact, founded on equivocations. He began with the prevailing assumption that Greek drama is deliberate art whereas the plays of Shakespeare are spontaneous effusions of natural talent (the "warbling of wood-notes wild"). Upon it he imposed the idea that classical tragedies are realistic whereas Elizabethan dramas are pieces of unbridled fantasy. Note the intricate cross-weaving of critical terms: art is now expressive of common-sense realism, while nature has been traduced into the realm of the fantastic. Beneath this inversion of traditional critical values, we find hints of a subtle and compli-

35

cated aesthetics. To Rymer, Greek tragedy is at once formal and realistic. It is natural to the mind because it imitates life when life is in a condition of extreme order. Its "rules" or technical conventions are the means of such imitation; order in action can only be reflected by order in art. Lacking this coherent framework, Shakespeare's naturalism in fact leads to extravagant license and improbability (Gloucester leaping off Dover Cliff). The bias of Elizabethan drama is that of realism, but the image of life which it enacts is far less real than that put forward by Sophoclean tragedy. In short: true realism is the fruit of intense stylization. These are not Rymer's terms, and it is doubtful whether anyone but Racine fully grasped the paradox on which neo-classical theories were built. But the contrary notions in Rymer's dialectic—art–nature, common sense–imagination, reason–fantasy—were to exercise great influence. They haunt the theory of drama from the age of Dryden to that of Shaw and Brecht.

It is one of Rymer's merits that he did not evade the difficulties inherent in the neo-classic view. Having assumed that Athenian tragedy should be the governing ideal of modern practice, he faced the awkward question of how myths and beliefs central to Greek art could be carried over to a Christian or secular playhouse:

Some would laugh to find me mentioning *Sacrifices, Oracles,* and *Goddesses:* old Superstitions, say they, not practicable, but more than ridiculous on our Stage.

These have not observ'd with what Art *Virgil* has manag'd the Gods of *Homer*, nor with what judgment *Tasso* and *Cowley* employ the heavenly powers in a Christian Poem. The like hints from *Sophocles* and *Euripides* might also be improv'd by modern Tragedians, and something thence devis'd suitable to our Faith and Customes.

The question is more searching than the answer. Again it was Racine who grasped the nettle and perceived that the underlying conventions of neoclassical tragedy are myths emptied of active belief.

Rymer is on firmer ground when he argues that the Sophoclean ideal implies the use of a chorus: "The *Chorus* was the root and original, and is certainly always the most necessary part." He touches here on the essential distinction between the open and the closed theatre. The encircling presence of the chorus is indispensable to certain modes of tragic action; it renders other modes, such as those of Shakespearean drama, impossible. The problem of the chorus will arise continually in European drama. It preoccupied Racine, Schiller, and Yeats; it plays a role in the theatre of Claudel and T. S. Eliot. Rymer, moreover, acutely notes that the intervention of a chorus carries with it the possibility of music drama. The lyric element may undermine the vital force of the spoken word. Choral drama can be a halfway house to opera. Sir Robert Howard, a contemporary of Rymer, regarded this peril as imminent: "Here is the *Opera* . . . farewell *Apollo* and the Muses!" It is a prophetic cry, and we shall hear it again in the age of Wagner and Richard Strauss.

The critical language of Rymer and his contemporaries is no longer that of our own usage. But the controversies in which they engaged are with us still. For since the seventeenth century, the history of drama has been inseparable from that of critical theory. It is to demolish an old theory or prove a new one that many of the most famous of modern dramas have been written. No other literary form has been so burdened with conflicts of definition and purpose. The Athenian and the Elizabethan theatre were innocent of theoretical debate. The *Poetics* are conceived after the fact, and Shakespeare left no manual of style. In the seventeenth century, this innocence and the attendant freedom of imaginative life were forever lost. Henceforth, dramatists become critics and theoreticians. Corneille writes astringent critiques of his own plays; Victor Hugo and Shaw preface their works with programmatic statements and manifestoes. The most important playwrights tend to be those who are also the most articulate of purpose. Dryden, Schiller, Ibsen, Pirandello, Brecht are working within or against explicit theoretic forms. Over all modern drama lies the cast of critical thought. Often it proved too heavy for the underlying structure of imagination. There are many plays since the late seventeenth century more fascinating for the theory they represent than for their art. Diderot, for example, was a third-rate playwright, but his place in dramatic history is of high interest. This dissociation between creative and critical value begins with Dryden. It makes of him the first of the moderns.

His situation was artificial. He was required to restore that national tradition of drama which had been broken by the Cromwellian interlude. At the same time, however, he was compelled to take into account the new fashions and sensibility which the Restoration had brought with it. With the Restoration came a strong neo-classic impulse. Ideas such as those of Rymer were in the ascendant. How, then, could Dryden carry forward from Shakespeare and the Jacobeans? Should the English theatre not look to France from which the court of Charles II had taken so much of its style and colouring? Dryden, who possessed a catholic taste and a critical intelligence of the first rank, was aware of these conflicting claims. He knew that there towered at his back the divided legacy of Sophocles and Shakespeare. To which should he turn in his endeavour to re-establish a national theatre? In seeking to hammer out a compromise solution, Dryden imposed on his own plays a preliminary and concurrent apparatus of criticism. He is the first of the critic-playwrights.

His attempt to reconcile the antique and the Elizabethan ideals led to a complex theory of drama. This theory, moreover, was unstable, and the balance of Dryden's judgement altered perceptibly between the *Essay of Dramatic Poesy*

(1668) and the preface to *Troilus and Cressida* (1679). Dryden's point of departure was itself ambiguous. The bias of his own temper, and the example of Tasso and Corneille, inclined him toward a neo-classic observance of dramatic unities. At the same time, however, Dryden was profoundly responsive to the genius of Shakespeare and felt drawn to the richness and bustle of the Elizabethan stage. He thought that he had found in Ben Jonson a *via media*. In contrast to Rymer and Milton, Dryden was prepared to allow a mixture of tragic and comic modes: "A continued gravity keeps the spirit too much bent; we must refresh it sometimes, as we bait in a journey, that we may go on with greater ease." But the type of drama which resulted from this compromise, the heroic play, followed neither Corneille nor Jonson. It is, in fact, a continuation of the romantic tragicomedies of Beaumont and Fletcher and shows the influence of the dramatic masques of the Stuart and Caroline court.

Yet Dryden was clearly dissatisfied with his own work. In the preface to *All for Love* (1678), he seems determined to restore a Shakespearean tradition. The confines of neo-classical drama "are too little for English tragedy; which requires to be built in a larger compass. . . . In my style I have professed to imitate the divine Shakespeare." But only a year later, he again shifted his critical ground. Much of the essay which precedes Dryden's version of *Troilus and Cressida* is a gloss on the *Poetics* ac-

cording to the strict canons of Boileau and Rymer.
Yet in the midst of the argument, we find praise
for that most unclassical figure, Caliban. The entire essay is a strenuous attempt to show that
Shakespearean drama does accord with Aristotle,
and that there is a necessary conformity between
Aristotelian "rules" and a just rendition of nature.
The inherent instability of such a critical view also
affected Dryden's use of verse. He vacillated between a belief in the natural propriety of Shakespearean blank verse and an adherence to the
rhymed couplets of the French neo-classical theatre. At times, his arguments end in total confusion.
Thus he declared that heroic rhyme was "nearest
Nature, as being the noblest kind of modern verse."

These theoretical doubts and conflicting ideals
are reflected in Dryden's plays. He wrote for the
stage during a period of some thirty years and composed or collaborated in twenty-seven plays. The
finest are the comedies—*Marriage à la Mode*, in
particular. Dryden had many of the virtues of a
great comic writer. He had a quick ear for the social shadings of language. He measured the distance
from the centre of conduct to its eccentric verge—
a distance that is the classic ground for comedy. He
had a robust but tactful insight into the skirmishes
of sexual love. *Marriage à la Mode* has the pace
and cool intelligence of vintage comedy. By comparison, Sheridan's work is coarse-grained. It is in
his treatment of political and tragic motifs that
Dryden failed. The heroic plays live best in parody.

They are great edifices of rhetoric and flamboyant gesture built on a void of feeling. Where we are moved at all, as in certain scenes of *Aureng-Zebe,* the delight is technical. One marvels at Dryden's ability to sustain in rhymed couplets long flights of passion and fury. Nor are the later, "straight" tragedies satisfactory. The finest are other men's work redone. This is a decisive point. The history of great drama is full of inspired plagiarism. The Elizabethans, in particular, had plundered freely wherever their eyes roamed. But what they took, they took as conquerors, not as borrowers. They mastered and transformed it to their own measure with the proud intent of surpassing what had gone before. In Dryden, this is no longer the case. When he "adapts" *Anthony and Cleopatra, Troilus and Cressida,* and *The Tempest,* he does so in complete awareness of the original. He is assuming that the earlier work lives in the remembrance of his public. His own version acts as a critique or variation on a given theme. It is "literary" in the narrow sense. In short, what we have here is pastiche, not re-invention. After the seventeenth century the art of pastiche will play an increasing role in the history of drama. Barren of invention, poets start pouring new sauces over old meats. In dealing with Dryden, we are still worlds away from such miseries as *Mourning Becomes Electra* or Cocteau's *Machine infernale,* but we are on the road.

This does not detract from the virtues of *All for Love.* No other English play after Shakespeare uses blank verse to such advantage. Dryden was a great master of his instrument:

> 'Tis time the World
> Should have a Lord, and know whom to obey.
> We two have kept its homage in suspense,
> And bent the Globe on whose each side we trod,
> Till it was dented inwards: Let him walk
> Alone upon't; I'm weary of my part.
> My Torch is out; and the World stands before me
> Like a black Desert, at th' approach of night.

But behind the grave nobility of these lines, we hear the richer, more close-knit music of Shakespeare's Anthony. Between the two, moreover, there has taken place a perceptible diminution of the pressure of feeling upon language. The effect is that of a skillful transcription for piano of a complete orchestral score. Dryden designated the play as *A Tragedy Written in Imitation of Shakespeare's Style*. Even if he was referring mainly to his use of certain Elizabethan conventions, the touch is ominous. Great theatre is not conceived in imitation.

Dryden saw reality in the light of dramatic encounter and dialectic. In a poem such as *The Hind and the Panther*, we "hear" the thrust and parry of ideas as we do in Ibsen. If Dryden failed to produce plays to match his talent, it is because he was working at a time when the very possibility of serious drama was in doubt. The Athenian and the Elizabethan past threw a lengthening shadow over the future of the dramatic imagination. Dryden was the first of numerous playwrights who found

43

between themselves and the act of theatric invention a psychological barrier. The greatness of past achievement seemed insurmountable. Saintsbury is right when he judges that Dryden never attained that "absolute finality, which makes the reading of all the greatest tragedies, whether Greek or English, a sort of finished chapter of life."

But we may ask in turn: has any tragic dramatist attained such finality since the seventeenth century?

III

In the *Essay of Dramatic Poesy*, Dryden remarked that "no French plays, when translated, have, or ever can succeed on the English stage." He was referring to French neo-classical tragedy, and to this day his judgement remains in force. Yet the fact itself is startling and it poses one of the most difficult problems in literary history. To an educated Frenchman it is a self-evident truth that Corneille and Racine are among the master poets of the world. A critic as broadly civilized as Brunetière can say that a study of drama must include the Spanish seventeenth century and the Elizabethans; but a study of tragedy need concern itself only with the Greeks and the French classicists. The *alexandrin* in which Corneille and Racine wrote their plays has given to French speech some of its strong yet delicate bone structure and to French public life much of its rhetorical cadence. The romantics tried to pull Corneille and Racine off the pedestal from which they dominate the French inner landscape. But they failed, and in retrospect the war whoops of Victor Hugo and the epigrams of Gautier read like the invectives which frightened schoolboys scrawl on monuments. Comparing Racine with Shakespeare, André Gide, by no means a chauvinist, reversed the judgement which Stendhal had made in his romantic period. He felt that the author of *Phèdre* should be preferred over the author of *Hamlet* as the more total dramatic poet. Gide meant by this that in Elizabethan drama the poetry is often in excess of the action. In Racine nothing whatever is extraneous to the tragic purpose.

But the wine will not travel. Outside France the enjoyment of Corneille and Racine is generally reserved to individual poets and scholars. *Le Cid*, *Horace, Phèdre*, or *Athalie* are performed occasionally, but as museum pieces rather than living theatre. In what foreign literature has French classicism acted as a shaping force? No body of work of comparable importance and intrinsic splendour has been so parochial in its field of action. This cannot be a matter only of poor translation. Great literature continually crosses frontiers, even in the guise of parody or misunderstanding. The *Oresteia, Hamlet,* and *Faust* are world possessions although their essential poetry is untranslatable. The elements of plot, character, and argument seem to retain sufficient power to "come across" in languages alien or inferior to the original. Even a prose version in modern speech of *Antigone* or *Macbeth* holds the imagination spellbound. No doubt the absence of physical action in French classical tragedy places the entire burden of meaning on language. But this is true also of much of Greek drama. It is difficult to believe that there should be in French verse an inherent resistance to translation. True, all good poetry can only be approximated when it is transposed into another langauge. But Stefan George and Rilke have shown how beautifully some of the most national of French poetry can be rendered into German, a language whose own habits of syntax are totally different. Or consider the recent advance into English of the exotic, fluid style of that much overrated poet, St. John Perse.

In his *Introduction à la poésie française*, Thierry Maulnier argues that French poetry is more remote than any other from universal elements of folklore and vernacular. It uses material refined by preceding literary tradition. The predominant matter of French poetry is poetry which has gone before. It is art addressing itself to art. The medium is rigorously pure and abstract, and it has beneath it none of the rich soil of myth and archaic feeling which make *Oedipus*, *King Lear*, or *Faust* resonant beyond their geographic and temporal borders.

But even if we allow for the special austerity of French poetic practice, why is it that actual per-

47

formances of Corneille and Racine are so rarely convincing outside the framework of the Comédie Française? *Cinna* and *Iphigénie* require extreme stylization, but so does a performance of Sophocles or of Mozart's operas. Dryden believed that the plays of Corneille were too rhetorical. The London audience wanted action on the stage. But there are many examples of "inactive" drama which have held their grip on the imagination. There is no less action in *Britannicus*, for example, than in the plays of Euripides, and no more rhetoric than in those of Schiller.

The problem lies deeper. French literature has shaped much of western sensibility. The *Essays* of Montaigne, Rousseau's *Confessions*, and *Madame Bovary* are in the general blood stream. All of us are, in some measure, descendants of Voltaire. But that body of work which the French themselves regard as supreme remains a national rather than a universal possession.

Many reasons are given for this. It is argued that the art of Corneille and Racine depends more than that of other playwrights on a special political and social milieu. Only in France have certain of the necessary conditions of understanding survived. General de Gaulle speaks the language of *Horace*, and when he offers to his adversaries a "peace of the brave," he is making a gesture familiar to the statecraft of Racine. Elsewhere in western culture these modes of rhetoric have not endured. Outside the Comédie Française, the perspectives of neo-classic tragedy seem terribly dated. But why should a comparable argument not pertain to Shakespeare? It is difficult to assert that the world of the Elizabethans is more alive in ours than is that of Louis XIV. The question is more intricate. The great moments in Corneille and Racine are the ones which fare worst in translation. The most sensitive translation, for example, can get nowhere with the famous injunction in *Horace: qu'il mourût*. The French language and the French style of life, which is closely related to it, include a range of pomp and grandiloquence which other cultures do not share. French solemnity becomes English pompousness and German rant.

In Racine, the case is somewhat different. His supreme effects are obtained by deliberate "thinning out" of all superfluous matter. It is because the stage is so naked that Phèdre's use of a chair conveys such intense disturbance. But it is the superfluous elements in drama—the excess emotion, the stage business, the humour, the melodramatic gestures—that travel best. The gorgeous claptrap of Rostand has enchanted audiences to whom Racine is inaccessible.

But even this difficulty—and no doubt it accounts for much of the isolation of French classical drama—has been surmounted in comparable cases. The sobriety of Greek tragedy or the surface calm of Goethe's *Torquato Tasso* have not proved a barrier to audiences schooled in more robust theatrical traditions. Why should an audience who are willing to abide by the conventions of immobility in the *Three Sisters* balk at the lack of sound and fury in *Phèdre* or *Bérénice?* Perhaps French neo-classicism came too near its ideals. Perhaps we neglect Racine because we can turn directly to Euripides.

We say "Corneille and Racine" because the dates say so and the schoolbooks, but we are wrong. We should not bracket two poets whom personal outlook and their conception of drama kept severely apart. Criticism has a weakness for neat appositions: Lope de Vega–Calderón, Goethe–Schiller. It supposes analogies where there are, in fact, sharp edges of difference. The reasons why Racine is difficult of access do not really apply to Corneille. The two writers differ in sensibility and in dramatic technique. We must learn to keep them distinct.

Corneille was of the theatre, *un homme de théâtre,* which Racine emphatically was not. Corneille was a natural dramatist who did not regard the artifice and flummery of the stage as an affront to poetic dignity. He was a provincial whose *terroir* remained Rouen and not Paris. He brought to the Parisian scene an old-fashioned savour of plain dealing. Set beside the swift, bending rapier of Racine, Corneille gives the aspect of a massive walking stick. His plays, moreover, did not originate in a formal or theoretic vision. They represent a concurrence of learned, professional, and popular theatric traditions. There is a Senecan element which carries over from the late decades of the sixteenth century (Corneille makes his provincial debut around 1625). This Senecan trait has persisted in French drama. The metallic resonance and ceremonious cruelty of the Senecan theatre live again in Montherlant. It accorded also with the role of Spain in the French imagination of the seventeenth century. When Corneille came to Paris, Spain and Spanish fashions were the rage. Paradoxically, the French-Spanish war gave to the Castilian tone an even greater prestige than hitherto. This fascination, moreover, has never ceased. The *Cid* is only an early example of a brilliant lineage which extends to *Don Juan*, *Hernani*, *Ruy Blas*, Claudel's *Le Soulier de satin* and Montherlant's *Le Maître de Santiago*. To the Senecan tradition and the habit of looking toward Spanish drama, Corneille brought his own knowledge of the provincial stage. No doubt he knew the work of the theatrical troupes which toured France, performing at fairs and on festive occasions. These kept sharply alive forms of pre-literary drama which can be traced back to medieval farce and to the improvisations of the *commedia dell' arte*. The lesson of vivacious action and stringent repartee was not lost on the future author of *Le Menteur* and *Rodogune*.

One must join to these elements the fact of a flourishing Parisian theatre. Today, only specialists ever glance at one or another of the six hundred plays reputedly written by Alexandre Hardy. But Hardy was no mere hack. He embodied that part of the baroque which is a kind of pure, joyous energy. His range is fairly described by the repertoire of the Players in *Hamlet*: "tragedy, comedy, history, pastoral, pastoral-comical, historical-pastoral, tragical-historical, tragical-comical-historical-pastoral; scene indivisible, or poem unlimited." His dominant style is that of baroque romance. Most of his plays are made up of wild imbroglios and rely shamelessly on the use of stage machinery to bring off fantastic mythological and scenic effects. But Hardy contrived a certain poetry of action and can, at his best, be compared with Calderón or the more artful practices of Beaumont and Fletcher.

Corneille's arrival in Paris at the time when Hardy's star was beginning to pale marks a parting of the ways in the history of European drama. Corneille might have chosen to carry on in the manner of his exuberant predecessors, a manner close to the natural mode of his talent, rather than put his art at the service of the new classicism. One can plausibly argue that had he done so, the French theatre would have taken a richer and more universal course. In the stagecraft of Hardy there is implicit the kind of drama in which the tragic and the comic, the realistic and the fantastic, the poetic and the prosaic, can coexist. French neo-classicism denies itself this duality and spaciousness. It gained a marvellous economy of form and purity of language, but they were bought at the cost of a great sum of life. The roots of neo-classicism, moreover, were as much political as literary. The world of Hardy is that of declining feudalism. It reflects the mutinous, quixotic gaiety of the aristocrats who, during the *Fronde*, delivered a final challenge to the centralized power of the modern state. The vision of neo-classical drama is that forged by Richelieu and imposed by Mazarin: there had to be order in life as in art.

In the theatre of Corneille, the non-classical tradition is nearly always present below the surface. His first tragedy, *Médée*, ends in baroque style, with Medea winging off on her dragon-chariot and Jason committing suicide on stage. After the *Cid*, Corneille took no such liberties. But even the mature poet experimented with forms of drama more open and "impure" than those of official classical doctrine. *Don Sanche d'Aragon* is characteristic of Corneille's natural bent. Part tragicomedy, part heroic pastoral, it is a play unlike any other in the classic repertoire (one finds nothing quite like it before Kleist and the *Prinz von Homburg*). In the late Corneille, the return toward the complicated intrigues of baroque drama is accentuated. In a real sense, his greatest work, the row of severe tragedies from the *Cid* to *Polyeucte*, was achieved against the grain.

None of this is relevant to Racine. Setting aside one of his early plays, we find in him little trace of the Senecan tradition. He looked neither to Spain nor to Hardy and the baroque theatre. The ideal of classic order was native to his genius.

It was the celebrated "quarrel of the *Cid*" which compelled Corneille to become a master of classic form. In itself, this piece of literary cabal is of no importance. Critics will always be jealous of poets and find elaborate reasons for their acrimony. But Corneille's harriers drove him away from the natural direction of his dramatic talent toward more exacting ideals. In the finest of Corneillian drama there is an unmistakable tension: the instinct for involved intrigue and tragicomic solutions seems to press against the confining barriers of neo-classic tragedy.

Corneille was too proud an artist to spend time refuting the quibbles which the neo-Aristotelians urged against the *Cid*. He withdrew to Rouen. The manoeuvre is characteristic of him; it is Antaeus touching the earth to regain strength. In Rouen, he conceived a play of utmost unity and nakedness of action. *Horace* is a brilliant refutation of Corneille's academic critics. But it is more, for in it the poet hit upon the theme which was to dominate his creative life: the theme of Rome. In his character and upbringing, there was the strong Latin trait of post-renaissance humanism. Corneille realized, moreover, that Roman history could be made illustrative of the political conditions which prevailed during the late years of Louis XIII and at the beginning of the autocracy of Louis XIV. Like Machiavelli and Montesquieu, he made of Rome an explicit counterpart to contemporary history. In an encomium addressed to Mazarin in 1644, Corneille built an elaborate conceit on the analogies between France and Rome. He saw in

royal France the direct inheritor of the dignities
of imperial and papal Rome:

> C'est toi, grand Cardinal, âme au-dessus de
> l'homme,
> Rare don qu'à la France ont fait le ciel et Rome,
> C'est toi, dis-je, ô héros, ô coeur vraiment romain,
> Dont Rome en ma faveur vient d'emprunter la
> main.[1]

It is fair to say that Corneille envisioned Rome with
something of the imaginative intensity which we
find in Dante.

The Rome motif dominated the dramas of Corneille from *Horace* to *Suréna*. These plays constitute the main body of political tragedy in western
literature. In Shakespeare, there are tragedies with
a strongly marked political background, but there
is not, I think, a complete realization of the tragic
nature of political power. Modern critics have read
into Shakespeare complex political insights, and in
certain plays, such as *Measure for Measure* and
Coriolanus, the bending force of politics upon human lives is closely observed. But in the major part
of Shakespearean drama, the conception of politics
is not far removed from medieval thought, and the
treatment of political action is subordinate to that
of the individual dramatic characters. Thus Shakespearean kings project onto a larger canvas of pub-

---

[1] 'Tis you, great Cardinal, soul more than human,
Rare gift to France from heaven and from Rome,
'Tis you, I say, O spirit truly Roman,
Through whom this bounty came to me from Rome.

lic affairs their private conflicts and ambitions. The actions of Henry V are private vivacities and awakenings magnified to a scale of national war. What matters is the psychological ripening of Prince Hal into a mature king. It is himself he seeks to govern in the act of kingship. *Richard II* is a kind of passion play, a meditation on the vices of the poetic temper when it is exposed to the seductions of material power. The vision of the play is allegoric, and perhaps for that very reason references to Elizabethan politics could be read into the plot. The conflict is rendered entirely through the personal clash between the king and Bolingbroke. It is a feudal tournament enlarged. Richard III casts his foul shadow across the body politic. But the affair is one of private lust and personal hatreds. It has political relevance only because the individuals concerned are of royal blood. The War of the Roses is seen entirely in terms of dynastic antagonism; Shakespeare hardly hints at a larger economic or political confrontation.

Corneille, on the contrary, possessed a modern grasp of the autonomous nature of political life. And he had struck upon a central truth: politics are a translation of rhetoric into action. Like Pascal, Corneille was haunted by the destructive role of rhetoric in political affairs. The personages of Corneillian drama literally talk themselves into irreconcilable hatreds. The formal pronouncement (the *tirade*) draws the mind into excessive rigour. Words carry us forward toward ideological confrontations

from which there is no retreat. This is the root
tragedy of politics. Slogans, clichés, rhetorical abstractions, false antitheses come to possess the mind
(the "Thousand Year Reich," "Unconditional Surrender," the "class war"). Political conduct is no
longer spontaneous or responsive to reality. It
freezes around a core of dead rhetoric. Instead of
making politics dubious and provisional in the manner of Montaigne (who knew that principles are
endurable only when they are tentative), language
encloses politicians in the blindness of certainty or
the illusion of justice. The life of the mind is nar-
rowed or arrested by the weight of its eloquence.
Instead of becoming masters of language, we become its servants. And that is the damnation of
politics. Corneille knew exactly how this process
takes place. No dramatist is his equal in rendering
the "feel," the complication, and the cancerous vitality of political conflict. Only Tacitus can rival
Corneille in showing how men are embedded in the
constricting, mind-clouding matter of political circumstance.

He achieved his particular mastery at the first
stroke, in Act V of *Horace*. In point of theatric design, this entire act is unnecessary (the main conflict has been resolved and the murder of Camille
is a gratuitous outrage). But it demonstrates how
political rhetoric can drive out humane reason. Horace has become a kind of public colossus. His language is sonorous and hollow like that of trumpets.
At every moment, he invokes heroic abstractions in

order to justify the destruction of life. When he offers to kill himself in order to expiate his crime, suicide is given the dignity of patriotism:

Permettez, ô grand roi, que de ce bras vainqueur
Je m'immole à ma gloire, et non pas à ma soeur.[2]

The juxtaposition of the abstract notion (*gloire*) against the reality of human life (*ma soeur*) is profoundly Corneillian.

Next came *Cinna*, a play which is primarily an analysis of the strategies of absolutism. Napoleon admired it for its fidelity to political truth. He heard in it the imperial note. In *Horace*, Rome is archaic; in *Cinna*, it is Augustan. The change in historical time is important. Henceforth, Corneille dramatized incidents from the period of the Civil Wars and the late empire. And he brought into the repertoire of the imagination a new geography: Syria in *Rodogune*, the Lombard kingdom in *Pertharite*, Parthia in *Suréna*. Corneillian drama has a natural bias toward obscure intrigue and violent disaster. The history of the declining empire and its bizarre settings gave Corneille precisely the kind of plots he needed.

Criticism (with the brilliant exception of Brasillach) has ignored Corneille's later plays. Yet our age, in which political rhetoric has wrought so much havoc, should recognize the force of Corneille's vision. *Pompée, Nicomède, Sertorius,* and

---

[2] Allow, great king, that I atonement make
Not for my sister's but my glory's sake.

Suréna are major accomplishments. There is no political drama more acute or tough-minded.

The theme of *Pompée* is identified with the origins of French tragedy. It had already been dramatized by Garnier, Chaulmer, Jodelle, and Benserade. Corneille chose a most difficult approach: Pompey is slain at the outset and never appears on stage. But his presence dominates every moment of the play (even as the shadow of Hannibal falls over the whole of *Nicomède*). "As for the style," writes Corneille, "it is loftier than in any other of my poetic compositions, and the verse is, undeniably, richer in pomp (*pompeux*) than any I have ever produced." There is more than a Joycean pun in the association between *Pompée* and *pompeux*. The idea of pomp does not commend itself to modern usage. But to Corneille, the term conveys the values of high rhetoric, of sonority, of ceremonious bearing. The implied conception of drama is closer to that of Handel's oratorios than it is to the modern stage. But that is natural, for it belongs to a world in which pomp, whether at the royal court of France or in the religious eloquence of Bossuet, was a virtue.

The tragic action in *Pompée* derives from the manner in which the characters assume abstract positions and abide by them to the point of ruin. Their free will is mastered and corrupted by political rhetoric. In *Cinna*, Augustus makes a famous boast: "Je suis maître de moi comme de l'univers." In fact, he is servant to the heroic style. In *Pompée*, we are shown how the outward elegance and apparent logic of the grand verbal manner can conceal or glorify even the shallowest and most murderous of political schemes.

The play is built around a series of orations and formal rhetorical encounters. Like the set arias in eighteenth-century opera, these long and ceremonious flights of language are the principal mode of dramatic action. Events are not acted; they are recounted. Thus the neo-classical ideal of propriety —horrible or bloody deeds must not be shown upon the stage—is relevant to the entire drama. No doubt there are situations and motifs to which a theatre of language rather than of action is inappropriate (in Corneille's more baroque plays the incessant recital of horrendous events becomes funny). But the kind of theatre in which language is supreme, accords precisely with political tragedy. We must learn to listen to these plays as we would to music; we must be audience rather than spectator.

The opening scene is superb. Ptolemy and his councilors are debating on how to receive the vanquished and fugitive Pompey. The dominant chord is struck with cruel, metallic insistence:

> le droit de l'épée
> Justifiant César, a condamné Pompée.[3]

"The right of the sword" against the claims of humanity. Photin argues that Pompey must be mur-

---

[3] the right of the sword,
Justifying Caesar, has doomed Pompey.

dered, but adds that his view is animated by no personal hatred: "J'en veux à sa disgrace, et non à sa personne." The evil of politics lies precisely in this separation of the human person from the abstract cause or the strategic necessity. Photin declares: "La justice n'est pas une vertu d'Etat." And nearly always in Corneille the word is capitalized. "Reason of state" is held in spurious balance against individual life. The term has its German equivalent, *Staatsraison*, but there is no exact concordance for it in the more sceptical and provisional grammar of English politics. Ptolemy yields to murderous counsel and invokes one of the ever recurring clichés which politicians use to justify their crimes, "the stream of history": "Et cédons au torrent qui roule toutes choses." When rulers begin talking of "streams" and "things," humanity has lapsed from both their language and their intent.

This kind of scene is rare in English drama. We find it, I think, only in the Roman plays of Ben Jonson. The dramatic tension is extreme, but derives entirely from cold and intricate argument. We come nearest to it in the Infernal Consultation in Book II of *Paradise Lost*. Corneille and Milton, unlike Shakespeare, have a direct, nearly sensuous apprehension of the tone of politics in high places.

The entire play exhibits Corneille's grasp of the Roman temper. Asked by Caesar what he thinks of Cleopatra, Anthony replies: "Et si j'étais César, je la voudrais aimer." But the most memorable figure is Cornélie, Pompey's avenging widow. In her attitude toward Caesar there is a touch of that *galanterie* which prevailed between adversaries during the battles of the *Fronde*. Cornélie is sworn to Caesar's destruction; but they are now in Egypt, and because they are Romans they experience a feeling of solidarity nearly as powerful as their mutual hatred. Their final meeting is one of the great splendours of neo-classical drama. Divided between enmity and admiration, Cornélie bids defiance and farewell to the victorious Caesar. Her closing speech must be studied as a whole. It shows how the forms of rhetoric can concentrate the utmost of dramatic feeling. Cornélie enters bearing an urn with the ashes of murdered Pompey:

> Je la porte en Afrique; et c'est là que j'espère
> Que les fils de Pompée, et Caton, et mon père,
> Secondés par l'effort d'un roi plus généreux,
> Ainsi que la justice auront le sort pour eux.
> C'est là que tu verras sur la terre et sur l'onde
> Les débris de Pharsale armer un autre monde;
> Et c'est là que j'irai, pour hâter tes malheurs,
> Porter de rang en rang ces cendres et mes pleurs.
> Je veux que de ma haine ils reçoivent des règles,
> Qu'ils suivent au combat des urnes au lieu d'aigles;
> Et que ce triste objet porte en leur souvenir
> Les soins de le venger, et ceux de te punir.
> Tu veux à ce héros rendre un devoir suprême;
> L'honneur que tu lui rends rejaillit sur toi-même:
> Tu m'en veux pour témoin; j'obéis au vainqueur;
> Mais ne présume pas toucher par là mon coeur.
> La perte que j'ai faite est trop irréparable;
> La source de ma haine est trop inépuisable;

A l'égal de mes jours je la ferai durer;
Je veux vivre avec elle, avec elle expirer.
Je t'avouerai pourtant, comme vraiment Romaine,
Que pour toi mon estime est égale à ma haine;
Que l'une et l'autre est juste, et montre le pouvoir,
L'une de ta vertu, l'autre de mon devoir;
Que l'une est généreuse, et l'autre intéressée,
Et que dans mon esprit, l'une et l'autre est forcée.
Tu vois que ta vertu, qu'en vain on veut trahir,
Me force de priser ce que je dois haïr:
Juge ainsi de la haine où mon devoir me lie,
La veuve de Pompée y force Cornélie.
J'irai, n'en doute point, au sortir de ces lieux,
Soulever contre toi les hommes et les dieux,
Ces dieux qui t'ont flatté, ces dieux qui m'ont
            trompée,
Ces dieux qui dans Pharsale ont mal servi Pompée
Qui, la foudre à la main, l'ont put voir égorger;
Ils connaîtront leur faute et le voudront venger.
Mon zèle, à leur refus, aidé de sa mémoire,
Te saura bien sans eux arracher la victoire;
Et quand tout mon effort se trouvera rompu,
Cléopâtre fera ce que je n'aurai pu.[4]

[4] I carry this to Lybia; there, I hope,
My father, Cato, and the valiant troupe
Of Pompey's sons, to a brave king allied,
Shall find both fate and justice on their side.
Mark well, and you will see on earth and brine
Fresh legions rising from Pharsalia's ruin;
From rank to rank, to hasten your defeat,
I'll show these ashes and my broken heart.
My hatred shall give emblems to our host,
Let urns, not eagles, ride upon their crest;
Let this grim object keep before their eyes
A double task: to venge and to chastise.
You wish to pay this hero final due;

63

No change in our habits of feeling and language can detract from the magnificence of this oration. Only a complete master of dramatic statement could have brought on the natural yet startling progress from defiance to esteem or gathered all the complex strands of argument into that final taunt. Politics has produced no greater poetry.

> All honour done him merely honours you.
> At your command, I must attend these shows,
> But do not fancy they shall calm my woes.
> The loss I bear exceeds all remedy,
> The wells of hatred never shall run dry,
> And I will hate so long as I draw breath:
> My life be hatred—hatred be my death.
> Yet, being Roman, I cannot deny
> That my esteem equals my enmity.
> Either is just; together they proclaim
> Your virtue's merit and my duty's claim.
> Hate is my office; praise I freely grant;
> To both these passions must my heart consent.
> Your greatness, which these idle plots would mar,
> Makes me give praise to what I must abhor;
> My duty binds me, Caesar, to my fate:
> 'Tis Pompey's widow bids Cornelia hate.
> Doubt not that when I leave this shore
> I go to summon men and gods to war—
> Those selfsame gods who flatter or deride,
> Who at Pharsalia turned from Pompey's side,
> Who saw him slaughtered and no lightning sped,
> Those gods may sorrow and avenge the deed.
> My zeal, enhanced by Pompey's high renown,
> Should the gods fail me, still shall tear you down;
> And when my force is spent, what I could not,
> Shall wanton Cleopatra bring about.

There is some padding in lines 20–29. Corneille rings rhetorical changes on the contrasting pairs, hatred and esteem, duty and spontaneous feeling. Being in any case a more constrained version, a translation tends to emphasize the momentary weakness

Nicomède (1650) reflects the atmosphere of the *Fronde*. This insurrection marked the final protest of the baroque spirit in politics against modern, centralized statecraft. It was an episode of very real violence, but with an odd note of frivolity. The play exactly renders the aura of intrigue and heroic romance that surrounded the politics of Condé and the Grande Demoiselle. Although the action lies under the shadow of the recent murder of Hannibal, the play is not essentially tragic. It is tragicomedy in the baroque style. But beneath the froth of plot, counterplot, and happy resolution, there is a genuine Corneillian conflict. Once again, *raison d'état* seeks to overthrow natural feeling and grace of heart. These are designated by *galanterie*, a complex, elusive word which implies personal valour, gracious bearing, and the pursuit of love. Flaminius is a cold Roman politician in whom civilized manners are the outward mask of cruelty. Nicomède is a "barbarian" prince and forerunner of the myth of the noble savage. The struggle between them concentrates two areas of feeling: the political and the amorous. This conjunction, or rather the attempt of politics to usurp love, became the major theme of Corneille's late tragedies. Flaminius regards sen-

---

of the original. I have also failed to render the muted ferocity and sarcasm of the final couplet. Cornélie says: "And when all my efforts shall have been repulsed, Cleopatra will accomplish what I could not." She means that Caesar will be undermined and defeated by Cleopatra's seductive and treacherous wiles. But the taunt is not made explicit. Pope would have found precisely the right equivalent.

sual passion as a pure instrument of political and strategic manoeuvre. At times, he foreshadows Laclos and Stendhal in using interchangeably metaphors of military and erotic life. Marriage is a form of dynastic expansion or political alliance. The sexual element is a mere servant to the mind's considered purpose. Nicomède, on the contrary, embodies the integrity of desire. He cannot dissociate the truth of love from a general truth of moral conduct. The one is rooted in the other. Corneille seems to have felt this with a particular vividness. The conditions of his argument differ immensely from those of D. H. Lawrence. but the intent is comparable. The play is centred on the image of fire. Where love is made the agent of political necessity, its fires are literally put out:

> L'amour entre les rois ne fait pas l'hyménée,
> Et les raisons d'Etat plus fortes que ses noeuds,
> Trouvent bien les moyens d'en éteindre les feux.[5]

Behind the duel of the proconsul and the young prince, like a shadow thrown on a wall, Corneille evokes the larger combat between Rome and the unvanquished spirit of Carthage. *Nicomède*, as one French critic has said, is "nearly a masterpiece."

The three plays that followed, *Pertharite*, *Oedipe*, and *La Toison d'or*, were bad failures. Two of them dealt with Greek mythology, and that fact alone

[5] It is not love makes royal marriages,
Reasons of state can loose a lover's knot
And find swift means to put love's fires out.

nearly suffices to account for their deficiencies. Corneille, in whom emotion is cleansed and heightened so that it works upon us as a kind of abstract energy, was never at ease on Greek ground. The Greek myths are too manifold for orderly reduction. *Oedipe* is wide of the mark not only because Corneille encumbered the plot with amorous intrigue, but because the struggle for material power between Oedipus and Creon is seen as the most vital part of the legend. Greece belonged to Racine as Rome to Corneille. There is no more trenchant sign of the difference in the character of the two poets.

In 1662, Corneille returned to his proper sphere. He combined the two elements which had brought him his surest success. *Sertorius* is a Roman action in a Spanish setting. It is a superb play. Sometimes poetry leaves in the mind a sense of colour; *Sertorius* has a dark redness, as of burnished copper. And its style has precisely the harshness and ornateness of Latin as it was written by poets and rhetoricians in Roman Spain during the late empire. Nowhere was Corneille's imagination in more complete possession of the historical fact. He conceded with wry pride: "Do not look in this play for the pleasures (*les agréments*) which can ensure theatrical success." Once more, we have here a tragedy of politics and military encounter. Having seen it, the great strategist Turenne asked: "Where has Corneille learnt so much about the arts of war?"

Sertorius unfolds relentlessly from the initial

67

premise that "civil war is the reign of crime." And
even more forcibly than in *Nicomède*, the impulses
of love are corrupted by the exactions of power.
Marriage is defined as "un pur effet de noble politique," and we are meant to discern in the word *pur*
the note of sterility. Again, fire is a dominant image
(and we must not forget that in the seventeenth-
century usage of *ardeur* there is still the connotation of literal flame):

> Ce ne sont pas les sens que mon amour consulte:
> Il hait des passions l'impétueux tumulte;
> Et son feu que j'attache aux soins de ma grandeur
> Dédaigne tout mélange avec leur folle ardeur.[6]

Observe how the traditional metaphor of love's fire
is inverted. Viriate claims that she can master the
fire of love and subject it to the sole aim of political
grandeur. She scorns the "mad ardours" of sensual
passion. Yet it is they that are true and humane.
The fires of premeditated, political affection are
cold; they burn only in the mind. Corneille excels
in rendering the false heat, one must nearly say the
chill heat, of ambition. Cunning and the thirst for
political power have their own frozen sensuality.

All the energies of the play gather toward the
meeting of Sertorius and Pompey in Act III. The

[6] The senses are not privy to my love;
  It scorns that tumult in which passions rave;
  Love's fire burns to serve my royal aim
  And does not mingle with a sensual flame.

68

scene magnificently justifies the neo-classical practice of articulating emotion; however violent,
through controlled rhetorical forms. We are shown
on what occasion the actions of the mind may be
given an architectural rather than a dynamic shape.
If only this episode survived from French neo-
classical tragedy, we should be able to discern in
the fragment much of the controlling design. Voltaire set this scene beside the night encounter of
Brutus and Cassius in *Julius Caesar*. The comparison is just, for both are summations of their respective dramatic traditions and the difference between
them is of kind, not of merit. Coleridge asserted
that nothing else in Shakespeare's work impressed
on him as strongly the belief that Shakespeare's
genius was "superhuman"; yet the comparison does
not detract from Corneille. In Brutus' tent, the actual words have around them the resonance of the
unspoken. We hear in them the reverberations of
weariness and concealed grief. In *Sertorius*, all is
said. These eloquent commanders are tacticians of
language in the manner of Cicero and Quintilian.
They marshal their words like legions, lie in ambush
for each other's proposals, and make of poetry an
assault upon reason. When Pompey holds up before Sertorius the image of distant Rome, we know
that he is advancing on the very citadel of his op-
ponent. But the fierce old man parries the blow:

> Je n'appelle plus Rome un enclos de murailles,
> Que ses proscriptions comblent de funérailles;

Ces murs, dont le déstin fut autrefois si beau,
N'en sont que la prison, ou plutôt le tombeau:
Mais, pour revivre ailleurs dans sa première force,
Avec les faux Romains elle a fait plein divorce;
Et, comme autour de moi j'ai tous ses vrais appuis,
Rome n'est plus dans Rome, elle est toute où je
    suis.[7]

The passage distills Corneille's constant meditation on Rome and its timeless majesty. One must be deaf to the pleasures of dramatic verse not to feel its grip. In Shakespeare, the words in their complex groupings accumulate meanings in excess of the actual statement. In Corneille as in Dryden, they signify exactly what they say, but they signify the whole of it. And thus the actual mode of expression has the kind of roundedness and precision which come only when a literary form has been used exhaustively. A Corneillian couplet leaves room neither for doubt nor stray sentiment. The principal tradition of the English poetic style, particularly since the romantic movement, is one of inference. But there is also a poetry of the explicit.

Othon (1664) is a cold piece of work. It recounts a palace intrigue in imperial Rome. The play is of interest only because it sharpened further Cor-

---

[7] Rome is to me more than a close of walls
Which Sylla's blood-laws crowd with burials;
Those walls, whose destiny was once so fair,
Are now Rome's prison—no, its sepulchre.
But to rise elsewhere in its pristine force,
From all false Romans, Rome has sought divorce;
Its true supporters being here at hand,
Rome is no more in Rome—it's where I stand.

neille's vision of the corruption of love through politics. The focal word is *civilité:*

> Mais la civilité n'est qu'amour en Camille,
> Comme en Othon l'amour n'est que civilité.[8]

"Civility" carries the full social and political implications of its root. Where it grows civil, love, which is the most private circumstance of life, grows public and spurious. Civility is a virtue of the mind and not of the heart.

Six years later, Corneille dramatized these contrary values in deliberate rivalry with Racine. Racine's *Bérénice* was first performed on November 21, 1670; *Tite et Bérénice* followed on November 28. Corneille was undeniably routed. Although it is made gentle by the absence of death, *Bérénice* is deeply tragic. The characters sacrifice the quick of their own being to the demands of outward glory and political power. Racine knows, and means us to know, that Bérénice's renunciation of Titus is achieved at too high a cost. Now it is this presumption which Corneille could not honestly accept. His judgement flinched from the implicit scale of values. The celebrated farewell of Bérénice—

> Adieu; servons tous trois d'exemple à l'univers
> De l'amour la plus tendre et la plus malheureuse
> Dont il puisse garder l'histoire douloureuse [9]

[8] In Camille, civility is love disguised,
   In Otho, love is mere civility.
[9] Adieu, let us be emblems to the world
   Of the most tender and ill-fated love
   Of which the tragic story shall survive.

—must have struck him as an abdication both of royalty and good sense. Corneille could not imaginatively penetrate that quality of mind which would renounce an empire for the privacy of love. Hence there is in his play no acute tension. The die is cast in advance. *Tite et Bérénice* is not a tragedy but, as Corneille himself entitled it, a *comédie héroique*. Throughout, Bérénice is concerned more genuinely with her glory than her passion. Even when her departure from Rome is imminent, she declares:

> Grâces au juste ciel, ma gloire en sûreté
> N'a plus à redouter aucune indignité.[1]

And her final statement is brilliantly revealing (both of her character and of Corneille's limitations):

> Votre coeur est à moi, j'y règne; c'est assez.[2]

In Corneillian drama, even the heart is a place for governance. To love is to rule.

But Racine's conception of the primacy of feeling was now in the ascendant. *Pulchérie* is a rearguard action. One cannot defend it as a work of art, but it gives proof of the constancy with which the aging poet clung to his special vision of human affairs. In fact, the play contains the most extreme statement of Corneille's dominant motif—one might nearly say of his obsession. A political marriage is concluded on the express proviso that it be left unconsummated. Power is bought with impo-

[1] Thanks be to heaven, I need have no fear
That on my glory there might be a slur.
[2] Your heart is mine; I rule there; 'tis enough.

tence. It is a cruel and memorable expression of the Corneillian insight into the tragedy of politics.

With *Suréna* (1674), Corneille took leave of the theatre.

It has often been noted that *Suréna* shows a strong awareness of the style and manner of Racine. This is true, but it tells us little of the merit of the play. Although *Suréna* is uneven, I wonder whether it does not come near to being Corneille's masterpiece. It takes from Racine certain tones and cadences of verse, but goes beyond them in a direction which is not that of Racine at all. The key to *Suréna* is its language. While abiding by the syntax of neo-classical French, that concentrated, lucid syntax which will carry over into eighteenth-century prose, Corneille returns to the vocabulary of the late baroque. The play is studded with the terminology of heroism and ornate passion of the poets and romancers who preceded neo-classic drama (*consume, tendresse, soupir, amertume, charmes*). It runs the risks of a certain enervation and preciousness, but in the main the strong articulation of the later grammar gives it the necessary force. The greatest measure of gathered emotion is transmitted through verbs whose infinitive ends in *ir*. The whole play turns on the assertion of Eurydice:

Je veux, sans que la mort ose me secourir,
Toujours aimer, toujours souffrir, toujours mourir.[8]

[8] Scorning the balm of death, 'tis my desire
Always to love, to suffer, to expire.

73

Suréna repeats the words at the end of the first Act:

> Où dois-je recourir,
> O ciel! s'il faut toujours aimer, souffrir, mourir?

They define the progress from love, through suffering, to death. And in the conventions of baroque *galanterie*, it is progress.

In *Suréna*, moreover, Corneille drew close to over-stepping the bounds of the rhymed couplet. The lines have a nervous, fluid movement which seems to carry them beyond their formal ending. They leave a residue of expressive silence in a manner exceedingly rare in French neo-classical drama. Corneille did not always succeed. Sometimes the complex motion—the attempt to maintain a free impulse beneath a rigid surface—produces in the verse a curious sag or concavity. Voltaire observed that there are moments in the play which fall far below Corneille's routine craftsmanship. But the failure arises directly from an effort to transcend the inherent limitations of the *alexandrin*. There is in *Suréna* an undeniable loosening of the heroic style, but that style was no longer appropriate to Corneille's purpose. This, I take it, was the creation of a kind of dramatic elegy—a drama of lament rather than of conflict.

The "softness" of the plot accords with the special quality of the language. At last Corneille allows love its long deferred supremacy. Eurydice, whose name is itself an emblem of the death-mastering power of love, reverses the traditional dialectic of

Corneillian tragedy. Her passion proves more tena-
cious than the demands of politics: "Mon amour
est trop fort pour cette politique." She must part
from Suréna, but the bond between them is intact.
Even in death the conceits of love are supreme.
Suréna falls with three arrows through his heart.
That is an ancient symbol of sensual ardour, and it
may be that Corneille was playing here, as do the
Elizabethans, on the dual insinuation of "death,"
the literal and the erotic. Eurydice follows her beloved in a movement as solemn and controlled as
that of a courtly dance:

Non, je ne pleure point, madame, mais je meurs.[4]

The tragic shock is deliberately muted by the profound elegance of the gesture.

Suréna is very nearly a great play. Perhaps the
action is too slight to sustain the elaboration and
the complexity of the poetic means. But it does
convey a kind of musical enchantment and autumnal light which are found nowhere else in neo-
classic art. And whereas Racine had no real successors, there are clear echoes to Suréna in the great
dialogues of unavailing love in the theatre of
Claudel.

Of all modern poets, Racine took most naturally to
the closed, neo-classical form of drama. There are
biographical and social reasons for it. Like Goethe,

[4] I weep not, madam, but I die.

Racine was a court poet who accepted the caste values of the aristocratic milieu. He worked for the stage, but not with it. There is the immense difference between him and Corneille or Molière. Racine is one of those great dramatic poets (Byron was another) who had no natural liking for the theatre. The history of Racine's relations to the stage is one of increasing fastidiousness. He moved from public drama to private performance and then to silence. In accepting the post of historiographer royal, he followed his own temper and social bias.

Racine chose the purest, most elegant, most uncompromising style of drama so as to achieve the greatest possible independence from the material contingencies of stagecraft. His sensitivity to adverse criticism and his religious scruples regarding the morality of the theatre were a part of his essential fastidiousness. Always in Racine's mind was the ideal of a ritual or court theatre, of a theatre of solemn occasion, as there had been in Athens. He tended to identify himself with the Greek tragedians not because of any particular affinity in world view, but because the theatre for which he imagined that Sophocles and Euripides had written had possessed a unique dignity. This is the thought expressed in the Preface to *Iphigénie*:

I have recognized with pleasure, by virtue of the effect which all that I have imitated from either Homer or Euripides has had on our stage, that reason and good sense are the same in all centuries. Parisian taste showed itself to be in accord with that of Athens.

76

Racine fully realized his ideal in *Esther* and *Athalie*, plays not even intended for performance in the usual sense. Acted by the young ladies of Saint-Cyr in 1689, *Esther* reached the open theatre only in 1721; presented in Mme. de Maintenon's rooms at Versailles in 1691, *Athalie* was not publicly performed by the Comédie Française until 1716. Despite their special character, these are the plays in which Racine's art is most deliberately expressed. Their use of the chorus is the outcome of a theory of drama implicit in the entirety of Racine's work.

The art of *Bérénice*, *Iphigénie*, and *Phèdre* solicits perfect attention, not a strong disorder of emotion or the spectator's identification with the action. For poor creatures like us to identify ourselves with these royal and ceremonious personages would be psychologically stupid and socially impudent. They are of rarer stuff than we. Thus we may say that Racine, like Brecht, is deliberately seeking to deepen the gulf between audience and stage. "This is a play," says Brecht when defining his famous concept of alienation (*Verfremdung*); "it is not real life at all or intended to be." "This is a tragic drama," says Racine; "it is purer and more significant than ordinary life; it is an image of what life might be like if it were lived at all times on a plane of high decorum and if it were at all instants fully responsive to the obligations of nobility." Both dramatists require a severe distinction between realness and realism.

This is the key to Racine's unworried, persuasive use of the unities. Unity of time and place were to him a natural condition of drama, whereas they had been to Corneille a tightrope on which to perform perilous acrobatics. The disorder of life, the material grossness of things, cannot be excluded from human affairs for more than twenty-four hours at a stretch. Even a Bérénice or a Phèdre must surrender to the vulgarity of sleep. We cannot make of more than one room at a time a place appropriate to the solemnity and purity of tragic action. Take a whole house and somewhere in it there is bound to be laughter. Outside the doors of the Racinian stage life waits with all its chaotic bustle. When the characters walk through those doors, they release their pent-up agony. We may imagine them screaming or weeping. The close of *Bérénice* should be acted quickly, as if in a race against an approaching thunderstorm. The wires are stretched to the breaking point, and at the fall of the curtain they will snap. We cannot conceive of Bérénice enduring an instant longer the suppressed agony of her spirit. She must hurry out.

Or to put it figuratively: the space of action in the dramas of Racine is that part of Versailles in the immediate vision of the king. Here decorum, containment, self-control, ritual, and total attentiveness are enforced. Even the uttermost of grief or hope must not destroy the cadence of formal speech and gesture. But just beyond the door, life plummets back to its ordinary brutishness and spontaneity. Racine is the historian of the king's chamber; Saint-Simon is the historian of the anteroom which is the world. Both are great dramatists.

Bérénice embodies the essential design of Racine's poetics. There occurs in it more than a renunciation of love. The tragedy arises from a refusal of all disorder; a final elegance of action is achieved at the expense of life. The miracle is that so special and closed a view of art and conduct should have produced some of the most superbly exciting drama known to literature. Vast energies are compressed to a flash point and then released with an explosive, murderous finality. The close of *Phèdre* or *Athalie* has in it as much fury as the battle in *Macbeth* or the massacre in *Hamlet*. The difference is simply this: the great bang takes place off stage. It is related to us in the formal *récit* of the messenger or confidant. But that does not make it a jot less exciting. On the contrary; the outward formality of the recital conveys the ferocity of the event. It impels our imaginings toward the scene of disaster:

> Déjà de traits en l'air s'élevait un nuage;
> Déjà coulait le sang, prémices du carnage.[5]

Precisely because Shakespearean and romantic dramas show the deed of violence on stage, they lack this particular mode of conveying the magnitude of a crisis. It is nearly a musical device; the echo suggests the immensity of the distant clamour.

[5] A cloud of javelins already rose in the air;
Already blood was flowing, first fruit of carnage.

The art of Racine is that of calculated tension. All manner of images spring to mind: the tension between the inherent repose of marble and the swiftness of depicted motion in Greek sculpture, the flying buttress, the in-pent power of a steel spring. Racine is of that family of genius which works most easily within restrictive conventions. The sense of drama we experience when listening to the Goldberg variations is of a related order: intense force being channelled through narrow, complex apertures. A controlling poise is maintained between the cool severity of the technique and the passionate drive of the material. Racine poured molten metal into his unbending forms. At every moment, one expects the structure to yield under stress, but it holds, and this expectation is itself conducive to excitement. Sometimes the preoccupation with structure can lead to artifice. The role of Eriphile in *Iphigénie* is rendered necessary by the counterpoint and balance of forces. But it is theatrically and psychologically unconvincing. In Racine, this kind of failure is rare. He is nearly always able to accord the design of tragic action to the demands of classic form.

Racine's four greatest plays are studies of women: *Bérénice*, *Iphigénie*, *Phèdre*, and *Athalie*. *Bérénice* is a magnificent but special case, for in it the quality of the tragic is muted. Terror is kept in a minor key. It was in his two Euripidean dramas and in *Athalie* that Racine set himself the most difficult task. In each of these three plays there is tremendous tension between the classic, rational form of the actual drama and the daemonic, irrational character of the fable. Racine opposed a secular mode of art to a world of archaic or sacred myth. It is here, I feel, that his Jansenism is important. At the heart of the Jansenist position is the effort to reconcile the life of reason to the mysteries of grace. This effort, sustained at fearful psychological cost, produced two tragic images of man, that of Racine and that of Pascal. In Pascal, an austere, violent compulsion toward reason plays against a constant apprehension of the mystery of God. In Racine, the language and gestures of a Cartesian society are required to enact sacred and mythological fables. We could not be further from the world of Corneille. The essential myth of Corneillian drama is that of history. Racine invokes the presence of Jehovah and the Minoan sun-god. He releases archaic terrors upon a court theatre.

In *Iphigénie*, there is still a measure of compromise, an attempt to evade some of the implications of irrationalism. Racine suggests that the Athenian view of miracles and supernatural happenings was already conventional, that "reason" and "good sense" made the same allowances in Athens as they did in Paris when confronted with the ancient materials of legend. Racine's predilection for Euripides is founded on just this assumption. He supposed that Euripidean *skepsis* and the stylization of mythology in Euripidean drama could be accounted for by the fact that the poet took a rationalistic view of his material. In a very real sense, the distance from the Aeschylean vision of myth to that of Euripides is greater than that which separates Euripides from Racine. Nevertheless, Racine cannot quite evade the root dilemma. He cannot assume in his audience the necessary sophistication of disbelief. Underlying Racine's handling of myth is a complex convention: ritual and action take place without a necessary implication of belief. It is on our acceptance of this convention that *Iphigénie* depends.

The matter of the play is that of legend. We find ourselves in a world of oracles, daemonic winds, and human sacrifice. The traditional *dénouement* (like that of the Medea plays) is wildly fantastic. Operatic composers and choreographers of the baroque and neo-classical period could handle Iphigenia's wondrous rescue from the altar. Diana descending from the clouds is one of the recurrent feats of seventeenth-century stage machinery. The logic of a musical crescendo or ballet finale justified, indeed required, this kind of climax. But for a psychological dramatist such as Racine the problem is far more difficult. In order to avoid it, he departed from the original myth and from Euripides:

How would it have seemed if I had sullied the stage with the horrid murder of someone whom I had shown to be as virtuous and amiable as Iphigenia? And how would it have seemed if I had resolved my tragedy by means of a goddess and a piece of stage machinery, and by a transformation which may still have found some credence in the age of Euripides but would have appeared to us as too absurd and incredible?

Later in his preface, Racine adds that the modern spectator will not accept miracles. But this evades the issue. If the audience is prepared to accept the mythical conditions of the play as a whole, why should it balk at the final motif of supernatural intervention? Moreover, in Ulysses' narration of Iphigenia's rescue, all the elements of miracle re-enter by the back door:

> Les dieux font sur l'autel entendre le tonnerre,
> Les vents agitent l'air d'heureux frémissements,
> Et la mer leur répond par ses mugissements.
>
> . . . .
>
> Le soldat étonné dit que dans une nue
> Jusque sur le bûcher Diane ets descendue,
> Et croit que, s'élevant au travers de ses feux,
> Elle portait au ciel notre encens et nos voeux.[6]

Note how adroitly Racine plays the game of reason; the miracle has been reported by a simple soldier. Ulysses, in turn, recounts it. He does not vouch for its veracity. It seems to be a matter of degree of plausibility. Racine retains the substance of the legend and discards some of its more spectacular im-

---

[6] The gods make thunder growl above the altar,
  The winds quicken the air to joyous motion,
  And hear the roaring answer of the ocean.
  . . . .
  The amazèd soldier says that in a cloud
  Diana lit upon the burning wood,
  And claims that rising through the very fire
  She bore aloft our incense and our prayer.

probabilities. But at a price; Iphigenia is saved, for what are essentially reasons of decorum and *galanterie*. In her place, Eriphile finds death. But the consequent absurdities of the plot (Eriphile's descent from Helen and Theseus, her passion for Achilles) are far more disturbing than the affront to reason implicit in Diana's appearance from the clouds. Thus Racine's solution to the problem of the irrational in *Iphigénie* is an unsatisfactory compromise. He was still trying to reconcile the claims of good sense and Cartesian logic to those of mythology. The transition from *Iphigénie* to *Phèdre*, three years later, marks the end of such conciliation.

Phèdre is the keystone in French tragic drama. The best that precedes it seems in the manner of preparation; nothing which comes after surpasses it. It is *Phèdre* which makes one flinch from Coleridge's judgement that Shakespeare's superiority to Racine is a flat truism. The genius of the play is specific to itself (it defines the reaches of its own magnificent purpose), yet it is representative in the highest measure of the entire neo-classic style. The supremacy of *Phèdre* is exactly commensurate to the greatness of the risks taken. A brutal legend of the madness of love is dramatized in theatric forms which rigorously suppress the possibilities of wildness and disorder inherent in the subject. Nowhere in neo-classic tragedy is the contrast between fable and treatment more drastic. Nowhere is the enforcement of style and unity more complete. Racine imposed the shapes of reason on the archaic blackness of his theme.

He took that theme from Euripides, accepting its whole savagery and strangeness. He made only one significant change. In the legend, Hippolytus is consecrated to extreme chastity. He is a cold, pure hunter who spurns the powers of love. Aphrodite seeks vengeance on her disdainer; hence the catastrophe. This is how Euripides and Seneca presented the myth, and in his *Hippolyte* (1573) Garnier followed closely on their example. Racine, on the contrary, makes of the son of Theseus a shy but passionate lover. He repulses the advances of Phèdre not only because they are incestuous but because he loves elsewhere. The original conception of Hippolytus accords perfectly with the dark quality of the legend; Euripides shows him as a forest creature, drawn from covert and enmeshed in human affairs of which he has no complete grasp. Why should Racine have changed him into a courtier and *galant homme?* Mainly, one supposes, because the image of a royal prince fleeing at the approach of women would have struck the contemporary audience as ridiculous. But that is the only concession Racine makes to the claims of decorum. For the rest he lets the furies cry havoc.

He tells us that Phèdre is committed to her tragic course "by her destiny and by the rage of the gods." The mechanism of fatality can be variously interpreted; the gods here may be themselves or what later mythologies of consciousness would call heredity. Ibsen speaks of "ghosts" when he means that our lives may be haunted to ruin by an inherited infection of the flesh. So Racine invokes the gods to account for the eruption in Phèdre of elemental passions more wanton and destructive than those habitual to men. In *Iphigénie*, such invocation gave ground for awkwardness, there being a margin of discord between the presumptions of the fable and the rational bias of the dramatic conventions. In *Phèdre*, Racine avails the imagination of all possible orders of "truth," allowing the sphere of reason to shade imperceptibly into larger and more ancient apprehensions of conduct. The difference is more than a richening of talent. Behind the tremendous force of the play seems to lie a cruel Jansenist conjecture. The action of *Phèdre* transpires in a time before Christ. Those who then fell into damnation did so in a manner more terrible than any thereafter, having available to them no occasion of redemption. Before Christ's coming, the descent into hell of a being such as Phèdre had a special horror, being irredeemable. Phèdre belongs to the world of those for whom the Saviour had not yet given His life. In that world, tragic personages cast shadows deeper than ours; their solitude is more absolute, being previous to grace. Their blood has not yet mingled in sacrament with that of a Redeemer. In it the taint of original sin burns pure and inhuman. That is the dominant note of the play.

Hippolyte strikes it in the first scene:

> Tout a changé de face
> Depuis que sur ces bords les dieux ont envoyé
> La fille de Minos et de Pasiphaé.[7]

The line is superb not only for its exotic sonority; it opens the gates of reason to the night. Into the courtly setting, so clearly established by the formal notations and cadences of the neo-classic style, bursts something archaic, incomprehensible, and barbaric. Phèdre is the daughter of the inhuman. Her direct ancestor is the sun. In her veins run the primal fires of creation. This fact is deliberately heightened by the tranquil formality, the elegance, of Hippolyte's pronouncement. He goes on to evoke the legendary prowess of his absent father, Theseus. And again, the sense of an archaic, bloodstained, daemonic world is loosed upon the drama:

> Les monstres étouffés et les brigands punis,
> Procruste, Cercyon, et Sciron, et Sinnis,
> Et les os dispersés du géant d'Épidaure,
> Et la Crète fumant du sang du Minotaure.[8]

Smoke, fire, and blood are the dominant images throughout the action.

Phèdre's subjection to the brutish wilfulness of

---

[7] All things are changed
Since the gods sent to these shores
The daughter of Minos and Pasiphaë.
[8] The monsters strangled and the thieves cast down,
Procrustes, Sciron, Sinis, and Cercyon,
The Epidaurian giant massacred,
Crete smoking with the Minotaur's blood.

the flesh is perfectly conveyed at her first entrance. There is a famous piece of stage business. Wearied by the weight of her ornaments and of her hair, Phèdre sits down. It is a momentous gesture of submission; the spirit bends under the gross tyranny of the body. Elsewhere in Racine and in neo-classic drama, tragic personages do not sit down. The agonies they suffer are of a moral and intellectual order; they leave the mind bruised or mortally hurt but still in command. Indeed, they seem to lessen the role of the flesh by exalting the outward bearing of the sufferer. If Bérénice sits down under the weight of her grief, it will only be off stage. Phèdre is different. She carries within her an obscure heaviness and fury of blood. It drags at her soul and she sits down. This minute concession spells out her greater yielding to unreason. It is precisely the nakedness of the neo-classic stage, the abstraction of technical form, which allows a dramatist to derive implications so rich and violent from the mere presence of a chair. The stricter a style, the more communicative is any departure from its severity. When Phèdre sits down she lets slip the reins of reason.

In these opening scenes, the word "blood" is pronounced again and again to accentuate the organic, involuntary nature of her predicament:

OENONE: Que faites-vous, Madame? Et quel mortel ennui
Contre tout votre sang vous anime aujourd'hui?

PHÈDRE: Puisque Vénus le veut, de ce sang
déplorable
Je péris la dernière et la plus misérable.
****

OENONE: Juste ciel! tout mon sang dans mes
veines se glace.
****

PHÈDRE: Je reconnus Vénus et ses feux redouta-
bles,
D'un sang qu'elle poursuit tourments
inévitables.[9]

The whole blood–fire motif is then contracted into
a single image:

De victimes moi-même à toute heure entourée,
Je cherchais dans leurs flancs ma raison égarée.[1]

[9] OENONE: What are you doing, madam, and what mortal
grief
Rouses you today against those of your own
blood?
PHÈDRE: Since Venus will have it so, of that lamentable
blood
I shall perish the last and most miserable.
******
OENONE: Just heavens! all my blood is freezing in my
veins.
******
PHÈDRE: I recognize Venus and her dreadful fires,
Inescapable torments of those whose blood she
pursues.

The meaning throughout hinges on the twofold sense of "blood":
the immediate physiological sense and the meaning "race,"
"lineage," "family." Both are implied at the same time, as in
the English word, "consanguineous."

[1] PHÈDRE: Surrounded at every hour by burnt offerings.
I sought out my distracted reason in their entrails.

Phèdre is at the altar (fire) surrounded by sacrificial victims (blood). She seeks reason and foresight in their entrails, the word *flancs* carrying all the relevant weight of erotic and animalistic implication. Again the ornateness and formality of the rhetoric seem to set off, and thereby heighten, the brutish ferocity of the myth.

The discipline imposed on the movement of the play by the solemnity of discourse and the containment of outward action allows the poet to exhibit at the same time the literal and figurative aspects of his material. Racine demands of us a constant awareness of both. Phèdre is possessed by Venus, and Theseus is wandering in the realms of the dead; a woman yields to extremity of love and her husband's absence stands for persistent infidelity. The difference is one of notation. In the first instance, we use the notation of classical mythology; in the latter, that of rational psychology (which is, perhaps, also a body of myths). It is the function of neo-classical rhetoric to keep both conventions of meaning equally in sight. "Ce n'est plus une ardeur dans mes veines cachée," says Phèdre; "C'est Vénus toute entière à sa proie attachée." *Ardeur* is both intensity of passion and material fire; Venus is a

This is the literal translation. Phèdre is referring, of course, to the Greek and Roman practice of seeking omens and guidance in the entrails of animals sacrificed to the gods. The shock of the image depends on the contrast between "reason" and the blood-reeking loins of beasts. Racine could make his statement so succinct because he knew that his audience were familiar with classical antiquities.

metaphor of obsession, but also the literal goddess
devouring her prey. The special quality of *Phèdre*
derives from the fact that the literal, physical connotations are always somewhat the stronger. Even
as Phèdre is compelled to sit down by the mastering
weariness of her flesh, so the language of the play
seems to bend toward grosser modes of expression
such as gesture or outcry. But neo-classical drama
allows no such alternatives. The violence is all in
the poetry. And it is because the unfolding and containment of it in *Phèdre* are so complete that the
economy of Racine has seemed to some even more
persuasive than Shakespeare's largess.

Having at his disposal no looseness of form, no
adjuncts of pageantry or outward music, Racine
makes of his language a constant summation of
energy and meaning. Images recur in counterpoint.
Phèdre has seen herself as a prey, helpless in the
grip of Venus. Hearing the false news of Theseus'
death, she declares:

> Et l'avare Achéron ne lâche point sa proie.[2]

As in *Tristan*, the images of love and death are in-
terchangeable; both consume men with similar ra-
pacity. And as the action strides forward, the *leit-
motiv* of fire and blood grows more insistent. It is
the gods, says Phèdre to Hippolyte, who have kin-
dled "le feu fatal à tout mon sang."

When Phèdre learns that her illicit passion has a
rival (Hippolyte loves Aricie), the last authority of

[2] Greedy Acheron does not release its prey.

reason is shattered. We have imagined the theatre
of Racine to be an enclosed place, fortified against
disorder by the conventions of the neo-classic style.
At the start of the play, however, Hippolyte warns
us that the atmosphere has altered, as if there was a
dimness in the air. The coming to Athens of the
daughter of Minos has opened the gates of reason
on to an alien and barbaric world. Now they are
flung wide. By force of incantation, the maddened
queen brings into the seventeenth-century playhouse presences begotten of chaos and ancient
night. She is a daughter of the sun; the whole of
creation is peopled with her monstrous and majestic ancestry. Her father holds the scales of justice
in hell. In the tremendous closing scene of Act IV,
the play shifts into a wilder key. Once more, Phèdre
invokes the twin powers of fire and blood:

> Mes homicides mains, promptes à me venger
> Dans le sang innocent brûlent de se plonger.
> Misérable! et je vis? et je soutiens la vue
> De ce sacré Soleil dont je suis descendue?
> J'ai pour aïeul le père et la maître des dieux;
> Le ciel, tout l'univers est plein de mes aïeux;
> Où me cacher? Fuyons dans la nuit infernale.
> Mais que dis-je? Mon père y tient l'urne fatale;
> Le sort, dit-on, l'a mise en ses sévères mains:
> Minos juge aux enfers tous les pâles humains.[3]

[3] My murdering hands, intent upon vengeance,
Burn with eagerness to plunge in innocent blood.
Wretch that I am! yet I live! and bear the sight
Of that sacred sun from whom I am descended!

Not since the blood-streaming heavens in Marlowe's *Faustus* has nature presided with more animate fury over a scene of human damnation. If I were to stage the play, I should have the background grow transparent to show us the dance of the Zodiac and Taurus, the emblematic beast of the royal house of Crete.

This unleashing of the forces of myth prepares us for the preternatural fatality of the *dénouement*. There is no need here for the equivocations practised in *Iphigénie*. Every touch adds to our awareness that the action has been invaded by elemental and daemonic presences. Oenone hurls herself into the sea across which she and her royal mistress came from Crete, and we are reminded of a splendid, barbarous image in Garnier's *Hippolyte*:

> Qu'il t'eut bien mieux valu tomber dessous les
> ondes,

The father and master of the gods is my ancestor;
The heavens and the entire universe are filled with my
forebears;
Where shall I hide? Let us flee into the night of hell.
But what am I saying? There my father holds the fatal
urn;
It is said that destiny has placed it in his severe hands:
In the underworld Minos passes judgement on all pallid
mortals.

In the urn of Minos are the lots or tokens that determine whether the dead soul goes to bliss or damnation. Phèdre, contemplating suicide, is terrified at the thought that her guilty shade shall appear for judgement before her own, implacable father.

Et remplir l'estomac des Phoques vagabondes,
Lors qu'à ton grand malheur une indiscrète amour
Te fait passer la mer sans espoir de retour.[4]

As Phèdre enters after Hippolyte's death, Theseus
says to her: "Il est mort, prenez votre victime." We
accept the intimation of inhumanity; a being half-
goddess and half-daemon has exacted a blood of-
fering. Dying, Phèdre proclaims her kinship with
that other barbarian queen who came from a world
of witchcraft beyond the Hellenic pale to wreak
havoc in Greece. Phèdre's veins have burnt with the
venom of love; now they are consumed by a poison
which Medea brought to Athens:

J'ai pris, j'ai fait couler dans mes brûlantes veines
Un poison que Médée apporta dans Athènes.[5]

But now, at last, the fire is out, and her closing
words tell of light without flame (*clarté, pureté*).

The death of Hippolyte affirms the savage quality
of the fable. Theseus, who has rid Greece of wild
beasts, summons a monster from the sea for the
destruction of his son. The blood and smoke to
which Hippolyte refers when recounting the ex-
ploits of his father—Et la Crète fumant du sang du
Minotaure—surround his own hideous death:

[4] 'Twere better you had fallen o'er the rail
   To glut the stomach of a roving seal,
   When careless love, the agent of your ruin,
   Made you cross seas whence there is no return.
[5] I have infused into my burning veins
   A poison which Medea brought to Athens.

94

De rage et de douleur le monstre bondissant
Vient aux pieds des chevaux tomber en mugissant,
Se roule, et leur présente une gueule enflammée
Qui les couvre de feu, de sang, et de fumée.[6]

Theseus slew the Minotaur, Phèdre's monstrous half-brother; now a horned beast (in Garnier's version he even has the face of a bull) slays his son. The cycle of horrors is brought to ironic completion.

In these final scenes of the tragedy, the literal violence of the myth carries all before it. It is difficult to interpret these wild, preternatural occurrences as allegories for some more decorous mythology of conduct. The monster springs from the moral blindness of Theseus, but the fire it breathes is real. That we should feel no discord between such realness and the conventions of the neo-classic theatre is supreme proof of Racine's art. The modulation of values, from the figurative to the literal, from the shapes of reason to those of archaic terror, is carefully prepared for. Throughout *Phèdre*, the part of the beast seems to encroach on the fragile bounds of man's humanity. In the end it erupts in a monstrous form, half dragon and half bull, coming from the ungoverned sea to wreck destruction on the ordered, classic land (Il suivait tout pensif le chemin de Mycènes).

[6] Leaping with pain and rage, the monster falls
Before the horses' feet, and bellowing rolls
Around; he fronts them with his flaming throat
Whence fire, blood, and reeking smoke pour out.

95

But the change of key and the descent of the
play into a kind of primal chaos are effected entirely inside the closed, neo-classic form. I have
spoken of the way in which the rear wall of the
stage seems to crumble at the end of Act IV. Actually, of course, it does not. There is not even a
change of scene. The infernal presences which
darken the air are made real by the sole force of
Phèdre's incantation. The monster that slays Hippolyte has a nauseating reality, but, in fact, we see
no trace of the beast. The horror is conveyed to us
through the formal narration of Théramène (the
messenger of Greek and Senecan tragedy making
one of his final and most effective appearances in
modern drama). All that happens, happens inside
language. That is the special narrowness and grandeur of the French classic manner. With nothing
but words—and formal, ceremonious words—at his
disposal, Racine fills the stage with the uttermost
of action. As nothing of the content of *Phèdre* is
exterior to the expressive form, to the language, the
words come very near the condition of music,
where content and form are identical.

Phèdre gives occasion to show this as it is among
the few plays which another dramatist of genius
did render into his own language:

> Ich Elende! und ich ertrag' es noch,
> Zu dieser heiligen Sonne aufzublicken,
> Von der ich meinen reinen Ursprung zog.
> Den Vater und den Oberherrn der Götter

> Hab ich zum Ahnherrn, der Olympus ist,
> Der ganze Weltkreis voll von meinen Ahnen.

Schiller conveys the outward meaning perfectly, and something of the cadence. But the sense of the violence inside the classic measure is gone. Rob Phèdre's incantation of its music (of the speech uniquely appropriate to it) and the rest is mere outcry.

After *Phèdre*, Racine, so far as drama is concerned, observed twelve years of silence. The poet's fastidiousness toward the ambiguous social status of the theatre deepened and he grew more pious. But a contemporary tells us that the true cause was Racine's unwillingness to jeopardize by any new venture the pre-eminence assured him by *Phèdre*. There may be something in that. It is difficult to conceive how he could have gone beyond *Phèdre* while retaining the conventions of neo-classic drama, how greater risks could have been equally or more finely met. When Racine did return to the theatre, it was in a special and private mode.

In *Esther* and *Athalie* the tension between fable and rational form, which is the mainspring of energy in Racine's previous plays, is resolved. Deriving from Scripture, the truth of the dramatic action is no longer conventional or figurative. It is actual. Racine's notes in the Toulouse copy of *Esther*, and what we have of the preliminary sketches for *Athalie*, show that the poet regarded sacred history as materially true. There are in both plays elements of miracle, but they afford no difficulty of treatment, being rational manifestations of the will of God. Paradoxically, therefore, it is these cantata-dramas, these courtly miracle plays, which most completely embody the stage-craft of the "theatre of reason." Written, moreover, for private performance by the young ladies of Saint-Cyr, *Esther* and *Athalie* fulfil an ideal latent in much of Racine's art—that of a festive playhouse of special occasion, removed from the contingencies and vulgarities of commercial drama. In concert with this ideal, Racine for the first time uses a chorus, though the possibilities of that device seem long to have glowed in his imagination.

The two plays are of dissimilar weight. *Esther* is probably unique in that it is a serious, full-length drama intended for presentation by young people and wholly in accord with that intent. (There are remarkable children's operas, but I can think of no comparable children's play.) The softness of tone, the ease with which the tragic crisis is averted, the swift, illustrative punishment of Aman, suggest a Christmas pantomime. One has difficulty in seeing why Racine should entitle *Esther* "a tragedy."

Athalie is very different. It is the fourth of Racine's full-length portrayals of women, and not even in *Phèdre* is there a greater mastery of classic form. The setting of the play is like a parable of enclosedness. The precincts of the Temple are surrounded by a wall on the other side of which lies the corrupt and misgoverned city. The boy-king,

Joas, is hidden inside the Temple. Athalie vainly seeks to draw him out on to profane and open ground. At the heart of the sanctuary are the places of high holiness to which only the Levites have access. Formally, the play is surrounded by a chorus, setting it off from more realistic imitations of action. Enclosure within enclosure. The actual dramatic conflict has the linear simplicity of Aeschylus' *Suppliants*. Athalie tries to break through the successive bounds in order to get at her hidden rival and in order to desecrate God's house. The key words of the drama denote the enclosed places (*parvis, limites, enceintes, lieu redoutable*). The angry queen invades the outer defences:

> Dans un des parvis, aux hommes réservé
> Cette femme superbe entre le front levé,
> Et se préparait même à passer les limites
> De l'enceinte sacrée ouverte aux seuls lévites.[7]

In the end, she does invade the sanctuary itself and finds that she has entered a deadly trap. There is no retreat from God's presence:

> Tes yeux cherchent en vain, tu ne peux échapper,
> Et Dieu de toutes parts a su t'envelopper.[8]

It is a simple but marvellously expressive design. Unity of place acquires a double significance: it is

[7] Into one of the precincts which are reserved to men,
This haughty woman enters, her head high,
And was even making ready to transgress the bounds
Of the holy enclosure to which only Levites are admitted.
[8] Thine eyes search vainly, for thou canst not flee,
On every side God has encompassed thee.

both a convention of the neo-classic form and the prime motive of action. In *Athalie*, as in the *Suppliants*, a place of sanctuary is preserved against incursions of violence. One of the last of the great formal tragedies in western literature seems to look back explicitly to the first.

The play is shadowed by the solemnity and half-light of the interior of the Temple. But the language has a rare glitter, as of burnished metal. "In the gloom," writes Ezra Pound, "the gold gathers the light against it." The entire drama turns on a dialectic of light and darkness. On the plane of appearance there is light in the outside world and darkness inside the Temple. In reality, the darkness lies on the idolatrous city, and the Temple is luminous with the radiance of God. Athalie is enveloped in darkness of soul and of royal vestment; the Levites are clothed in white linen. Their weapons blaze with light as they step out of the shadows to surround Athalie. The play is tragic because we know that Joad's vision will be accomplished and Joas will become an evil king. But beyond the blackness of the fate of Israel is the light of the greater redemption. In his prophetic trance, the High Priest sees a new Jerusalem arising from the desert. It is a city of light, "brillante de clartés."

After *Athalie* (1691), Racine wrote no more for the theatre. He was only fifty-two, yet his silence had nothing of the quality of defeat which marked the end of Corneille's career. It was the crowning

repose of a playwright who had loved drama but
never trusted the stage.

Let us return, for a moment, to our initial concern: the "untranslatability" of Corneille and Racine into any theatrical milieu or literary tradition
outside France. Given the power and variousness
of their work, the parochialism of its reach still
seems to me baffling. But part of the answer must, I
think, lie with the limitations of the neo-classical
ideal. The total action of a neo-classic play occurs
inside the language. The elements of stage business
and setting are reduced to barest necessity. But it is
precisely the sensuous elements in drama that
translate best; they belong to the universal language
of eye and body and not to any particular national
tongue. Where speech has to convey the totality of
the intended effect, miracles of translation, or
rather of re-creation, are called for. In the case of
the French classics, these have not been forth-
coming.

But with regard to Corneille, this lack seems a
matter of negligence rather than of technical im-
possibility. We have been kept from Corneille
partly because French criticism has itself not taken
his full measure. An age that has been roused to the
call of Churchillian rhetoric, and which is aware of
the cancer of violence endemic in affairs of state,
should have an ear for Corneille. The great stride
of argument in his plays carries beyond the baroque
conventions of the plot. He is one of the very few

masters of political drama that western literature
has produced. What he can tell us of power and
the death of the heart is worth hearing outside the
confines of the Comédie Française. And an effective translation is at least conceivable. I imagine it
to be a mixture of prose and verse. The parts of intrigue and background matter could be conveyed
in a formal and Latinate prose (something in the
manner of Clarendon). The flights of rhetoric, the
great confrontations of discourse, could be rendered
in heroic couplets. This would require a master of
that exacting form, one who could give back to the
couplet both the pace and the weight which it has
in the best of Dryden. Mr. Yvor Winters might do
it beautifully.

Racine poses a different problem, and it may well
be insoluble. Being a presenter of reality in language alone, Racine invested his words with such
responsibility that no other words will conceivably
do the job. Even the finest translation (Schiller's,
for example) brings dispersal and dissolution to the
tightness of Racine's style. On the naked stage of
Bérénice and *Phèdre,* minute shifts in tonality are
the prime movers of the drama. The crises which
reverberate through the muted air are crises of syntax. It is a change of grammatical number which
marks the point of no return in *Phèdre.* The queen
has nearly confessed her love to Hippolyte. He shies
back in horror:

> Dieux! qu'est-ce que j'entends? Mad-
> ame, oubliez-vous

>   Que Thésée est mon père, et qu'il est
>   votre époux?
> PHÈDRE: Et sur quoi jugez-vous que j'en perds
>   la mémoire,
>   Prince? Aurais-je perdu tout le soin
>   de ma gloire?
> HIPPOLYTE: Madame, pardonnez. J'avoue, en
>   rougissant,
>   Que j'accusais à tort un discours in-
>   nocent.
>   Ma honte ne peut plus soutenir votre
>   vue,
>   Et je vais . . .
> PHÈDRE: Ah, cruel! tu m'as trop entendue.
>   Je t'en ai dit assez pour te tirer d'er-
>   reur.[9]

The entire shock of revelation lies in the shift from the formal *vous* to the intimate *tu*. The change is marked three times in the two lines which convey

[9] HIPPOLYTE: Ye Gods! what do I hear? Madam, do you forget
>   That Theseus is my father, and that he is
>   your husband?
> PHÈDRE: And what ground have you to suppose that
>   I forget it,
>   Prince? Could it be that I have abandoned
>   all regard for my place and renown?
> HIPPOLYTE: Forgive me, madam. Blushing, I confess
>   That I falsely judged innocent words.
>   My shame no longer can endure your sight,
>   And I go. . . .
> PHÈDRE: Ah, cruel one! thou hast understood me all
>   too clearly.
>   I have told thee enough to dispel thy error.

In French, particularly in seventeenth-century usage, *entendre* means both to hear and to understand.

Phèdre's desperate confession. Decorum is gone and with it all possibility of retreat. But the English translator is helpless before the fact, for a change from "you" to "thou" renders nearly nothing of the immense crisis. The only counterpart is the way in which a change of key can alter the entire direction of a piece of music.

Or consider Bérénice's question to Titus:

> Rien ne peut-il charmer l'ennui qui vous dévore? [1]

It is the fragile tonality of *charmer* and *ennui*, the courtly lilt of the phrase, which communicate the intimations of anguish. But how is one to translate the two words or convey in any other language the ominous cadence of the final vowels? The art of Racine shows us what Valéry meant when he said, "of two words, choose the lesser." But nothing in a language is less translatable than its modes of understatement.

This dilemma of translation exists even within French. Racine is studied in the schools and acted in the Comédie. I wonder, however, whether he still speaks to many of his countrymen. The role

---

[1] Can nothing soothe the fret that ravens you?

This won't really do. *Charmer* is "soothe" but also more: it implies relief through elegance and gracious seduction. "Charm," as the Elizabethans used it, connotes actual magic. Bérénice seeks to dispell Titus' grief only through her entrancing presence. Nor is *ennui* adequately rendered by "fret." Used today, the English word seems weak and archaic; in Defoe, it still carries the right overtones of deep-gnawing irritation. Finally, there is *dévorer*, a verb intentionally excessive and out of proportion with *ennui*. What is one to do? But that is my whole point.

he plays in French life is monumental rather than
vital. You cannot derive from Racine's plays those
larger conventions of romantic action or historical
pageant which have helped carry over so much of
Shakespeare. In no art is the principle of life more
completely that of style. What there is in *Andro-
maque* and *Iphigénie* and *Phèdre*, is totally expressed in the noble intricacy of seventeenth-
century speech. That speech does not translate well,
either into other languages or even into the loosened fabric of colloquial French.

Italians say this of Leopardi, and Russians of
Pushkin. But such judgement carries no diminution. In some poets, universality is a matter of
breadth—breadth of range and influence. In others,
it is an attribute of intrinsic height. And it may well
be the untranslatable poet who strikes nearest the
genius of his own tongue.

IV

WE HAVE, so far, dealt with tradition. Required to construe a tradition out of rival precedents—the antique and the Elizabethan—Dryden committed himself to neither entirely, and failed. Racine, on the contrary, derived from the actual practice of classic and more precisely of Euripidean tragedy, elements of tone and form beautifully appropriate to a theatre at once Cartesian and baroque. In French neo-classical drama there is that successful retranslation of a past ideal into a present form which we call tradition.

But if we consider the twenty-five hundred years which separate us from Greek tragedy, the history of tragic drama will strike us as having in it little of overt continuity or tradition. What impresses one is a sense of miraculous occasion. Over wide reaches of time and in diverse places, elements of language, material circumstance, and individual talent suddenly gather toward the production of a body of serious drama. Out of the surrounding darkness, energies meet to create constellations of intense radiance and rather brief life. Such high moments occurred in Periclean Athens, in England during the period 1580–1640, in seventeenth-century Spain, in France between 1630 and 1690. After that, the necessary encounter of historical setting and personal genius seems to have taken place only twice: in Germany in the period 1790 to 1840 and, much more diffusely, around the turn of our century, when the best of Scandinavian and Russian drama was written. Not elsewhere, nor at other times. In the long view, therefore, it is the existence of a living body of tragic drama, not the absence of it, that calls for particular note. The rise of the necessary talent to the possible occasion is rare. The material conditions of the theatre are rarely favourable to tragedy. Where the fusion of appropriate elements is realized, we do find more than the individual poet: Aeschylus is followed by Sophocles and Euripides; Marlowe, by Shakespeare, Jonson, and Webster; Corneille, by Racine. With Goethe came Schiller, Kleist, and Büchner. Ibsen, Strindberg, and Chekhov were alive in 1900. But these constellations are splendid accidents. They are extremely difficult to account for. What we should expect, and actually find, are long spells of time during which no tragedies and, in fact, no drama of any serious pretensions is being produced.

But although this is a reasonable view of the matter, it is distinctly modern. It reflects the problem we are concerned with: the long pursuit of the tragic ideal. It is because there have been in English drama no successors to the Elizabethans, nor in French drama any later rivals to Corneille and Racine; it is because the Spanish theatre after Calderón falls into dusty silence and because the death of Büchner seems to date so precisely the close of the high period of German tragedy, that we now look on the creation of great drama as a rare and rather mysterious piece of good fortune. We are probably right in doing so. But our realism springs from disappointment, and we must not make the mistake of assuming that so disenchanted a view prevailed earlier.

We cannot understand the romantic movement if we do not preceive at the heart of it the impulse toward drama. The classical imagination seeks to impose on experience attributes of order and accord. The romantic imagination injects into experience a central quality of drama and dialectic. The romantic mode is neither an ordering nor a criticism of life; it is a dramatization. And at the origins of the romantic movement lies an explicit attempt to revitalize the major forms of tragedy. In fact, romanticism began as a critique of the failure of the eighteenth century to carry on the great traditions of the Elizabethan and baroque theatre. It was in the name of drama that the romantics assailed neo-classicism. Not only did they see in the dramatic the supreme literary form; they were convinced that the absence of serious drama arose from some specific failure of understanding or some particular material contingency. The modern view that a dearth of dramatic poetry is a natural state of affairs, remedied by rare and unpredictable good fortune, would have struck the romantics as absurd and self-defeating.

The defeat, moreover, was of a kind which no society could safely endure. The romantics believed that the vitality of drama was inseparable from the health of the body politic. That is the crux of Shelley's argument in his *Defence of Poetry*:

And it is indisputable that the highest perfection of human society has ever corresponded with the highest dramatic excellence: and that the corruption or extinction of drama in a nation where it has once flourished, is a mark of a corruption of manners, and an extinction of the energies which sustain the soul of social life.

This is an important idea. It arises from the recognition that the eminent periods of classic, Spanish, Elizabethan, and French drama did coincide with periods of particular national energy. It is an idea which will enlist the ambitions of the entire romantic movement and culminate in the social philosophy of Wagner and Bayreuth.

When Shelley made his point, the situation of drama seemed critical in the extreme. Throughout European literature, the close of the seventeenth century appeared to mark a collapse of the dramatic imagination. What had come thereafter were the cold, declamatory exercises of the neo-classical tragedians, the dramas of Voltaire and Samuel Johnson's *Irene*. The romantics looked back to Calderón, Shakespeare, and Corneille over a gap of years which seemed to them inadmissibly long and sterile. "It is impossible to mention the word tragedy," wrote Leigh Hunt, "without being struck by the exceeding barrenness which the stage has exhibited of late years in everything that concerns the tragic department." He felt that there had been no English play that could even be regarded as tragedy "since the time of Otway" (a span of one hundred and thirty years).

Why should this be? The romantics were certain that reasons could be found and indeed must be found if tragic drama was to be restored to its former glory. Romanticism is a complex movement, with complex national particularities. Thus the problem of the decline of tragic drama posed itself somewhat differently in England, France, and Germany.

Let us consider England first. Here the sense of preceding failure was sharpest, for there had occurred after Shakespeare and the Jacobeans so drastic and obvious a break. There was nearly a century and a half to account for. Why the decline of tragedy after 1640? The reasons might be practical; English drama could have been silenced simply by the closing of the playhouses during the Civil

War and Cromwell's rule. Or there might be deeper, philosophic reasons. But reasons there must be.

To discover them, poets and critics of the early nineteenth century took an anxious look at the actual conditions of the contemporary stage. Romantic thought was Hegelian in that it saw beneath the seemingly autonomous life of artistic forms the practical workings of historical circumstance. If the English stage had failed to produce tragic drama since the seventeenth century, the empirical facts of theatrical life could well be the cause. The fault might lie with the fact that three theatres—Covent Garden, Drury Lane, and the Theatre Royal in the Haymarket—enjoyed a virtual monopoly in the production of legitimate drama. Patents and licenses first issued in the 1680's had now become archaic obstructions. As one "reformer" noted in 1813:

All the success of a Dramatist depends on the taste, caprice, indolence, avarice, or jealousy of three individuals, the Managers of three London Theatres.

By challenging contrast, the Elizabethan spectator could see drama performed in any of fifteen playhouses. To justify their privileged role, moreover, Covent Garden and Drury Lane had to be very large. As John Philip Kemble pointed out, even a very powerful and sensitive actor (such as himself) had to coarsen his art in order to reach an audience running into the thousands. Inevitably, the theatre moved away from drama and toward spectacle. Kemble's production of *Julius Caesar* attracted far less enthusiasm than *Timour the Tartar*, an "equestrian melodrama" or *The Cataract of the Ganges*, an extravaganza on which the manager of Drury Lane lavished £5,000.

In the course of the eighteenth century, the stature of the individual actor had greatly increased. This made of the late eighteenth and early nineteenth centuries a golden age of English acting (Kemble, George Frederick Cooke, Edmund Kean, Macready, the incomparable Mrs. Siddons). But the primacy of the actor seemed to be achieved at the expense of the play. Sir Walter Scott asserted that it was no longer the poetry or the plot which drew an audience to *Hamlet*; it was the wish to compare some turn of gesture or intonation in Kemble's performance with one's remembrance of Garrick. The very style of the romantic actors, moreover, their predilection for the moment of extreme passion and wild lyricism, further increased the general drift toward the melodramatic. And because it was the actor who drew the public rather than the play, dramatists tried to write plays exactly tailored to the tastes or technical resources of a particular actor. They produced "monodramas" in which only one role mattered, all lesser parts serving as foils to the star. This is what Keats did in *Otho the Great*, in the hope that Kean might become interested in the main part: "If he smokes the hotblood character of Ludolph—and he is the only actor that can do it—He will add to his own fame, and improve my fortune."

These problems of commercial control and stage-craft led inevitably to a larger question. Drama is the most social of literary forms. It exists fully only by virtue of public performance. Therein lies its fascination and its servitude. This means that one cannot separate the condition of drama from that of the audience or, in a larger yet strict sense, from that of the social and political community. Has European literature after the seventeenth century failed to produce tragic drama because European society has failed to produce an audience for it? This argument was widely advanced in the romantic period. Erich Heller puts it in a modern form:

In spite of all the unavoidable cleavages, disharmonies, animosities and antagonisms which are the perennial lot of human beings and human societies, there is a possibility—and this possibility is called culture when it is realized—of a community of men living together . . . in a state of tacit agreement on what the nature and meaning of human existence really is. . . . Such must have been the society for which the performances of the tragedies of Aeschylus and Sophocles were national celebrations; such were wide stretches of what we rather vaguely call the Middle Ages; such were, to judge by their artistic creations, the days of the Renaissance and of Elizabeth. The age of Goethe, however, was not of this kind.

I believe that there is in this a great deal of truth. I shall often come back to the notion that certain essential elements of social and imaginative life, which had prevailed from Aeschylus to Racine, receded from western consciousness after the seventeenth century—that the seventeenth century is the "great divide" in the history of tragedy.

But it must be noted that theories of artistic change which are founded on the nature of the relevant audience are immensely difficult to document. We know next to nothing of the social composition and temper of the Athenian audience. Did any but a very small number of those who sat on the tiers of the Theatre of Dionysus actually enjoy seeing the tenth or twentieth version of the Orestes myth? Or did they participate in the event because it was a ritual chore enforced by the habits of the *polis*? Nor do we know very much about the Elizabethan public. There is evidence to suggest that the Elizabethan playwrights were exceptionally fortunate, the audience for which they wrote being both representative of great variety and yet homogeneous. Socially, it appears to have spanned the entire range from aristocrat to menial and to have been richly illustrative of the diverse energies and imaginative traditions abroad in Elizabethan life. At the same time, the Shakespearean audience seem to have constituted a community, in the sense of Heller's argument. They shared certain orders of value and habits of belief which made it possible for the dramatist to rely on a common body of imaginative response. The nobleman and his lackey may have found very different sources of delight in *Hamlet*. But neither needed footnotes or a special gloss to prepare him for the possibility of ghostly action and for the implicit reference of human conduct to a scale of values reaching from the angelic down to brute matter.

Or so, at least, we suppose. When we use the work of art itself to prove anything about its audience, we are judging after the fact. We do not really know.

Yet there are a number of things that can be said of the nineteenth-century public. Having become more democratic, it had deteriorated in literacy. The audience of Racine were, in the main, a closed society to which the lower orders of social and economic life had little entry. Throughout the eighteenth century, the centre of social gravity shifted toward the middle classes. The French Revolution, essentially a triumph of the militant *bourgeoisie*, accelerated the shift. In his *Essay on the Drama*, Sir Walter Scott shows how the liberalization of the audience led to a lowering of dramatic standards. The theatrical managers and their playwrights were no longer catering to a literate aristocracy or *élite* drawn from the magistracy and high finance; they were trying to attract the *bourgeois* family with its lack of literary background and its taste for pathos and happy endings.

Even more important is the sharp diminution in the role of the theatre in the community. When going to the theatre, the nineteenth-century spectator was not participating in a religious or civic exercise as had the Athenians; he was not aware of

any of the elements of festive ritual which seem to
have carried over into the Elizabethan playhouse
from the Middle Ages; he was not even attending
an occasion of high ceremony in the manner of
Versailles. He was simply choosing one from an increasing number of rival pastimes. Drama was becoming what it is today: mere entertainment. And
the middle-class spectator of the romantic period
did not want more. He was not prepared to take
the risks of terror and revelation implicit in tragedy.
He wished to shudder briefly or dream at ease.
When coming from the street into the playhouse,
he was not leaving the real for the more real (as
does any man who is willing to encounter the imaginings of Aeschylus, Shakespeare, or Racine); he
was moving from the fierce solicitations of current
history and economic purpose into the repose of
illusion.

This is a crucial point. The French Revolution
and the Napoleonic wars plunged ordinary men
into the stream of history. They laid them open to
pressures of experience and feeling which had, in
earlier times, been the dangerous prerogatives of
princes, statesmen, and professional soldiers. Once
the great levies had marched and retreated across
Europe, the ancient balance between private and
public life had altered. An increasing part of private
life now lay open to the claims of history. And that
part grew with the expansion in the means of communication. Short of neighbouring catastrophe, the

Elizabethan and neo-classic spectator had come to *Hamlet* or *Phèdre* with a mind partially at rest, or at least unguarded against the poetry and shock of the play. The new "historical" man, on the contrary, came to the theatre with a newspaper in his pocket. In it might be facts more desperate and sentiments more provocative than many a dramatist would care to present. The audience had within itself no quality of silence, but a surfeit and tumult of emotion. Goethe complains bitterly of this fact in the Prologue to *Faust*:

> Gar mancher kommt vom Lesen der Journale.
> Man eilt zerstreut zu uns, wie zu den Masken-
>   festen,
> Und Neugier nur beflügelt jeden Schritt.[1]

Neugier: literally, the hunger for the new. How was the playwright to satisfy it, to rival the drama of actual news? Only by crying even louder havoc, by writing melodrama.

But the challenge came from more than journalism and the quickened tempo of life. In the past, drama had occupied that central place which Hamlet ascribes to it. It had held up to nature a spacious mirror. Dramatists and players had been the abstract and brief chronicles of the time. They had taught their countrymen history, in the manner of Shakespeare, or conduct, in that of Jonson and

[1] Many a one comes straight from reading the gazette.
They hasten to us, scatterbrained as to a carnival,
And mere curiosity claps wings upon their heels.

117

Molière. This was no longer the case. Other literary forms were reaching an audience much greater than that drawn to the theatre. The history of the decline of serious drama is, in part, that of the rise of the novel. The nineteenth century is the classic age of low-cost mass printing, of serialization, and the public reading room. The novelist, the popularizer of humane and scientific knowledge, the satirist, or the historian now had far readier access to the public than the playwright. To see mirrors held up to nature by expert hands, the literate public had no particular need of theatrical performance. A man could stay by his own fire with the latest part-issue of a novel, with the newest number of the *Edinburgh Review* or the *Revue des deux mondes*. The spectator had become the reader. In the seventeenth century, a Dickens and a Macaulay would most likely have been playwrights. Now the greater audience lay elsewhere.

Thus we find dramatists, from the time of Goethe's administration of the Weimar stage down to the age of Brecht and the contemporary "little theatres," trying to re-create for themselves the lost audience. The most sumptuous attempt was Wagner's. He sought at Bayreuth to invent or educate a spectator adequate to his own vision of the role and dignity of drama. What matters at Bayreuth is not so much the novel stage or orchestra pit. It is the auditorium destined for the kind of ideal audience which Wagner imagined to have existed in antiquity. Since Racine, serious dramatists and serious critics of drama have been men in search of a public.

This search necessarily leads away from an inquiry into the technical conditions of drama. It involves a theory of history and social change. But such theorizing lay close to the romantic temper. Given the empirical fact of the decline of tragedy, and the belief that there lay at the root of it an ascertainable cause, the romantics embarked on deep waters of conjecture.

In a letter to Byron (October 1815), Coleridge spoke of "the tragic Dwarfs, which exhausted Nature seems to have been under the necessity of producing since Shakespeare." The notion probably would not have arisen before the nineteenth century. It expresses a strain of melancholy historicism which leads directly from the romantics to Spengler. The sense of a downward drift in human affairs was aggravated by the apparent failure of the ideals of the French Revolution. Hazlitt felt that there had occurred in the spirit of the age some great disillusion; the nervous, paradoxical temper of the times could produce lyric poetry; it lacked the breadth and confidence required for drama. Half in earnest, Peacock declared in the *Four Ages of Poetry* that literature itself would be replaced by more positive forms of intelligence:

the day is not distant, when the degraded state of every species of poetry will be as generally recognized as that of dramatic poetry has long been: and this is not from any decrease either of intellectual power, or intellectual acquisition, but because intellectual power and intellectual acquisition have turned themselves into other and better channels.

Poetry was man's "mental rattle," argued Peacock. He would soon relinquish it in favour of the natural sciences. Shelley's *Defence* addresses itself directly to Peacock's prophecy. It is not poetic genius which has faltered or turned to other pursuits; it is society. There can be no great tragic drama under the political oppression and social hypocrisy of the age of Castlereagh. The Athenian tragic poets "coexisted with the moral and intellectual greatness of the age." If we are to re-create a living theatre, we must reform the "soul of social life." This will be the doctrine of Wagner and, in a certain measure, of Ibsen.

With the long failure of nineteenth-century poetic drama, these speculations grew more sombre and irrational. They seem to culminate, nearly a century later, in the dark brooding of Hardy's Preface to *The Dynasts*:

Whether mental performance alone may not eventually be the fate of all drama other than that of contemporary or frivolous life, is a kindred question not without interest. The mind naturally flies to the triumphs of the Hellenic and Elizabethan theatre in exhibiting scenes laid "far in the Unapparent," and asks why they should not be repeated. But the meditative world is older, more invidious, more nervous, more quizzical than it once was, and being unhappily perplexed by

Riddles of Death Thebes never knew,

may be less ready and less able than Hellas and old England were to look through the insistent, and often grotesque, substance at the thing signified.

Again, one feels that there is in these gloomy meditations a significant truth. A century apart, Hazlitt and Hardy both discern in the spirit of the modern age a prevailing nervousness, a falling away of the imaginative. Something is lacking of the superb confidence needed of a man to create a major stage character, to endow some presence within himself with the carnal mystery of gesture and dramatic speech. What remains obscure is the source of failure. Do art forms have their prescribed life cycle? Perhaps there is in poetic energy no principle of conservation. Manifestly, the Greek and the Elizabethan achievement seem to lie on the back of all later drama with a wearying weight of precedent. Or is the heart of the crisis within society? Did the dramatic poets of the nineteenth century fail to produce good plays because there were available to them neither the necessary theatres nor the requisite audience?

In the early decades of the romantic period, such queries and doubts were much in the air. But the writers themselves were in no way ready to concede the game. On the contrary, the more they dwelt on the dreary state of contemporary drama, the more certain did they become that it would be one of the tasks and glories of romanticism to restore tragedy to its former honours. The thought of such restoration preoccupied the best poets and novelists of the century. In many it grew to obsession. Consider even a partial list of the tragic plays written or planned by the English romantics.

William Blake wrote a part of an *Edward III*; Wordsworth wrote *The Borderers*; Sir Walter Scott composed four dramas; Coleridge collaborated with Southey in *The Fall of Robespierre*, then went on to write *Remorse* and *Zapolya*; Southey himself put together *Wat Tyler*. In addition to his dramatic sketches, Walter Savage Landor wrote four tragedies. Leigh Hunt published *Scenes from an Unfinished Drama* in 1820, and his *Legend of Florence* was performed at Covent Garden in 1840. Byron is the author of eight dramas. Shelley wrote *The Cenci, Prometheus,* and *Hellas,* and translated scenes from Goethe and Calderón. Keats placed great hopes on *Otho the Great* and began *King Stephen.* Thomas Lovell Beddoes wrote a number of strange Gothic tragedies, at least one of which is carried near mastery by its unflagging wildness and stress.

I do not set down this list in antiquarian pedantry (though such registers have a certain dusty fascination). I enumerate only to suggest the magnitude of implied aspiration and effort. Here we find some of the masters of the language producing tragedies which are, with few signal exceptions, dismally bad. In nearly each of the writers listed there lived at some moment the ideal of tragic drama, the thought that modern literature must achieve in the dramatic mode a work to set beside

Sophocles or Shakespeare. There is something at once moving and depressing in the glaring contrast between the quality of the talent and that of the work. In the midst of his miraculous year of lyric invention, Keats turned to *Otho the Great:*

Were it to succeed . . . it would lift me out of the mire. I mean the mire of a bad reputation which is continually rising against me. My name with the literary fashionable is vulgar—I am a weaver boy to them—a Tragedy would lift me out of this mess.

This, from the author of the *Eve of St. Agnes* and the Odes.

Yet as the sum of failure grew, so did the ambition. We can hardly refer to a poet or novelist of the nineteenth century without finding somewhere in his actual writings or intent the mirage of drama. Browning, Dickens, Tennyson, Swinburne, George Meredith; Stendhal, Balzac, Flaubert, Zola; Dostoevsky; Henry James. In each there burnt on occasion the resolve to master the stage, the determination to add something to the literary form which had in antiquity, in the renaissance, and in the baroque marshalled the best of poetic genius. But consider the plays these writers actually turned out; the incongruity is baffling. There appears to be no relationship between the stature of the artist and the bleak conventionality or total mechanical failure of the work.

There is here some need of explanation. And the problem is not solely one of theatrical history.

For only if we come nearer to the causes of the downfall of romantic drama, can we get into focus the question of what it was that had receded from western sensibility after Racine. And it was the failure of the romantics to restore to life the ideal of high tragedy which prepared the ground for the two major events in the history of the modern theatre: the separation between literature and the playhouse, and the radical change in the notion of the tragic and the comic brought on by Ibsen, Strindberg, Chekhov, and Pirandello. We cannot judge the extent of their victory without knowing something of the previous *débâcle*.

Romanticism and revolution are essentially related. In romanticism there is a liberation of thought from the deductive sobriety of Cartesian and Newtonian rationalism. There is a liberation of the imagination from the ferule of logic. There is, both intuitively and practically, a liberation of the individual from predetermined hierarchies of social station and caste. Romanticism is the shaking into motion of the atoms of the mind and society provoked by the decay of the *ancien régime* and by the decline from imaginative vitality of classic rationalism. Hair is allowed to fall freely where once sat the confining majesty of the powdered wig. Carried over into politics, romanticism became the French Revolution, the chain reaction of the Napoleonic wars, and the tremors that ran through the structure of Europe in 1830 and 1848. The first romantic decades were "a dawn," said

Wordsworth, in which it was bliss to be alive. For at the heart of their liberating energy lay a conviction inherited from Rousseau. The misery and injustice of man's fate were not caused by a primal fall from grace. They were not the consequence of some tragic, immutable flaw in human nature. They arose from the absurdities and archaic inequalities built into the social fabric by generations of tyrants and exploiters. The chains of man, proclaimed Rousseau, were man-forged. They could be broken by human hammers. It was a doctrine of immense implications, signifying that the shape of man's future lay within his own moulding. If Rousseau was right (and most political systems are, to this day, heirs to his assertion), the quality of being could be radically altered and improved by changes in education and in the social and material circumstances of existence. Man stood no longer under the shadow of original corruption; he carried within him no germ of preordained failure. On the contrary, he could be led toward tremendous progress. He was, in the vocabulary of romanticism, perfectible. Hence the glow of optimism in early romantic art, the feeling of ancient gates broken open and flung wide to a luminous future. In the final chorus of *Hellas*, Shelley celebrated the rise of the new sun:

> The world's great age begins anew,
>   The golden years return,
> The earth doth like a snake renew
>   Her winter weeds outworn:

Heaven smiles, and faiths and empires gleam,
  Like wrecks of a dissolving dream.
A brighter Hellas rears its mountains
  From waves serener far;
A new Peneus rolls his fountains
  Against the morning-star.
Where fairer Tempes bloom, there sleep
  Young Cyclads on a sunnier deep.

After 1820, the glow faded from the air. Reactionary forces reimposed their rule throughout Europe, and the middle class, which had been the source of radical energy, turned prosperous and conservative. The romantics experienced profound dejection (the word is decisive in Coleridge). They suffered a sense of betrayal, and Musset gave a classic account of their disillusion in the *Confession d'un enfant du siècle*. Romanticism developed qualities of autumn and afternoon: the stoicism of the late Wordsworth, the wild sadness of Byron, the autumnal, apocalyptic *tristesse* of the later Victor Hugo. There ripened in the romantic temper those elements of melancholy and nervous frustration which characterize post-romantic art. Symbolism and the Decadent movements of the later nineteenth century are a nightfall to the long decline of day.

But these darkenings were hardly perceptible in the period in which the romantics were trying to create a new dramatic tradition. And even when the light had grown lurid and uncertain, the original premise of romanticism retained much of its force. The Rousseauist belief in the perfectibility of man survived the partial defeats of liberalism in 1830 and 1848. Autocracy and *bourgeois* greed were fighting momentarily victorious rear-guard actions. But over the longer view, the human condition was one of destined progress. The city of justice lay in distant sight. Call it democracy, as did the romantic revolutionaries of the west, or the classless society as did Marx. In either case, it was the dream of progress first dreamt by Rousseau.

The Rousseauist and romantic vision had specific psychological correlatives. It implied a radical critique of the notion of guilt. In the Rousseauist mythology of conduct, a man could commit a crime either because his education had not taught him how to distinguish good and evil, or because he had been corrupted by society. Responsibility lay with his schooling or environment, for evil cannot be native to the soul. And because the individual is not wholly responsible, he cannot be wholly damned. Rousseauism closes the doors of hell. In the hour of truth, the criminal will be possessed with remorse. The crime will be undone or the error made good. Crime leads not to punishment, but to redemption. That is the *leit-motiv* in the romantic treatment of evil, from *The Ancient Mariner* to Goethe's *Faust*, from *Les Misérables* to the apotheosis of redemption in *Götterdämmerung*.

This redemptive mythology may have social and psychological merit, freeing the spirit from the black forebodings of Calvinism. But one thing is clear: such a view of the human condition is radically optimistic. It cannot engender any natural form of tragic drama. The romantic vision of life is non-tragic. In authentic tragedy, the gates of hell stand open and damnation is real. The tragic personage cannot evade responsibility. To argue that Oedipus should have been excused on grounds of ignorance, or that Phèdre was merely prey to hereditary chaos of the blood, is to diminish to absurdity the weight and meaning of the tragic action. The redeeming insight comes too late to mend the ruins or is purchased at the price of irremediable suffering. Samson goes blind to his death, and Faustus is dragged howling to perdition. Where a tragic conception of life is in force, moreover, there can be no recourse to secular or material remedies. The destiny of Lear cannot be resolved by the establishment of adequate homes for the aged. The dilemma which dooms Antigone lies deeper than any conceivable reform of the conventions that govern burial. In tragedy, the twist of the net which brings down the hero may be an accident or hazard of circumstance, but the mesh is woven into the heart of life. Tragedy would have us know that there is in the very fact of human existence a provocation or paradox; it tells us that the purposes of men sometimes run against the grain of inexplicable and destructive forces that lie "outside" yet very close. To ask of the gods why Oedipus should have been chosen for his agony or why Macbeth should have met the Witches on his path, is to ask for reason and justification from the voiceless night. There is no answer. Why should there be? If there was, we would be dealing with just or unjust suffering, as do parables and cautionary tales, not with tragedy. And beyond the tragic, there lies no "happy ending" in some other dimension of place or time. The wounds are not healed and the broken spirit is not mended. In the norm of tragedy, there can be no compensation. The mind, says I. A. Richards,

does not shy away from anything, it does not protect itself with any illusion, it stands uncomforted, alone and self reliant. . . . The least touch of any theology which has a compensating Heaven to offer the tragic hero is fatal.

But it is precisely a "compensating Heaven" that romanticism promises to the guilt and sufferings of man. It may be a literal Heaven as in *Faust*. More often, it is a state of bliss and redemption on earth. By virtue of remorse, the tragic sufferer is restored to a condition of grace. Or the ignorance and social injustice which have brought on the tragedy are removed by reform and the awakening of conscience. In the poetics of romanticism, the Scrooges turn golden.

The theme of remorse resounds through the entire tradition of romantic drama, from Coleridge to Wagner. The fable varies, but the characteristic *clichés* are constant. The tragic hero or hero-villain has committed a terrible, perhaps nameless, crime. He is tormented by his conscience and roams the earth, hiding an inward fire which reveals itself by

his feverish aspect and glittering eye. We know
him as the Ancient Mariner, Cain, the Flying
Dutchman, Manfred, or the Wandering Jew. Sometimes he is haunted by a pursuing double, an avenging image of himself or of his innocent victim. At
the hour of mortal crisis or approaching death, the
soul of the romantic hero is "wrenched with a woe-
ful agony." Suddenly, there is a flowering of remorse—brought to the repentant Tannhäuser, the
Papal staff puts forth leaves. Salvation descends on
the bruised spirit, and the hero steps toward grace
out of the shadow of damnation:

> The self-same moment I could pray;
> And from my neck so free
> The Albatross fell off, and sank
> Like lead into the sea.

The murderous villain who is responsible for the
evils committed in Wordsworth's tragedy, *The
Borderers*, is told at the close of the play:

> Thy office, thy ambition, be henceforth
> To feed remorse, to welcome every sting
> Of penitential anguish, yea with tears.

John Woodvil, the hero of a wretched but entirely
characteristic play by Charles Lamb, recounts his
hour of illumination. Here the Rousseauist belief
in the redemptive powers of sentiment has become
pure *cliché:*

> I past into the family pew,
> And covering up my eyes for shame
> And deep perception of unworthiness,

Upon the little hassock knelt me down,
Where I so oft had kneel'd,
A docile infant by Sir Walter's side;
And, thinking so, I wept a second flood
More poignant than the first;
But afterwards was greatly comforted.
It seem'd, the guilt of blood was passing from me
Even in the act and agony of tears,
And all my sins forgiven.

In Coleridge's *Remorse*, the problem of the quality of repentance is made the centre of the drama:

Remorse is at the heart, in which it grows:
If that be gentle, it drops balmy dews
Of true repentance; but if proud and gloomy,
It is a poison-tree, that pierced to the inmost
Weeps only tears of poison!

Coleridge was far too perceptive not to realize that there is in the entire notion of redemptive remorse something fraudulent. The villain of the play, Ordonio, gets to the heart of the matter:

ALVAR: Yet, yet thou may'st be sav'd—
ORDONIO: Sav'd? sav'd?
ALVAR: One pang!
       Could I call up one pang of true re-
       morse!
ORDONIO: .... remorse! remorse!
       Where gott'st thou that fool's word?
         Curse on remorse!
       Can it give up the dead, or recompact
       A mangled body? mangled—dashed to
         atoms!
       Not all the blessings of a host of angels

> Can blow away a desolate widow's
> curse!
> And though thou spill thy heart's blood
> for atonement,
> It will not weigh against an orphan's
> tear!

A superb answer, and one that cuts to the heart of the distinction between romanticism and a tragic sense of life. But the prevailing mythology proved too strong, and the drama ends on a note of redemption. Ordonio perishes crying: "Atonement!"

The theme of the "poison-tree," remorse turning to venom because the mind does not accept the possibility of redemption, obsessed Byron. Manfred is wracked by

> The innate tortures of that deep despair,
> Which is remorse without the fear of hell.

He knows there is no future pang

> Can deal that justice on the self-condemned
> He deals on his own soul.

And because he has determined, in his mad pride, that his punishment must be commensurate to his mysterious crime, Manfred will not give himself absolution. He says to the avenging Spirit:

> I have not been thy dupe, nor am thy prey—
> But was my own destroyer, and will be
> My own hereafter.

There is in this final arrogance a grim justice, and it gives to the close of *Manfred* an element of real tragedy.

But what we find in most romantic dramas and in Wagnerian opera is not tragedy. Dramas of remorse cannot be ultimately tragic. The formula is one of "near tragedy." Four acts of tragic violence and guilt are followed by a fifth act of redemption and innocence regained. "Near-tragedy" is precisely the compromise of an age which did not believe in the finality of evil. It represents the desire of the romantics to enjoy the privileges of grandeur and intense feeling associated with tragic drama without paying the full price. This price is the recognition of the fact that there are in the world mysteries of injustice, disasters in excess of guilt, and realities which do constant violence to our moral expectations. The mechanism of timely remorse or redemption through love—the arch-Wagnerian theme—allows the romantic hero to partake of the excitement of evil without bearing the real cost. It carries the audience to the brink of terror only to snatch them away at the last moment into the light of forgiveness. "Near-tragedy" is, in fact, another word for melodrama.

I have insisted on this theme of remorse because it exhibits clearly that evasion of the tragic which is central to the romantic temper. It is relevant, moreover, to more than the bad plays of poets who may, for a multitude of reasons, have been bad playwrights. The evasion of tragedy is decisive in Goethe's *Faust*. Marlowe's Faustus descends to hell-fire with a terrible, graphic awareness of his condition. He pleads: "My God, my God, look not so fierce on me." But it is too late. In his lucid mind, he is aware of the possibility of repentance, but he knows also that the habits of evil have grown native to his heart: "My heart is harden'd, I cannot repent." It is precisely because he can no longer cross the shadow line between the thought of remorse and the redemptive act, that Faustus is damned. But his awareness of the truth, his assumption of complete responsibility, make of him a tragic and heroic personage. His last contact with the secular world is to bid his disciples move away from him, "lest you perish with me."

Goethe's Faust, on the contrary, is saved. He is borne away amid falling rose-petals and the music of angelic choirs. The Devil is robbed of his just reward by a cunning psychological twist. Faust's intellect is corrupted by his commerce with hell, but his will has remained sanctified (this being the exact reverse of Dr. Faustus who wills evil even when he retains a knowledge of the good). The supreme bliss for which Faust bargained with the infernal powers turns out to be an act of Rousseauist benevolence—the draining of marshes toward the building of a new society. It is Mephistopheles who loses the wager. The heavens stream not with blood, as in Marlowe, but with redemptive hosannas. Nor is this a concession of the aged poet to his long ripening belief in the progressive, sanctified quality of life and the world. The idea of the "happy ending" is explicit in the first sketches of a Faust play set down by the young Goethe in the

1770's. Marlowe's *Faustus* is a tragedy; Goethe's *Faust* is sublime melodrama.

This bias toward the "near-tragic" controls the romantic theatre even where the subject seems least susceptible to happy resolution. In Schiller's *Jungfrau von Orleans*, the lady is not for burning. Joan dies near the battlefield in an apotheosis of victory and forgiveness. The curtain falls on her jubilation:

> Hinauf—hinauf—Die Erde flieht zurück—
> Kurz ist der Schmerz, und ewig ist die Freude! [2]

It is a glorious assertion. We hear it celebrated in Beethoven's setting of Schiller's *Ode to Joy*. It has in it the music of revolution and the sunrise of a new century. But it is a denial of the meaning of tragic drama. Schiller, who discriminated carefully between literary genres, was aware of the contradiction. He entitled the play *Eine romantische Tragödie*, and this is, I believe, the first time the antithetical terms "romanticism" and "tragedy" were conjoined. They cannot honestly go together. Romanticism substituted for the realness of hell which confronts Faustus, Macbeth, or Phèdre, the saving clause of timely redemption and the "compensating Heaven" of Rousseau.

In large measure, we are romantics still. The evasion of tragedy is a constant practice in our own contemporary theatre and films. In defiance of fact

---

[2] Aloft—aloft—The earth recoils from me—
Pain is short-lived, and joy is everlasting!

and logic, endings must be happy. Villains reform, and crime does not pay. That great dawn into which Hollywood lovers and heroes walk, hand in hand, at the close of the story, first came up on the horizon of romanticism.

If the romantic movement inherited from Rousseau his presumption of natural goodness and his belief in the social rather than metaphysical origins of evil, it inherited also his obsession with the self. The famous opening statement of Rousseau's *Confessions* struck the major chord in romantic literature:

Je veux montrer à mes semblables un homme dans toute la vérité de la nature; et cet homme, ce sera moi. Moi seul. Je sens mon coeur, et je connais les hommes. Je ne suis fait comme aucun de ceux que j'ai vus; j'ose croire n'être fait comme aucun de ceux qui existent.[3]

Rousseau was right to declare that his enterprise had no precedent. In Montaigne, the meditation on the self is intended toward knowledge of the generality of the human condition. To a classical temper such as Pascal's, the self is "hateful," interposing random claims and infirmities between the spirit and its communion with God. Rousseau and the romantics place the ego at the centre of the intelligible world. Byron remarks ironically in *Don Juan:*

[3] I want to show to my fellow men a man in all the truth of nature; and that man will be I. I alone. I feel my own heart, and I know men. I am not made up like any that I have seen; I venture to believe that I am unlike any that exist.

> What a sublime discovery 't was to make the
>   Universe universal egotism,
> That's all ideal—*all ourselves*.

Whereas Boileau censured a work of art if the author revealed in it his own person or private sensibility, the romantics sought in art the rapture of self-consciousness. Behind Coleridge's judgement of Milton lies a veritable revolution of values:

> his Satan, his Adam, his Raphael, almost his Eve—are all John Milton; and it is a sense of this egotism that gives me the greatest pleasure in reading Milton's works. The egotism of such a man is a revelation of spirit.

The classic image of man is one that places him within a stable architecture of custom, religious and political tradition, and social caste. He accords his individual person to the style of his temporal station. The romantic man is Narcissus in exalted pursuit and affirmation of his unique identity. The surrounding world is mirror or echo to his presence. He suffers and glories in his solitude:

> Mais moi, Narcisse aimé, je ne suis curieux
>   Que de ma seule essence;
> Tout autre n'a pour moi qu'un coeur mystérieux,
>   Tout autre n'est qu'absence.[4]

Being the natural voice of self-awareness, the lyric is the dominant mode of romantic literature.

---

[4] But I, Narcissus loved, would plumb
  Only my essence;
All other hearts to me are dumb,
  All else is absence.

It is in lyric verse and in the prose of reverie or first-person narrative that romanticism gained its eminent glories. The life and candour of the private spirit in the art of Wordsworth, Keats, Shelley, Lamartine, Vigny, Heine, Leopardi, or Pushkin give to their poetry a kind of incandescence. It burns to the touch. Our awareness of the range of prose would be narrower if we did not know *Werther, The Confessions of an English Opium Eater*, or Dostoevsky's *Notes from the Underground*. Romanticism taught prose the arts of intimacy.

But the lyric mode is profoundly alien to the dramatic. Drama is the supreme practice of altruism. By a miracle of controlled self-destruction, which we can only dimly apprehend, the dramatist creates living characters whose radiance of life is precisely commensurate to their "otherness"—to their not being images, shadows, or resonances of the playwright himself. Falstaff lives because he is not Shakespeare; Nora, because she is not Ibsen. Indeed, their power of life is greatly superior to that of their begetters. Even if Sophocles were only a name whereby to designate an unknown, as is that of Homer, Oedipus and Antigone would be indestructably vital. Who but the scholar is aware of the identity of the poet who first put Don Juan on a stage? What knowledge need we have of Racine to experience the extreme life of Iphigénie or Phèdre? Doubtless, the creation of a dramatic character is related to the private genius of the dramatist. But we do not really know how. Characters

are, perhaps, those parts of shadow or independent
vitality within the psyche which the poet cannot
integrate to his own person. They are cancers of
the imagination insisting on their right to live outside the organism from which they are engendered
(how long could a man endure with an Oedipus or
a Lear locked inside him?). But whatever their relationship to the source of invention, dramatic
personages assume their own integral being. They
lead their own life far beyond the mortality of the
poet. We have not, and need not have, adequate
biographies of Aeschylus or Shakespeare.

All classic art strives for this ideal of impersonal-
ity, for the severance of the work from the contingency of the artist. Romanticism aims at the
contrary. It seeks to render the poem inseparable
from the voice of the poet. In the romantic imagination, expression invariably tends toward self-
portrayal.

Such a conception is radically inappropriate to
drama. Yet the romantics sought to bring the dramatic form within the scope of egotism. Heine
glories in asserting that his tragedies are intimate
revelations of his own heart:

> Meine Qual und meine Klagen
> Hab ich in dies Buch gegossen,
> Und wenn du es aufgeschlagen,
> Hat sich dir mein Herz erschlossen.[5]

[5] Both my anguish and outrage
Have I poured into my art,
As you turn the printed page,
You are reading in my heart.

In fact, neither *Almansor* nor *Ratcliff* has any spark
of independent life. They exist solely by the grace
of our interest in Heine himself. In *Les Contempla-
tions*, Victor Hugo compares the dramatist to a
creature—half pelican, one supposes, and half
phoenix—which pours out its lifeblood to create
characters all of whom are reflections of its own
identity. The whole passage is a romantic credo:

> Dans sa création, le poète tressaille;
> Il est elle, elle est lui; quand dans l'ombre il
>   travaille,
> Il pleure, et s'arrachant les entrailles, les met
> Dans son drâme, et, sculpteur, seul sur son noir
>   sommet
> Pétrit sa propre chair dans l'argile sacrée;
> Il y renaît sans cesse, et ce songeur qui crée
> Othello d'une larme, Alceste d'un sanglot,
> Avec eux pêle-mêle en ses oeuvres éclot.
> Dans sa genèse immense et vraie, une et diverse,
> Lui, le souffrant du mal éternel, il se verse,
> Sans épuiser son flanc d'où sort une clarté.[6]

[6] The poet is quiveringly alive inside his own creation;
He is his creation, it is he; when he labours in darkness,
He weeps, and tearing out his insides, puts them
Into his drama; the sculptor, alone on his black mountain-
     top,
Kneads his own flesh into the hallowed clay;
From it, he is constantly reborn; and the dreamer who
     creates
Othello from a tear, Alceste from a sob,
Flourishes within his creation, inseparable from those he
     shapes.
In his true and immense creative act, unique and manifold,
The artist, suffering from an eternal wound, expends him-
     self,

Not all poets of the romantic period were blind to the contradiction between an egotistical theory of art and the nature of drama. Byronism signifies a wild, lyric expression of self-consciousness. Yet with respect to drama, Byron himself held classic convictions. He tried to write a number of tragedies in which the voice of the poet would fall silent behind that of the personages. Keats went even further. He developed an explicitly antiromantic ideal of drama founded on a rejection of what he called "the egotistical sublime." Inspired by Hazlitt's view of Shakespeare, Keats asserted that "Men of Genius are great as certain ethereal Chemicals operating on the Mass of neutral intellect—but they have not any individuality, any determined Character." In October 1818, he arrived at his conception of the true poet. The passage is famous, but so charged with meaning that one cannot cite it too often:

As to the poetical Character itself (I mean that sort of which, if I am any thing, I am a Member; that sort distinguished from the wordsworthian or egotistical sublime; which is a thing per se and stands alone) it is not itself—it has no self—it is every thing and nothing—It has no character—it enjoys light and shade; it lives in

---

Without exhausting his loins, from which radiance streams forth.

Victor Hugo is here at his worst; the text is turgid bombast. Often, the old trumpeter wrote his poorest verse when he was being most urgent and sincere. For, unquestionably, this passage embodies his inmost vision of art and the artist.

gusto, be it foul or fair, high or low, rich or poor, mean or elevated—It has as much delight in conceiving an Iago as an Imogen. . . . A poet is the most unpoetical of any thing in existence; because he has no Identity. . . . When I am in a room with People if I ever am free from speculating on creations of my own brain, then not myself goes home to myself: but the identity of every one in the room begins so to press upon me that I am in a very little time annihilated.

In the same month, Keats wrote to his brother:

I do not live in this world alone but in a thousand worlds. . . . According to my state of mind I am with Achilles shouting in the trenches, or with Theocritus in the Vales of Sicily. Or I throw my whole being into Troilus . . . I melt into the air.

Keats's recognition of the manner in which the dramatic poet is "annihilated" within his work is superbly classical. It refutes the entire Rousseauist and romantic conception of the primacy of the self. These letters of 1818 are a beautifully articulate programme for a renascence of English tragedy. Instead, Keats produced a wretched melodrama, *Otho the Great.* And the reason, this time, lies not in a failure to comprehend the function of the dramatic poet. The reason is one of technical form. Though Keats saw much deeper than other romantics into the nature of drama, he shared the prevailing belief that the future of tragedy was inseparable from the Shakespearean ideal.

Admiration for Shakespeare predates the ro-

mantic period. Dryden repeatedly expressed a sense
of the poet's unique eminence:

> But Shakespeare's Magick could not copy'd be;
> Within that Circle none durst walk but he.

Even where he made formal reservations, Samuel
Johnson saw in Shakespeare a titan superior to any
neo-classic dramatist and, at times, to the Greek
tragedians. Some thirty-five editions of Shakespeare's plays appeared between 1766 and 1799,
and the editorial scholarship of Johnson, Steevens,
and Malone laid the foundations for much of our
modern text. As early as 1786, an essayist could
write of Shakespeare in a tone close to that of the
higher flights of romantic exaltation: "But, say you,
we have never seen such a thing. You are in the
right; Nature made it, and broke the mould."

But the romantic relationship to Shakespeare
runs deeper. Nowhere in eighteenth-century criticism would we find the comparisons between
Shakespeare and Scripture drawn by Coleridge, or
that conception of Shakespeare as the prime master
of the human spirit which is argued in Keats's letters. It was around Shakespearean drama that the
romantic sensibility gathered its main forces. The
romantic poets sought to cast their own person into
the mould of Romeo, Lear, or Macbeth. Hamlet
became their emblem and guardian presence. In
the lives of Charles Lamb, Hazlitt, Coleridge,
Keats, Victor Hugo, Musset, Stendhal, Schiller,

Pushkin—the list could be interminably extended
—the discovery of Shakespeare was the great
awakener of consciousness. In his *Mémoires*, Berlioz recounts the shock of Shakespearean recognition:

Shakespeare, en tombant sur moi à l'improviste, me
foudroya. Son éclair, en m'ouvrant le ciel de l'art avec
un fracas sublime, m'en illumina les plus lointaines pro-
fondeurs. Je reconnus la vraie grandeur, la vraie
beauté, la vraie vérité dramatique. . . . Je vis . . . je
compris . . . je sentis que j'étais vivant et qu'il fallait
me lever et marcher.[7]

He thereupon entered into an ill-fated marriage
with a Shakespearean actress in order to live closer
to the radiance of Juliet and Ophelia. In the history
of the romantic artist, whether he be a poet, a
composer, or a painter such as Delacroix, it is the
volume of Shakespeare found in the library on a
winter's night or in the bookstall, which rouses in
the soul the intimation of genius.

Thus, Shakespeare became to the romantic poets
more than an object of critical reverence. His works
were held up as a model to all later drama. Combine all, wrote Coleridge,

wit, subtlety, and fancy, with profundity, imagination,
and moral and physical susceptibility to the pleasurable

[7] Shakespeare, who fell upon me unawares, struck me like lightning. His bolt, in opening for me with a sublime thunderclap
the heaven of art, lit for me its furthest depths. I recognized
true grandeur, true beauty, true dramatic verity. . . . I saw
. . . I understood . . . I felt that I was alive and must rouse
myself and march forward.

—and let the object of action be man universal; and we shall have—O, rash prophecy! say, rather, we have— a Shakespeare!

If English tragedy was to be waked from its neo-classic slumbers, it could only be to the clarion call of Shakespeare. Here was to be found mastery of all arts, passions, and poetic styles. Advising a friend on the proper ordering of a tragic play, Lamb counseled:

I recommend a situation like Othello, with relation to Desdemona's intercession for Cassio. By-scenes may likewise receive hints. The son may see his mother at a mask or feast, as Romeo, Juliet. . . . Dawley may be told his wife's past unchastity at a mask by some witch-character—as Macbeth upon the heath, in dark sentences.

In his preface to *The Borderers*, Wordsworth points out that the figure of Iago and his bedevilling of the Moor are crucial to his own play. Coleridge called *Zapolya* a "humble imitation of the *Winter's Tale.*" Indeed, from Coleridge to Tennyson, nearly all English poetic dramas are feeble variations on Shakespearean themes.

But not exclusively. Shakespeare's contemporaries were also drawn into the circle of ardent imitation. English romanticism rediscovered Marlowe, Chapman, Marston, Tourneur, Middleton, Webster, and Ford. With the publication of Lamb's *Specimens of English Dramatic Poets* in 1808, a treasure house of rhetoric and tragic sentiment was opened to the romantic pursuit of drama. "When a Giant is shown to us," asked Lamb, "does it detract from the curiosity to be told that he has at home a gigantic brood of brethren, less only than himself?" Hence we find in Lamb's *John Woodvil* not only a slavish imitation of *As You Like It,* but passages modelled on Ford and on *Dr. Faustus.* In *The Cenci,* there are dozens of echoes of *Romeo and Juliet* and *Measure for Measure,* but Shelley drew also on the tone and plot of *The White Devil* and *The Duchess of Malfi.* The erudite Coleridge included in *Remorse* hints from the pre-Shakespearean *Spanish Tragedy* and from *The Two Noble Kinsmen,* a play traditionally ascribed half to the master and half to Fletcher. In short, English romantic drama is a veiled anthology of the Elizabethan and Jacobean playwrights.

This is the decisive point: the romantic imitation of Shakespeare and his contemporaries embraced not only matters of plot and dramatic technique—it was close, deliberate imitation of language. The eighteenth century had admired Shakespeare in spite of his archaic language. A critic such as Johnson held that English had gained in clarity and sobriety since the Elizabethans and Jacobeans. He had too much good sense to suppose that the language of a past literary period could be revived, language being the living mirror of historical change. The romantics, on the contrary, immersed themselves in Shakespearean speech, in the hope that they could thereby restore the lost glory of the English stage. They hung on their melodramatic plots and egotistical imaginings great streamers of words borrowed from Marlowe, Shakespeare, Webster, or Ford. The result is a dismal farrago. To cite more than one or two representative instances would be an exercise in mockery.

Perhaps because he knew the old dramatists even more intimately than did his contemporaries, Lamb was most helpless when it came to his own plays. Take the opening scene of *John Woodvil*:

PETER: A delicate song. Where did'st learn it, Fellow?

DANIEL: Even there, where thou learnest thy oaths and thy politics—at our master's table. Where else should a serving man pick up his poor accomplishments?

MARTIN: Well spoken, Daniel. O rare Daniel!—his oaths and his politics! excellent!

The episode derives from *Othello,* and the wholly inappropriate response is taken from *The Merchant of Venice.* The language as such is an archaic hodgepodge never spoken by living man or beast.

At the other extreme of imitation, we find *The Cenci.* Here pastiche is carried to the level of art. The play gives the impression of having been conceived by a poet of obvious talent as a stylistic exercise in the Elizabethan mode. At times, the invoked feelings are so strong as to master the borrowed tongue and make it natural:

> So young to go
> Under the obscure, cold, rotting, wormy ground!
> To be nailed down into a narrow place;
> To see no more sweet sunshine; hear no more
> Blithe voice of living thing; muse not again
> Upon familiar thoughts, sad, yet thus lost!
> How fearful! to be nothing! Or to be—
> What? O, where am I? Let me not go mad!
> Sweet Heaven, forgive weak thoughts! If there
>   should be
> No God, no Heaven, no earth in the void world;
> The wide, grey, lampless, deep, unpeopled world!

Beatrice Cenci's grief is so beautifully expressed that we can, momentarily, ignore how closely it is modelled on the outburst of Claudio in Act III of *Measure for Measure*. But even at the best, the fact of imitation intrudes. When Beatrice confronts her tormentors—

> Entrap me not with questions. Who stands here
> As my accuser? Ha! wilt thou be he,
> Who art my judge? Accuser, witness, judge,
> What, all in one?

we cannot help recalling the words of Vittoria Corombona in *The White Devil*:

> Who says so but yourself? if you be my accuser,
> Pray cease to be my judge: come from the bench,
> Give your evidence against me, and let these
> Be moderators.

Shelley wrote, observes Edmund Blunden, "with Lamb's *Specimens of the Dramatists* at his elbow." Seeing in Shakespeare his "patron saint" and the

148

ultimate incarnation of dramatic genius, Keats inevitably followed on Shakespearean traces when
writing *Otho the Great*. The play is Gothic melodrama; some of the wild plot derives from *Cymbeline* and *Much Ado About Nothing*, and one
scholar has counted borrowings from the language
of seventeen Shakespearean plays. Keats looked also
to Middleton, whose *Duke of Milan* he read shortly
before beginning on *Otho*, and to Marlowe. When
trying to be a dramatist, the poet of the Odes and
of *Lamia* was as defenceless as a schoolboy before
the rush and bombast of the Marlovian style:

> 'Stead of one fatted calf
> Ten hecatombs shall bellow out their last,
> Smote 'twixt the horns by the death-stunning
> mace
> Of Mars, and all the soldiery shall feast
> Nobly as Nimrod's masons, when the towers
> Of Nineveh new kiss'd the parted clouds.

It is as if Keats had set out to write a parody of
Tamburlaine.

What is puzzling about the abdication of the
romantic poets from their own voice and living
speech is the fact that they knew how wrong they
were. In his preface to *The Cenci*, Shelley declared
"that in order to move men to true sympathy we
must use the familiar language of men." Romantics
should study the Elizabethans only so as to do
"that for our own age which they have done for
theirs." No one in the nineteenth century wrote
plays more completely penetrated with the lan-

guage and technique of the Jacobeans than Thomas Lovell Beddoes. This fiery, minor figure was not a reviver of the past but, as Lytton Strachey remarked, "a reincarnation." Yet it was Beddoes who expressed most eloquently the need for independence:

Say what you will—I am convinced the man who is to waken the drama must be a bold trampling fellow—no creeper into worm-holes—no reviser even—however good. These reanimations are vampire-cold. Such ghosts as Marlowe, Webster &c are better dramatists, better poets, I dare say, than any contemporary of ours—but they are ghosts—the worm is in their pages—& we want to see something that our great-grandsires did not know. With the greatest reverence for all the antiquities of the drama, I still think that we had better beget than revive—attempt to give the literature of this age an idiosyncrasy & spirit of its own, & only raise a ghost to gaze on, not to live with—just now the drama is a haunted ruin.

Yet between this clear knowledge and the act of writing fell the Shakespearean shadow. And in English drama it falls still. The problem of dramatic verse remains largely unsolved. The language of English poetic drama is still seeking to free itself from the Shakespearean precedent. English blank verse seems to carry the mark of Shakespeare in its marrow. Today also, much of serious drama is "a haunted ruin," and I wonder whether we have moved very far since 1902, when Edmund Gosse said of the Elizabethan tradition: "It haunts us, it oppresses us, it destroys us."

V

SHAKESPEARE had cast his spell beyond England.
His name and work were a battle cry to the French
romantics. It was not *Hernani* which first brought
the romantic voice to the French theatre, but
Vigny's translation of *Othello* performed in October 1829. Victor Hugo regarded Shakespeare as his
patron spirit, and was resolved to break the neo-
classic mould with a Shakespearean hammer. In
the preface to *Cromwell*, he declared that it was
the essential genius of romanticism to associate the
"grotesque" with the "sublime," to combine in art
the drollery and rough shadow sides of life with
ideals of expressive beauty. This concordance of
rival energies had first been accomplished by Shakespeare, "the sovereign poet":

Shakespeare, c'est le drame; et le drame qui fond sous un même souffle le grotesque et le sublime, le terrible et le bouffon, la tragédie et la comédie.[1]

From his exile on the island of Jersey, Victor Hugo paid to the Elizabethan poet a wild, entrancing homage. *William Shakespeare* is not really a piece of literary criticism: it is an ecstatic cry of the romantic imagination. The book is filled with the grandiloquence of the sea which then surrounded the author. The scale of judgement is more than human. Shakespeare is a headland thrust into the waters of eternity; in his capacious soul storms of ultimate fury alternate with halcyon calm; in his works is mirrored the mystery of elemental creation. With Homer, Aeschylus, Job, Isaiah, and Dante, Shakespeare constitutes one of the lone summits of the human spirit. Those who precede him in time seem to lead toward his crowning magnificence. It is in the image of Shakespeare that the modern artist, such as Beethoven or Victor Hugo himself, must create his own ideal.

Victor Hugo's romantic contemporaries were possessed by a comparable wildness of admiration. Often, they knew little of Shakespeare's actual work. The name of the Elizabethan master sufficed as a catalyst to their own sense of the heroic, the passionate, and the sublime. What really mattered was the fact that neo-classicism in France had ig-

[1] Shakespeare is the drama; and the drama which mingles in one breath the grotesque and the sublime, the terrible and the clownish, tragedy and comedy.

nored or reviled the creator of Hamlet and Romeo. Voltaire, the *bête noire* of the romantics, had regarded Shakespeare as an uncouth barbarian redeemed by occasional flashes of primitive energy. Even Diderot, who had recognized in him a "colossus," found his work "gross" and "shapeless." Such errors of judgement were grist to the romantic mill. Through Victor Hugo's essay blows a hurricane of invective against the critics and poetasters of the eighteenth century who had sought to measure the daemonic freedom of Shakespeare's art by their own petty rules. Those who are against Shakespeare, says Victor Hugo, are against us. They are the reactionaries, the academics, the Philistines whom the young romantics battled in the theatre pit during the *première* of *Hernani*. Even Stendhal who knew his Shakespeare at first hand, saw in *Hamlet*, *Lear*, and *Macbeth* levers by which to remove Racine from the commanding place he held in the French sensibility. Stendhal's Shakespeare is great, in large measure, because he affirms values contrary to those of Racine.

Thus, the Shakespearean influence on French romantic drama was mainly strategic. The romantics appealed to the Shakespearean precedent when committing audacities which were already implicit in their own canons. They mingled the comic and the tragic in repudiation of the neo-classical doctrine of unity. They introduced grotesque and low-born personages into the sphere of high drama in order to subvert the neo-classic principle of decorum. They brought to the theatre themes of madness, of physical violence, of ghost-ridden and dreamlike fantasy. Their heroines were Ophelias or Desdemonas exhaling their anguish to the willows. Their heroes were princes out of Denmark; their villains, writhing Iagos. But the substance was that of romanticism itself. It had grown from the great movement toward pathos occurring in the late eighteenth century, from the egalitarian ideals of the French Revolution, and from the night world of the Gothic. If the romantic hero is Hamlet, he is also Werther and the "daemon-lover" of the German ballads.

Indeed, there is in the interpretation of Shakespeare by the French romantics much misunderstanding. They saw in Shakespeare complete licence of form, having no awareness of the elements of ritual and convention which are at work in Elizabethan drama. Their notion of Shakespearean realism was naïve. The historicism of Victor Hugo, Dumas, or Vigny, their passionate interest in local colour and authenticity of presentation, is entirely alien to Shakespeare. Nothing could be further from the spirit of Elizabethan drama than Victor Hugo's assurance that "there is not in *Ruy Blas* one detail of private or public life, of setting, of escutcheon, of etiquette, of biography . . . which is not scrupulously exact." The world of *Julius Caesar, Anthony and Cleopatra,* and the chronicle plays, is one in which the imagination is freed from

obligations of historical fidelity. When Victor
Hugo opens *Cromwell* with the notation—

> Demain, vingt-cinq juin mil six cent cinquante-
> sept—

he shows that he is of the century of Hegel. In both
Shakespeare and Racine there is a timelessness; and
where there is time, it is not chronology.

If the French romantics' vision of Shakespeare
has more fire than knowledge, the reason is obvious. Most of Victor Hugo's contemporaries did not
know their author in the original. They had read
the plays in the mediocre translations of Pierre Le
Tourneur, published between 1776 and 1782.
When the first troupe of English players came to
Paris in 1827 to perform *Romeo and Juliet*, *Hamlet*,
and *Othello* in their native tongue, the audience
were filled with enthusiasts who did not understand
a word of what was being said. Among them was
Berlioz whose idolatry of Shakespeare and whose
musical settings of Shakespearean themes were
founded on wretched translations. It is only in the
later nineteenth century, and with the critical work
of Taine, that the authentic Shakespeare becomes
accessible to the French reader.

The Shakespeare of the romantics, therefore, was
not primarily an Elizabethan poet with medieval
traditions in his art and world view. He was a
master of poetic sublimity and volcanic passion, a
proclaimer of romantic love and melancholy, a

radical who wrote melodramas. The difference between the false picture and the true can be clearly
shown in Verdi's operas. *Macbeth* dramatizes a
romantic reading of Shakespeare. *Otello* and *Falstaff*, on the contrary, exhibit a transfiguring insight
into the actual meaning of the two Shakespearean
plays.

To these facts there is a notable exception. Musset's *Lorenzaccio* is shaped by a direct awareness
of the quality of Shakespeare. It shows that a poet
is exceptionally fortunate when he can enter into
the spirit of Shakespeare without being able to
enter completely into the letter. Had Musset been
more steeped in the actual text of Shakespeare,
Lorenzaccio might have been one of a score of
pseudo-Shakespearean romantic dramas. Instead,
he borrowed from Shakespeare only what he could
recast into his own idiom. But I shall return to
Lorenzaccio later on.

In Germany and in German literature, the role
of Shakespeare was far more decisive than in
France. The reason is that, in a paradoxical sense,
Shakespearean influence was exercised from within.
Wieland's translation in the 1760's and the famous
version of the complete Shakespeare by Schlegel
and Tieck (1796–1833) did more than convey to
German awareness the genius of a foreign poet.
These formidable re-creations of the English text
coincided precisely with the time in which the
German language was coming of literary age. They
entered directly into the crucible. The Shakespear-

ean manner penetrated into the cadence and tonality of classic German. The German sensibility appropriated to itself the habits of rhetoric and dialectic inherent in Shakespearean tragedy. It was a true graft of the foreign branch to the native stem. During the nineteenth century Germany became a source of much of the finest in Shakespearean criticism and scholarship. Nowhere else were the plays performed with comparable frequency or fidelity to the text. German audiences were seeing authentic versions of *Hamlet* and *Lear* when most English stages were still using texts softened or truncated to suit neo-classic taste. Appropriately, the love affair between Germany and Shakespeare culminated in the attempt of certain Prussian scholars to show that Shakespeare had actually been a German.

But because Shakespeare's presence is so intrinsic to the German language and to the growth of German drama, it is difficult to point to precise derivations. In the Goethe–Schiller correspondence —that live commentary on the precariousness and possibilities of a national culture—the existence of Shakespearean drama is a prime assumption. It is the tuning fork by which the native theatre must try its note. The two masters adapted Shakespearean plays for the Weimar stage, and the Shakespearean example is vital in their own works. Goethe's *Götz von Berlichingen* and his *Egmont* are strongly coloured by the Shakespearean touch. In both, we find a tension characteristic of Shake-

spearean chronicle plays, the tragic life of the hero
being set off against the larger canvas of the crowd
and the historical moment. Encouraged by Goethe,
Schiller harboured the thought of writing a series
of dramas founded on German history. These
would waken German national consciousness by
giving it a vision of the past comparable to that
which Englishmen found in Shakespeare. He wrote
to Goethe in November 1797:

In the last days I have been reading the plays of Shakespeare which deal with the War of the Roses, and now
that I have finished *Richard III*, I am filled with true
amazement. This latter play is one of the noblest tragedies I know. . . . No Shakespearean play has so much
reminded me of Greek tragedy.

The letter concludes with the remark that *Wallenstein* is progressing satisfactorily. This train of
thought was no accident, for of all German drama
Wallenstein is most Shakespearean. The large design stretching over a dramatic prelude and two
massive plays, the lines of action winding and
crossing in elaborate patterns, the hero in whom
resolution alternates with weariness and introspec-
tion—all reflect Schiller's study of *Henry IV*,
Richard II, and *Richard III*. The most significant
debt lies in the handling of the crowd. Schiller's
convictions as a revolutionary and a historian made
him ascribe to the crowd a shaping role in political
events. But the presentation of a mass of soldiers
or citizens lay entirely outside the reach of the
antique and the neo-classical theatre. Goethe sug-

gested to Schiller that the solution lay with *Julius Caesar* and *Coriolanus*, where the conflict between individual and crowd was fully dramatized. So far as it transfers the life of the crowd to a special prologue, *Wallenstein* falls short of Schiller's intent. He was coming closer to the ideal of interaction in *Demetrius*, a great torso of drama which Schiller did not live to complete. Here as in Shakespeare, the crowd was to be actor, chorus, and elemental force.

The theme of Demetrius, the false czar, directs us to the finest of all the dramas produced by the romantic study of Shakespeare and to one of the very few genuine tragedies written in the nineteenth century. Exiled to his family estate in the year 1824–5, Pushkin turned from Byron to Shakespeare. He was acutely conscious of the fact that Russian literature had, so far, produced no drama. Shakespeare revealed to him the tragic poetry of the historical. *Boris Godunov* is a masterpiece. The jagged, nervous rhythm of successive scenes may be distantly indebted to *Götz von Berlichingen*, but Mussorgsky saw in it a quality which was peculiarly Russian. The dense gloom of the atmosphere, the hysteria which glares around the edges of the characters' minds, foreshadow the climate of Dostoevsky. The death agony of Boris, with the boyars gathering in on him like hooded bats, suggests what the theatre of Byzantium might have brought forth had there been Byzantine tragedians. It has the weight and ominous glitter of a mosaic.

Yet *Boris Godunov* would not exist in anything resembling its present form without *Macbeth*, *Henry IV*, and *Richard III*. Boris is a Shakespearean tyrant in whom evil is mitigated, as in Macbeth, by sheer vividness of imagination and moral awareness. He is haunted by Shakespearean visions of retribution. The noblemen who surround him are those fierce, scheming beasts of prey who fight for York or Lancaster in Shakespeare's histories. The scenes of battle are conducted in the Elizabethan style, and the Russian crowd seethes around the high personages as in the cauldron of *Richard III*.

But such was Pushkin's talent, and so great were the distances of language and atmosphere which divide the Russian play from its Shakespearean sources, that we feel no sense of mere imitation. What Pushkin took, he appropriated wholly to himself. Over *Boris Godunov*, as nowhere else in romantic drama, the presence of Shakespeare throws light rather than shadow.

Little else in European romantic drama rivals the tragic coherence of *Boris Godunov*. The reason does not, however, lie primarily with the arresting influence of Shakespeare. In England, that influence was overwhelming enough to crush the life out of poetic drama. Elsewhere, it could act only as a stimulant or partial seduction. The failure of romantic tragedy in Europe, or the deliberate evasion of the tragic, cannot be accounted for by any single, universal circumstance. The case, moreover, differs in France and in Germany.

In regard to French romantic drama, one's sense of artistic failure is drastic. The plays of Victor Hugo, Vigny, and the lesser romantics are not only hopelessly dated; they have about them an insidious flavour of decay. Yet why are *Hernani* and *Ruy Blas* so intolerable if looked at in any serious light? Victor Hugo was immensely possessed by a flair for the theatrical. He was a brilliant, cunning versifier. He had at his command what appears to have been some of the best acting in the history of the modern theatre. What makes of his plays such vehement trivialities? Surely, the reason is that in them the theatre triumphs so relentlessly over the drama. All is outward effect, and the effect is invariably in gross excess of the cause. A play such as *Ruy Blas* erects an edifice of incident, passion, rhetoric, and grand gesture on the most precarious of foundations. There is no core of intelligible motive; the issues engaged are, if we can unravel them at all, of the slightest interest. What is tremendously provided are the outward semblances of drama. For Victor Hugo is a master showman. Characters reveal themselves from behind voluminous cloaks; they drop out of chimneys; they draw murderous rapiers at the least provocation; they roar like lions, and die in long flourishes. The mechanics of excitement are superbly contrived. The curtain falls on successive acts like a thunderclap, leaving us breathless with expectation. Often, the situations themselves are unforgettably vivid. Even if one has only seen *Hernani* as a child (and later on it is difficult to last the distance), one remembers the great drum roll of words with which the hero discloses his identity in the crypt at Aix-la-Chapelle:

Puisqu' il faut être grand pour mourir, je me lève.
Dieu qui donne le sceptre et qui te le donna
M'a fait duc de Segorbe et duc de Cardona,
Marquis de Monroy, comte Albatera, vicomte
De Gor, seigneur de lieux dont j'ignore le compte.
Je suis Jean d'Aragon, grand maitre d'Avis, né
Dans l'exil, fils proscrit d'un père assassiné
Par sentence du tien, roi Carlos de Castille! [2]

[2] As only grandees have the right to die, I rise.
God who has wrought the scepter and who made you king,
Has made me twice a duke, in Cardóna and Segorbe,
Marquess of Monroy, Count Albatera, Viscount
Of Gor, I reck not of how many places lord.
I, John of Aragon, am Master of Avís;
Hunted, in exile born, my father done to death
By order of your sire, O Carlos of Castile!

The places named are towns or townships in Valentia and the surrounding provinces; the Order of Avis was a Portuguese chivalric order; by addressing the king as Carlos of Castile, Hernani seeks to emphasize the partial, local character of Spanish royal sovereignty. He, John of Aragon, implies that he is the equal of the king of Castile. There is no use in trying to render Victor Hugo's rhymed *alexandrins* into English couplets. In English as in French neo-classicism, the rhymed couplet conveys precisely those qualities of order and economy which Victor Hugo repudiated. The closest counterpart to Hugo's style would be Marlowe modernized. What counts in this passage from *Hernani* is the grand roar of vowels and the rhetorical flourish.

Who can forget the entrance of the masked figure
in the last act of *Ruy Blas?*

> RUY BLAS: Cet homme, quel est-il? Mais parle
> donc! j'attends!
> L'HOMME MASQUÉ: C'est moi!
> RUY BLAS: Grand Dieu!—Fuyez, madame!
> DON SALLUSTE: Il n'est plus temps.
> Madame de Neubourg n'est
> plus reine d'Espagne.[3]

Splendid, in its own special way, but completely
hollow to any touch of intelligence. The shapes of
drama are being invoked without the substance.
The forces which set the action in motion are those
of wild hazard and tenuous intrigue. There are
conflicts of abstract honour or dynastic privilege
(the recurrent Castilian note) but not of articulate
character or belief. Our entire interest is solicited
by the manner of contrivance, not by any intrinsic
meaning. Will the fatal horn blow before Hernani
can find bliss with Doña Sol? Will Ruy Blas kill
his satanic master in time to save the compromised
Queen? The limiting conditions are not those of
moral insight or intelligence, but clocks nearing
midnight, bolted doors, messengers racing toward
scaffolds. Even the verbal form is theatrical rather
than dramatic. The romantics retained the Alex-

[3] RUY BLAS: Who is this man? Speak! Speak! I wait!
THE MASKED MAN: It is I!
RUY BLAS: Great God!—Flee, madam!
DON SALLUSTE [now unmasked]: It is too late for that.
Madame de Neubourg is no longer queen of Spain.

andrine of their neo-classic predecessors and rivals.
But what had been in Racine dramatic form, is now
rhetorical formality. As the argument in Corneille
and Racine is close and rapid, the couplet forms a
natural unit. The rhyme accentuates the finality
of the thought, and few lines are broken. In the
dramas of Victor Hugo, the single verse is continually interrupted and scattered among several
speakers. This renders the form declamatory and
artificial. The rhyme is achieved by an acrobatic
leap over the void of logic. It serves no real purpose.
Like the action, the language is full of great empty
gestures.

Where the theatrical is allowed complete rule
over the dramatic, we get melodrama. And that is
what French romantic tragedies are: melodramas
on the grand scale. Having repudiated classic notions of the evil in man, Victor Hugo and his contemporaries replaced the tragic by the contingent.
The events of the plot are caused by fatalities of
chance encounter or affront. They articulate no
conflict natural to human affairs. Therefore they
provoke in us the momentary shock, the shiver in
the spine—what the romantics called *le frisson*—
—not the abiding terror of tragedy. And this distinction between horror and tragic terror is fundamental to any theory of drama. "Terror," as Joyce
reminds us, "is the feeling which arrests the mind
in the presence of whatsoever is grave and constant
in human suffering." There is neither gravity nor
constancy in the sufferings portrayed on the ro-

mantic stage, only a cloak-and-dagger frenzy. The difference is that between melodrama and tragedy.

The theatre of Victor Hugo culminates in the entrancing nonsense of Rostand. Cyrano is the true heir to all those masked and plumed figures who sweep past moonlit casements to the clash and tinkle of rhyme. But in its technique, a drama such as *Ruy Blas* clearly foreshadows the "well-made plays" of the later nineteenth century. Dumas's *Antony* (1831) is the bridge between pure romanticism and domestic melodrama. In it, the romantic cult of passion is rendered prosaic and given a *bourgeois* setting. Transposed into the sphere of domestic and psychological intrigue, the heroic imbroglios of *Hernani* or *Ruy Blas* become the mundane precisions of the drama of Sardou and Dumas fils. This is paradoxical, as these later playwrights claimed to be antiromantic and prided themselves on their cold realism. But, in fact, their techniques of suspense and revelation came directly out of romantic stagecraft.

French romantic tragedy led also in another direction: toward grand opera in the pre-Wagnerian style. Many of these dramas survive not in their own right but as libretti. In Verdi's rendition, *Hernani* has a certain noble amplitude. Victor Hugo's *Le Roi s'amuse* is an insufferable piece of *guignol*; as *Rigoletto*, it is enthralling. Eugène Scribe, a master technician of late romantic drama, became the preeminent contriver of operatic texts. The relationship is a natural one. In the French romantic theatre, the core of drama is buried beneath the mechanics of passionate presentation. The basic quality of the work suffers no violence through the addition of music. On the contrary, music rationalizes and completes the elements of pure gesture and fantasy inherent in the material. Melodic lines can safely carry a great burden of absurdity. Thus it is in the operas of Donizetti, Meyerbeer, and Verdi that Victor Hugo's conception of dramatic form was most fully realized.

The case of German drama in the nineteenth century is more various and complex. A literature which proceeded from Goethe and Schiller to Kleist, Büchner, Grillparzer, and Hebbel, and which ripened within it elements that led to Wedekind and Brecht, comes fairly to occupy much of one's consciousness of modern drama. At present, however, I want to consider only one aspect: the place of Goethe and Schiller in our particular theme of the tragic.

Goethe's avoidances in this domain are notorious. *Faust* is only the crowning example of a turn away from tragedy, which is everywhere apparent in his manifold creations. Goethe's own pronouncements are unmistakable: the tragic mode repelled certain governing dispositions of his genius. In his frequent meditations on Goethe, Thomas Mann put forward the thought that there was in the Olympian a decisive *Bürgerlichkeit*. The word is nearly impossible to translate. It argues notions of middle-class solidity, of enlightened decorum, of confidence in the way of the world. It points to that in Goethe which made of him a gifted civil servant, a satisfied courtier, and a patrician who nevertheless ascribed much of his good fortune to the solid virtues of his middle-class background. In tragedy, there is a wildness and a refusal running against the grain of middle-class sensibility. Tragedy springs from outrage; it protests at the conditions of life. It carries in it the possibilities of disorder, for all tragic poets have something of the rebelliousness of Antigone. Goethe, on the contrary, loathed disorder. He once said that he preferred injustice, signifying by that cruel assertion not his support for reactionary political ideals, but his conviction that injustice is temporary and reparable whereas disorder destroys the very possibilities of human progress. Again, this is an anti-tragic view; in tragedy it is the individual instance of injustice that infirms the general pretence of order. One Hamlet is enough to convict a state of rottenness.

There is in Goethe, moreover, a special roundedness. The energies, purposes, and acts of that great life seem to constitute a sphere around a radiant centre. No force is scattered, no end left loose. The jubilant close of *Faust* encloses the poet's entire creation. But it is a roundedness achieved neither by dogmatic assumption nor by a shallow disregard of moral and intellectual crisis. In Goethe's case, one has every evidence of doubt and bleakness strenuously overcome. We know how much there is in his early works of personal adventure ill digested and of remorse objectified in poetic form. There are zones of shadow in Goethe's personal life, and periods when that unbelievably productive mind lay fallow with depression. And because the creative serenity enjoyed by the mature Goethe had been achieved at a high cost, we find the poet wary of the abyss. Tragedy is a deliberate advance to the edge of life, where the mind must look on blackness at the risk of vertigo. Goethe was determined to proceed upward, and so he kept his eyes to the light.

These are, if we will, weaknesses, though of a rather exalted order. They invest Goethe's person with a certain awesome coldness. But Goethe's rejection of tragedy also had its positive aspects. His accomplishments in letters, science, and statecraft proclaim two principal values: growth and education. They are, of course, related. Goethe's tone glows with a particular excitement whenever he touches on the theme of organic growth, on the unfolding toward self-completion of matter, plant, poem, or historical process. He felt the energies of growth with a kind of sensuous directness. Life itself was for him the sum of growth, the capacity of the organism to perfect itself through accretion and change. Goethe's vision was Darwinian before the fact. A sense of the evolutionary inspired his botany, his mineralogy, his theories of literary form, and his political conservatism. He was conservative precisely because he believed that revolutions made by partisan interests merely distort or impede the great harmonies of progress which give to history its true and gradual shape.

Hence, Goethe's lifelong interest in education. Education is the ordering of natural growth. To Goethe the divine spark in man is the fact that he can be taught. Where that spark endures, as in the aging Faust, there is no ground for despair or damnation. Literature should educate, if not by explicit precept, at least by showing in actions and characters the quality of self-completion. That is the *leitmotiv* of *Wilhelm Meister*, of *Iphigenie*, of *Faust*. It is the hope held out at the end of *Torquato Tasso*.

Now, clearly there is in this ideal of growth and education an implicit refusal of tragedy. Tragedies such as *Oedipus* and *Lear* do show a kind of progress toward self-knowledge. But it is achieved at the price of ruin. Tragic personages are educated by calamity and they reach their fulfilment in death. Only the *Oresteia* (which Goethe preferred among Greek tragic dramas) ends in an affirmation of unequivocal progress, and the *Oresteia* is a very special case.

The extraordinary fact, therefore, is not that Goethe should have failed to write plays which strike us as distinctly and completely tragic, but rather that he should have written so much that draws near to the tragic mode. The first part of *Faust* is, after all, a grim business. Goethe's contemporaries saw in the Faust–Margarete story the very embodiment of romantic tragedy. Berlioz let Faust ride to damnation and thus derived from Goethe's drama a genuine tragic form. No one who has seen *Iphigenie* acted will forget how much anguish is gathered before the final twist of grace. Iphigenia herself invokes the gods in terms not distant from those of *Lear*:

> Es fürchte die Götter
> Das Menschengeschlecht!
> Sie halten die Herrschaft
> In ewigen Händen
> Und können sie brauchen
> Wie's ihnen gefällt.
>
> Der fürchte sie doppelt
> Den je sie erheben! [4]

The end of *Torquato Tasso* is one of repose, but it is a precarious repose accompanied by intimations of future disaster. If there is in the play a certain withdrawal from urgency, the reason is that here, more perhaps than anywhere else in literature, the drama has moved inward. The sole actions are those of mood and feeling. *Tasso* is a moving play, but in it Goethe commits, in his own lofty style, the romantic fallacy of egotism. The work acquires meaning by virtue of self-portrayal. It presents Goethe

[4] Let mankind
Fear the gods!
They hold sovereign power
In eternal grasp
And can use it
At their pleasure.

Whom sometime they exalt
Should fear them doubly!

animating a vision of his own dual nature. It is a lyric meditation given theatric form. And we experience no definite tragic shock because we know that Goethe, unlike Tasso, will not come to ruin, but go forward victoriously, being at once Tasso and Antonio. Were it less attached to the identity of its author, the play would exhibit a graver meaning.

One other drama of the Weimar period seems to move in tragic directions, but it is among the most baffling of Goethe's works. The blurred, rather artificial effect of *Die Natürliche Tochter* is wholly disproportionate to the skill and energies consumed. We find ourselves at the beginning of major conflicts; a tangle of private lives is thrown into high relief against a background of political turmoil. Goethe appears to be advancing toward some central dramatic statement regarding the French Revolution. But the drama veers away into a detour of intrigue and ends on a note of mystery. In part, this is because *Die Natürliche Tochter* is the first of an intended trilogy and Goethe never wrote the rest. But what clues there are lead one to suppose that the final resolution would have been one of progress and reconcilement. As elsewhere in Goethe, the tragic would have been preliminary to affirmation.

Yet even as a fragment, *Die Natürliche Tochter* is fascinating, for it directs us to a characteristic trait in Goethe's works. All his writings, even the most splendid, leave one with an intimation of the unfinished, as if they were partial realizations of an

inner design even more complete and conclusive.
In the observance of the finished statue, there
crowds upon one a sense of marble quarried but not
entirely used. Between Goethe's works there are
complex resonances, as if each found its echoing
completion in the sum. And in the last analysis, that
sum was the life of the man. Goethe's disposal of
his manifold energies was his greatest work of art,
making meaningful all the fragmentary expressions
of creative form. And, plainly, the tragic was one of
the modes of understanding which that life had
envisaged but subordinated to values more affirma-
tive and joyous. Even Goethe's incarnation of evil,
Mephistopheles, has a kind of sinister gaiety. The
fires of hell do not scorch him; he warms his hands
at them.

If the disparate ideals of romanticism and tragedy
are anywhere united, it is in the dramas of Schiller.
He is the richest playwright western literature produced between Racine and Ibsen, and one cannot
survey his massive achievement in any brief compass. Again, therefore, I will restrict myself to the
one particular aspect: Schiller and the concept of
tragedy. But in Schiller's case such a theoretic view
has some warrant, for in him flourished that dual
consciousness which we first observed in Dryden.
He was both poet and critic. He thought deeply
and acutely on problems of poetic form and left a
body of philosophic criticism of the first rank. The
dramatist in Schiller responded specifically to chal-
lenges posed by the critic.

Schiller was persistently aware of the fact that the modern spirit differed sharply from that which had engendered classic and Shakespearean drama. He experienced in its entire breadth, indeed he in part provoked, the crisis of feeling of the late eighteenth century, the turn toward the life of sentiment and pathos. His first drama, *Die Räuber*, followed eight years after *Werther* (1774 and 1781), and together with Goethe's novel became the password of romanticism. It proclaimed, in accents of lyric frenzy, the rights of passion against those of conventional morality and caste. And whereas romanticism was to Goethe a passing or occasional mood, one of the conditions of feeling into which he could translate his protean genius, it was to Schiller a natural setting. He was a romantic by virtue of his militant liberalism, of his love for the wild and picturesque in nature, of his keen sensitivity to local colour and the stress of history. In his dramas and heroic ballads, the romantic generation found its repertoire of emotion. Nearly to the close of his life, when illness shadowed him, Schiller retained a Rousseauist optimism. He regarded man as naturally virtuous and believed in the possibility of social justice. And like a true romantic, he projected himself into all that he fashioned. Even the historical works, the chronicles of the Thirty Years' War and of the rebellion of the Netherlands, carry the stamp of Schiller's ardent nature. They are the prose of his imagination. As we have seen, moreover, he had the characteristic romantic passion for Shakespeare.

The tones of Iago, Edmund, and Richard III resound in his first play; the theatric problems raised by *Coriolanus* and *Julius Caesar* are implicit in the fragments of the unfinished *Demetrius*.

Nevertheless, and particularly in his commerce with Goethe, Schiller felt the contrariety between romantic ideals and tragedy. He knew that there is no natural affinity between liberalism and the tragic. He was passionately versed in Greek drama, and his treatments of Greek mythology are among the sources of that special kind of Hellenism which cast its spell over the German mind from Winckelmann to Nietzsche. Schiller translated Racine and had far more understanding of French neo-classic drama than most of his romantic contemporaries. In one instance, he carried to an extreme pitch the notion of restoring to the modern stage the exact forms of antique tragedy.

Thus there is in Schiller's plays a tidal movement, an ebb and flow of romantic values. In *Die Räuber*, romanticism is in flood; in *Die Braut von Messina*, it has receded completely and we find ourselves in a cold, luminous Attic landscape. Where Schiller is at his best, the pressure of romantic sentiment against the ideal of dramatic objectivity and a tragic world view produces a characteristic tension. Schiller himself saw this so clearly that he tried to evolve a special mode of the tragic. He termed several of his plays "tragedies of reconciliation," seeking to find a modern counterpart to that progress from ruin to forgiveness which occurs at the end of the

Oresteia and in the *Oedipus at Colonus*. In short, it is with Schiller that began the explicit search for tragic forms appropriate to the rational, optimistic, and sentimental temper of post-Pascalian man.

Don Carlos, the first of the major dramas, is an unwieldy treasure. The full text is too long for tolerable performance, yet nearly everywhere it is charged with dramatic force. We find in it the lesser glories of romanticism, the straw of which Victor Hugo made his shiny bricks: the blood and velvet of the Spanish setting, the pomp of cloak and rapier, the scenes of revelation and despairing love. But there is far more than that. In the black personage of Philip II (the blackness of his garb staining every cold, sumptuous word), Schiller struck a distinctly modern note: the man of evil, but in whom evil is pitiable because it is an infirmity, a deadness at the core. Behind him, in the shadows of the Escorial, seem to wait John Gabriel Borkman and all the other characters of modern drama in whom there has occurred the death of the heart. One of the great moments in the play is that in which the Count of Lerma rushes from the royal presence with the news that the King is weeping. The courtiers are horror-stricken. For there is something horrible and obscene in such tears, as if the ghost of buried feeling had risen momentarily to haunt the ruthless mind.

Don Carlos is filled with such strokes. They translate the outward crises of romantic melodrama into authentic conflicts of character and ideals. The issues are real and the mechanics of theatrical excitement are there only to give them expressive shape. The defect in *Don Carlos* is not an excess of melodrama, but rather the sacrifice of poetic form to the claims of ideology. In defiance of historical fact, Schiller made of Don Carlos a victim in the political struggle between absolutism and liberty. And in the Marquis von Posa (the true hero of the play), he dramatized his vision of the ideal man: noble, liberal, immensely alive, yet prepared to sacrifice his life to the romantic ideals of freedom and masculine friendship. The marquis creates in the play a persistent unbalance. The plot is arrested by massive interludes of rhetoric and philosophic debate. No subsequent action can rival the intensity of emotion expended in the great encounter between Philip and Posa. Setting the voice of autocracy and pessimism against that of Rousseauist liberation, Schiller wrote some of the most renowned lines in German literature:

MARQUIS: Sehen Sie sich um
          In seiner herrlichen Natur! Auf Frei-
               heit
          Ist sie gegründet—und wie reich ist sie
          Durch Freiheit! Er, der grosse Schöpfer,
               wirft
          In einen Tropfen Tau den Wurm und
               lässt
          Noch in den toten Räumen der Ver
               wesung
          Die Willkür sich ergetzen—Ihre Schöp-
               fung,

Wie eng und arm! Das Rauschen eines
    Blattes
Erschreckt den Herrn der Christenheit
    —Sie müssen
Vor jeder Tugend zittern. Er—der Frei-
    heit
Entzückende Erscheinung nicht zu
    stören—
Er lässt des Übels grauenvolles Heer
In seinem Weltall lieber toben—ihn,
Den Künstler, wird man nicht gewahr,
    bescheiden
Verhüllt er sich in ewige Gesetze;
Die sieht der Freigeist, doch nicht ihn.
    "Wozu
Ein Gott?" sagt er, "die Welt ist sich
    genug."
Und keines Christen Andacht hat ihn
    mehr
Als dieses Freigeists Lästerung geprie-
    sen.

KÖNIG: Und wollet Ihr es unternehmen, dies
Erhabne Muster in der Sterblichkeit,
In meinen Staaten nachzubilden?

MARQUIS: Sie,
Sie können es. Wer anders? Weihen
    Sie
Dem Glück der Völker die Regenten-
    kraft,
Die—ach so lang—des Thrones Grösse
    nur
Gewuchert hatte!—Stellen Sie der
    Menschheit

Verlornen Adel wieder her! Der Bürger
Sei wiederum, was er zuvor gewesen,
Der Krone Zweck!—Ihn binde keine
Pflicht
Als seiner Brüder gleich ehrwürdge
Rechte!
Wenn nun der Mensch, sich selbst
zurückgegeben,
Zu seines Werts Gefühl erwacht—der
Freiheit
Erhabne, stolze Tugenden gedeihen—
Dann, Sire, wenn Sie zum glücklichsten
der Welt
Ihr eignes Königreich gemacht—dann
ist
Es Ihre Pflicht, die Welt zu unterwer-
fen.[5]

[5] THE MARQUIS: Look about you
At His resplendent Nature! It is built
On Freedom—and how rich it has through
Freedom
Grown! The great Creator gives unto the
worm
A house of dew; even in the dead places
Of decay, He lets the force of Nature
Freely work. How narrow and how mean
Is *your* creation! The rustle of a leaf
Affrights the lord of Christendom. You
quake
Before each virtue. But He—lest be ob-
scured
Freedom's design and radiance—allows
The dreadful hosts of Evil to consort
Wildly in His domain. He, the artist
Of creation, does not obtrude. Modestly,
He seeks concealment in eternal laws.
The sceptic sees the law but not the giver.

I have cited at some length to show what Thomas Mann meant when he said that not even Shakespeare was a greater master of dramatic rhetoric. But the rhetoric in *Don Carlos* comes to overshadow the drama. In the light of such ultimate

---

"Wherefore a God?" he asks, "The world suffices
To itself." No prayer from a Christian lip
Does Him more honour than this blasphemy.

PHILIP: And would you venture, sir, to imitate
This high design amidst mortality
And in my realms?

THE MARQUIS: You can do it, sire,
You. Who else? Henceforth devote your power—
Which, too long, alas, has been usurious
To the sole profit of the throne—devote
It to the happiness of men! Restore
To man his lost nobility! The subject
Shall be, as he was in former times, the care
And purpose of the crown! Let nothing bind him
Save his respect for others' equal rights!
And when mankind, unto itself restored,
Is roused to know its inborn dignity,
When Freedom's proud, exalted virtues flourish,
Then, sire—having made your own domain
The happiest on earth—then 'tis your duty
To subdue the world.

I have capitalized Nature, Freedom, and Evil to underline the element of personification. In Schiller's rhetoric these abstractions play a graphic role. The level of allegory is always near to that of realistic action.

179

philosophic conflicts, the characters tend to abstraction. Over their lives hangs too vivid a cast of thought. Schiller would be among the first of those whom Eric Bentley has referred to as "the playwright as thinker."

Ten years elapsed between *Don Carlos* and the *Wallenstein* trilogy (1787–96). During that time Schiller wrote many of his historical and philosophic essays. He turned to Aristotle's *Poetics*, to Greek tragedy, and to Shakespeare's history plays. In 1794 began his growing intimacy with Goethe and Goethe's ideals of classic form. He came to look on *Don Carlos* with dissatisfaction, seeing in it the excess of ideology and personal feeling. *Wallenstein* was to be "objective drama" in the Sophoclean and Shakespearean manner, exhibiting character solely through dramatic action. Above all, the poet was to deny himself the pleasures of romantic egotism; he was to stay distant from his invention. In November 1796, Schiller wrote proudly of *Wallenstein:* "I would nearly say that the subject does not interest me."

But again the sheer virtuosity of Schiller's historical knowledge and the breadth of his imaginative powers exceeded the limits of dramatic form. In the two parts of *Henry IV* the double plot is so devised as to unify the episodic structure. In the *Wallenstein* triad the lines of action are so complex and entangled as to disperse our interest. Now our attention is riveted to the hero, now to the elder or younger Piccolomini; matters of state alternate be-

wilderingly with those of private feeling. Only at
the close, in the last two acts of *Wallensteins Tod,*
are all the great elements gathered to fatality. The
drama ends in a mighty rush of Shakespearean action. But taken as a whole, *Wallenstein,* like *Don
Carlos,* is a play that is most vividly present when it
is read.

As if to show that he could bend his profuse powers to the necessary limitations of the stage, Schiller
proceeded, immediately after *Wallenstein,* to the
most tightly composed of all his dramas. *Maria
Stuart* is an incomparable work. It is, with *Boris
Godunov,* the one instance in which romanticism
rose fully to the occasion of tragedy. The noble
lady haunted the romantic imagination; in her were
united the appropriate virtues of mysterious guilt,
of a lost cause, and a passionate heart. The red of
her scaffold and the black of her gown were em-
blazoned on romantic fiction, from Sir Walter Scott
to Dumas. Swinburne wrote a *Mary Stuart*; Alfieri,
a *Maria Stuarda.* The music of her grief resounds
in forgotten romantic operas, including one by
Donizetti.

But no other treatment of her flamboyant, tragic
history compares with that of Schiller. For he perceived in her death a double tragedy. Queen Elizabeth is at last delivered of her rival, but in the
struggle she expends much of her humanity. Like
one of Corneille's statesmen, she delivers her conscience into the keeping of political necessity. At
the close of the play, she stands like a great edifice

through which fire has passed: charred and cold. The tragedy of Elizabeth matches that of her victim, and the action dramatizes at every moment the exact balance of doom. It is like a parable to Nietzsche's observation that if one looks into the abyss, the abyss looks back into one's own spirit.

The entire play, indeed all that had previously been achieved in romantic drama, seems to ascend toward the encounter of the two women in the garden at Fotheringhay. In historical fact, no such confrontation occurred, and Goethe wondered how Schiller would manage it. He managed it superbly. It is a scene in which one's awareness of the dialectical nature of reality, of the conflicts between self and "other," between mind and heart, between the enforced and the spontaneous, is given total expression. In that garden is brought home to us a sense of what is irreconcilable in the matter of our lives.

In *Don Carlos*, the debate between the King and the marquis engaged rival ideologies, the doctrine being more vital than the voice through which it spoke. The encounter of the two queens has a flagrant humanity; their blood is in their words. It is pure and magnificent theatre. Mary Stuart approaches her enemy in compelled submission. Elizabeth confronts her with the charge of conspiracy and restless intrigue. The captive lady renounces her dynastic claims. She asks only for release and the chance of ending her fiery chronicle in repose. The scene appears to be .moving toward a resolution of the great discord. But the woman rises in the triumphant Queen. A grim erotic irony possesses her. Having broken in Mary Stuart the spell of the crown, she seeks to break in her the quality of passion to which so many men have been drawn. Herself inviolate, she would cast out the sensual magic of her fallen rival. But Elizabeth flays too grossly, and Mary strikes back. She hurls at the Queen the notorious charge of bastardy and by this irreparable insult destroys her own chances of survival. The presence of the attendant lords has lit in the two women a sexual hatred which neither policy nor forgiveness can stifle.

Only by citing the entire scene, could one convey its mastery. In the meeting of Brutus and Cassius (one of the few moments in drama at all comparable for completeness of revelation), the movement proceeds from high tension to repose. Here it surges incessantly upward. Mary starts kneeling; she ends, immensely, on her feet. It is Elizabeth who hastens away. And as in any encounter of equal masses, both suffer hurt. In both queens the quick of life has been outraged. Mary Stuart cries after her foe: "She carries death in her heart." True, but it is also Mary's death.

The rest of the drama leads inexorably down from this summit. The tragedy bears increasingly on Elizabeth. Even as she signs the death warrant, she knows that the woman in her can never be wholly avenged or justified:

Maria Stuart
Heisst jedes Unglück das mich niederschlägt!
Ist sie aus den Lebendigen vertilgt,
Frei bin ich, wie die Luft auf den Gebirgen.
Mit welchem Hohn sie auf mich niedersah,
Als sollte mich der Blick zu Boden blitzen!
Ohnmächtige! Ich führe bessre Waffen,
Sie treffen tödlich, und du bist nicht mehr! [6]

The equilibrium between the two centres of tragic weight is sustained to the end. We see Mary Stuart going to the scaffold and Elizabeth into a barren solitude.

Short of close, literal study, there is not much one can usefully say of so obviously perfect a work. The economy of dramatic structure—note the pace of the last two acts—makes expressive the relentless character of real tragedy. When the curtain falls, we are left, as in the *Antigone*, with a sense of cruel yet natural havoc. The harvest of *Maria Stuart* is one of those rare visions of what Melville called "the final lore." We perceive in man, where he is most excellent, the nearness of destruction.

Neither *Die Jungfrau von Orleans* nor *Wilhelm Tell* are quite of this reach. Schiller remains a virtuoso of language and dramatic structure, but the

[6] Mary Stuart—
All my afflictions bear that cursèd name!
If she were from the living rooted out,
I should be free as is the mountain air.
She looked upon me with so harsh a scorn
As if her glance could strike me to the ground!
Powerless wretch! I carry sharper weapons,
Their stroke is mortal, and thou shalt be gone!

pamphleteer and the sentimentalist of the earlier plays reassert themselves. Both works are glittering fairy-tales. They point an emphatic moral of national consciousness and political freedom. The close of *Die Jungfrau* is a kind of Christmas pageant, the stage directions calling for a flush of roseate light in the sky. It crosses the thin line, inherent in romanticism, between sentiment and sentimentality. In the last act of *Wilhelm Tell* the logic and pace of the action are deliberately marred so that the poet may draw a moral distinction between two types of political crime, those committed in private hatred, and those justly carried out against tyranny.

These dispersals of tragic force are, however, intentional. After *Maria Stuart* Schiller became increasingly concerned with the idea of partial or arrested tragedy, in the manner of Goethe's *Iphigenie*. He stressed the moral and aesthetic values of reconciliation and believed that where it approached ideal form a work of art should express transfiguring joy. As his material life sickened, the exhilaration of his spirit mounted. He saw in the dramatist a creator of national epic and one who could present the claims of the ideal by virtue of myth. We shall meet these ideas again at Bayreuth and in the theatre of Brecht.

But *Don Carlos*, *Wallensteins Tod*, and, above all, *Maria Stuart* belong to the world of tragedy. True, romanticism was anti-tragic; but the romantic age is also that of Beethoven.

VI

THERE IS in every literary movement a part of revolt
and a part of tradition. Romanticism arose in rebellion against the ideals of reason and rational form
which had governed taste in the late seventeenth
and eighteenth centuries. In the mythology of Blake
the wings of imagination are liberated from the
cold blight of reason put upon them by Newton and
Voltaire. The poetics of romanticism were necessarily polemic, being elaborated in the course of an
attack on neo-classic principles. Wordsworth's Preface to the *Lyrical Ballads* and Victor Hugo's critical
manifestoes are at once proclamations of future intent and explicit condemnations of the immediate
literary past. Had Pope and Voltaire not existed the
romantics would have had to invent them in order
to articulate their own contrary values.

But at the same time the romantic movement

strove to establish for itself a majestic lineage. It
aspired not only to the heritage of Shakespeare and
the renaissance. It claimed for its ancestry Homer,
the Greek tragedians, the Hebrew prophets, Dante,
Michelangelo, Rembrandt—in short, all art in
which it discerned grandeur of proportion and the
high lyric tone. The romantic pantheon is like a
gallery of the sublime. Often Victor Hugo passed
through it, calling the roll of the Titans as if in invocation of his own future place:

> Homer, Job, Aeschylus, Isaiah, Ezekiel,
> Lucretius, Juvenal, St. John, St. Paul, Dante,
> Rabelais, Cervantes, Shakespeare.
> That is the array of the unmoving giants of the
> human spirit.
> Genius is a dynasty. There is none other. All who
> belong to it wear a crown, including one of thorns.

The barren ground of the eighteenth century had
broken the chain of sublime creation. The romantics saw themselves taking up the torch where it
had fallen after Shakespeare and Michelangelo.
That is how Delacroix conceived the role of the
painter, and Berlioz that of the musician. Romanticism signified the tradition of genius.

But such a view implied a startling paradox. How
could the romantics at the same time claim descent
from the Greek poets and repudiate neo-classicism?
When summoning to his inspiration the presence
of Aeschylus or Sophocles, how did the romantic
poet differ from Racine, and even from Voltaire?
How could the Shakespearean ideal be reconciled to

the antique? It was Lessing who first posed the problem. He gave to it a solution which immensely influenced all subsequent theories of drama and which is implicit in our own modern image of the shape of the past.

Lessing's immediate concern was the creation of a German national theatre. He found the German stage of the 1760's under the complete domination of French neo-classical drama and more particularly of French tragedies written after Racine. For whereas Racine had not crossed the frontiers, being too compact and autonomous in his supremacy, his pallid successors had. The court and city theatres of Germany were governed by the works of La Harpe and Voltaire, cold declamatory pieces in which the forms and rules of neo-classicism were observed with servile pedantry. Examining these plays, Lessing came upon his revolutionary insight.

He found that neo-classicism was not *new* classicism but *false* classicism. Castelvetro, Boileau, and Rymer were not the true interpreters of the classic ideal. They had seized on the dead letter of Greek drama but had failed to grasp its authentic spirit. Lessing rejected the belief that the quality of Aeschylus and Sophocles could be recaptured by adherence to the formal precepts of Aristotle and Horace. The genius of Greek tragedy lay elsewhere than in the convention of the three unities, in the use of mythological plots, or in the presence of the chorus. At one stroke Lessing challenged assumptions which had dominated two hundred years of poetic theory. Neo-classicism was not a continuation of the Attic tradition, but a travesty of it.

In Lessing's view the entire conflict between the classic and the Shakespearean was spurious. It had arisen from a great error of perspective. Milton was wrong when he dismissed Shakespeare in the name of Aeschylus. Dryden had been misled by a false image when he had attempted to choose between the Elizabethan and the antique ideal. The distinction which had largely controlled the theory of art and drama—Sophocles *or* Shakespeare—was erroneous. As early as 1759 Lessing implied a momentous kinship: he said, Sophocles *and* Shakespeare.

That is the core of his revaluation. It meant that the great divide in the history of western drama occurred not between the antique and the Elizabethan, but between Shakespeare and the neo-classics. The *Oresteia* and *Hamlet* belonged together, in the same sphere of tragedy.

In the *Hamburgische Dramaturgie* (1767–8), Lessing applied his revolutionary conception to practical criticism. He reviewed plays by Voltaire and Thomas Corneille (the illustrious Corneille's younger brother) and argued that they violated the true intent of the *Poetics*. It was not in these neo-classic works that the Aristotelian ideal of tragedy was realized, but in the dramas of Shakespeare. Lessing gives a persuasive example of his new approach when inquiring into the use of spectral apparitions on the modern stage. The ghost of Darius in *The Persians* convinces us for it has behind it the force of genuine religious belief. We experience a comparable realness in *Hamlet* as it is within the compass of the Elizabethan imagination to allow for the presence in the world of incarnate shadow. The ghost in Voltaire's *Semiramis* is rococo claptrap introduced by an unbelieving poet into an unbelievable plot. Having behind it neither ritual observance nor imaginative conviction, it is mere literary artifice.

Similarly it is not in the neo-classic theatre that we shall find a true version of the Aristotelian concept of pity and fear. The stately heroes of Corneille and Voltaire solicit from us cold admiration. These characters would bridle at our pity. To experience tragic compassion, we should look to Desdemona. To feel the kind of elemental terror provoked by the *Seven Against Thebes* or Euripides' *Medea*, we need only turn to *King Lear* and *Richard III*. And if we insist on unity of action, argues Lessing, it is not in neo-classic drama that we shall find it. Here there is outward unity achieved at the price of incredible dramatic coincidences and foreshortenings (the acrobatics to which Corneille saw himself compelled). What Aristotle meant by unity was inner coherence and poetic logic as it is exhibited in *Othello* or *Macbeth*. The emphasis of the *Poetics* on the lesser unities of time and place arose from the technical forms of the Athenian theatre. These forms possessed no eternal or exclusive authority.

Lessing's idea became one of the rallying cries of

French and German romanticism. The attempt to apply Aristotle's *Poetics* to Shakespeare was soon discarded. What mattered was the kinship of genius and tragic spirit between Greek and Elizabethan drama. It was in the name of Aeschylus and Shakespeare that the romantics asserted their conception of the sublime. They saw in neo-classicism an equal departure from both. Victor Hugo drew an exalted parallel between the two masters of tragedy:

Take away from drama the Orient and replace it by the North, take away Greece and put in England, take away India and put in Germany (that other immense mother Alemannia, All-men), take away Pericles and put in Elizabeth, take away the Parthenon and put in the Tower of London, take away the plebeians and put in the mob, take away fatality and put in melancholy; take away the Gorgon and put in the witch, take away the eagle and put in the cloud, take away the sun and put in the wind-swept heath under the pale moon— and you have Shakespeare.

Given the dynasty of genius—the originality of each being wholly preserved—the poet of the Germanic temper had to follow on the poet of Zeus, the Gothic mist on the antique mystery—and Shakespeare is Aeschylus the second.

Other poets expressed the same belief in more tranquil style. Schiller saw in the modern tragic poet the natural successor to both the Sophoclean and the Shakespearean achievement. Wagner's theory of drama and the vision of Bayreuth are rooted in the notion of a continuity of the tragic spirit which would unite the world of Oedipus to that of Lear while excluding the formality and rationalism of the neo-classics. In the imagination of the nineteenth century the Greek tragedians and Shakespeare stand side by side, their affinity transcending all the immense contrarieties of historical circumstance, religious belief, and poetic form.

We no longer use the particular terms of Lessing and Victor Hugo. But we abide by their insight. The word "tragedy" encloses for us in a single span both the Greek and the Elizabethan example. The sense of relationship overreaches the historical truth that Shakespeare may have known next to nothing of the actual works of Aeschylus, Sophocles, and Euripides. It transcends the glaring fact that the Elizabethans mixed tragedy and comedy whereas the Greeks kept the two modes severely distinct. It overcomes our emphatic awareness of the vast difference in the shape and fabric of the two languages and styles of dramatic presentation. The intimations of a related spirit and ordering of human values are stronger than any sense of disparity. Comparable visions of life are at work in *Antigone* and *Romeo and Juliet*. We see at once what Victor Hugo means when he calls Macbeth a northern scion of the house of Atreus. Elsinore seems to lie in range of Mycenae, and the fate of Orestes resounds in that of Hamlet. The hounds of hell search out their quarry in Apollo's sanctuary as they do in the tent of Richard III. Oedipus and Lear attain similar insights by virtue of similar blindness.

It it not between Euripides and Shakespeare that the western mind turns away from the ancient tragic sense of life. It is after the late seventeenth century. I say the late seventeenth century because Racine (whom Lessing did not really know) stands on the far side of the chasm. The image of man which enters into force with Aeschylus is still vital in *Phèdre* and *Athalie*.

It is the triumph of rationalism and secular metaphysics which marks the point of no return. Shakespeare is closer to Sophocles than he is to Pope and Voltaire. To say this is to set aside the realness of time. But it is true, nevertheless. The modes of the imagination implicit in Athenian tragedy continued to shape the life of the mind until the age of Descartes and Newton. It is only then that the ancient habits of feeling and the classic orderings of material and psychological experience were abandoned. With the *Discours de la méthode* and the *Principia* the things undreamt of in Horatio's philosophy seem to pass from the world.

In Greek tragedy as in Shakespeare, mortal actions are encompassed by forces which transcend man. The reality of Orestes entails that of the Furies; the Weird Sisters wait for the soul of Macbeth. We cannot conceive of Oedipus without a Sphinx, nor of Hamlet without a Ghost. The shadows cast by the personages of Greek and Shakespearean drama lengthen into a greater darkness. And the entirety of the natural world is party to the action. The thunderclaps over the sacred wood at Colonus and the storms in *King Lear* are caused by more than weather. In tragedy, lightning is a messenger. But it can no longer be so once Benjamin Franklin (the incarnation of the new rational man) has flown a kite to it. The tragic stage is a platform extending precariously between heaven and hell. Those who walk on it may encounter at any turn ministers of grace or damnation. *Oedipus* and *Lear* instruct us how little of the world belongs to man. Mortality is the pacing of a brief and dangerous watch, and to all sentinels, whether at Elsinore or on the battlements at Mycenae, the coming of dawn has its breath of miracle. It banishes the night wanderers to fire or repose. But at the touch of Hume and Voltaire the noble or hideous visitations which had haunted the mind since Agamemnon's blood cried out for vengeance, disappeared altogether or took tawdry refuge among the gaslights of melodrama. Modern roosters have lost the art of crowing restless spirits back to Purgatory.

In Athens, in Shakespeare's England, and at Versailles, the hierarchies of worldly power were stable and manifest. The wheel of social life spun around the royal or aristocratic centre. From it, spokes of order and degree led to the outward rim of the common man. Tragedy presumes such a configuration. Its sphere is that of royal courts, dynastic quarrels, and vaulting ambitions. The same metaphors of swift ascent and calamitous decline apply to Oedipus and Macbeth because they applied also to Alcibiades and Essex. And the fate of such men has tragic relevance because it is public. Agamemnon, Creon, and Medea perform their tragic actions before the eyes of the *polis*. Similarly the sufferings of Hamlet, Othello, or Phèdre engage the fortunes of the state. They are enacted at the heart of the body politic. Hence the natural setting of tragedy is the palace gate, the public square, or the court chamber. Greek and Elizabethan life and, to a certain extent, the life of Versailles shared this character of intense "publicity." Princes and factions clashed in the open street and died on the open scaffold.

With the rise to power of the middle class the centre of gravity in human affairs shifted from the public to the private. The art of Defoe and Richardson is founded on an awareness of this great change. Heretofore an action had possessed the breadth of tragedy only if it involved high personages and if it occurred in the public view. Behind the tragic hero stands the chorus, the crowd, or the observant courtier. In the eighteenth century there emerges for the first time the notion of a private tragedy (or nearly for the first time, there having been a small number of Elizabethan domestic tragedies such as the famous *Arden of Feversham*). In *La Nouvelle-Héloïse* and *Werther* tragedy is made intimate. And private tragedy became the chosen ground not of drama, but of the new, unfolding art of the novel.

The novel was not only the presenter of the new, secular, rationalistic, private world of the middle class. It served also as a literary form exactly appropriate to the fragmented audience of modern urban

culture. I have said before how difficult it is to make
any precise statements with regard to the character
of the Greek and Elizabethan public. But one major fact seems undeniable. Until the advent of rational empiricism the controlling habits of the western mind were symbolic and allegoric. Available
evidence regarding the natural world, the course of
history, and the varieties of human action were
translated into imaginative designs or mythologies.
Classic mythology and Christianity are such archi-
tectures of the imagination. They order the manifold levels of reality and moral value along an axis
of being which extends from brute matter to the
immaculate stars. There had not yet supervened between understanding and expression the new languages of mathematics and scientific formulas. The
poet was by definition a realist, his imaginings and
parables being natural organizations of reality. And
in these organizations certain primal notions
played a radiant part, radiant both in the sense of
giving light and of being a pole toward which all
perspectives converge. I mean such concepts as the
presence of the supernatural in human affairs, the
sacraments of grace and divine retribution, the idea
of preordainment (the oracle over Oedipus, the
prophecy of the witches to Macbeth, or God's covenant with His people in *Athalie*). I refer to the notion that the structure of society is a microcosm of
the cosmic design and that history conforms to patterns of justice and chastisement as if it were a

morality play set in motion by the gods for our instruction.

These conceptions and the manner in which they were transposed into poetry or engendered by poetic form are intrinsic to western life from the time of Aeschylus to that of Shakespeare. And although they were, as I have indicated, under increasing strain at the time of Racine, they are still alive in his theatre. They are the essential force behind the conventions of tragedy. They are as decisively present in the *Oresteia* and *Oedipus* as in *Macbeth*, *King Lear*, and *Phèdre*.

After the seventeenth century the audience ceased to be an organic community to which these ideas and their attendant habits of figurative language would be natural or immediately familiar. Concepts such as grace, damnation, purgation, blasphemy, or the chain of being, which are everywhere implicit in classic and Shakespearean tragedy, lose their vitality. They become philosophic abstractions of a private and problematic relevance, or mere catchwords in religious customs which had in them a diminishing part of active belief. After Shakespeare the master spirits of western consciousness are no longer the blind seers, the poets, or Orpheus performing his art in the face of hell. They are Descartes, Newton, and Voltaire. And their chroniclers are not the dramatic poets but the prose novelists.

The romantics were the immediate inheritors of

this tremendous change. They were not yet prepared to accept it as irremediable. Rousseau's primitivism, the anti-Newtonian mythology of Blake, Coleridge's organic metaphysics, Victor Hugo's image of the poets as the Magi, and Shelley's "unacknowledged legislators" are related elements in the rear-guard action fought by the romantics against the new scientific rationalism. From this action sprang the idea of somehow uniting Greek and Shakespearean drama into a new total form, capable of restoring to life the ancient moral and poetic responses. The dream of achieving a synthesis between the Sophoclean and the Shakespearean genius inspired the ambitions of poets and composers from the time of Shelley and Victor Hugo to that of Bayreuth. It could not really be fulfilled. The conventions into which the romantics tried to breath life no longer corresponded to the realities of thought and feeling. But the attempt itself produced a number of brilliant works, and these form a transition from the early romantic period to the new age of Ibsen and Chekhov.

The wedding of the Hellenic to the northern genius was one of the dominant motifs in Goethe's thought. His Italian journey was a poet's version of those perennial thrusts across the Alps of the German emperors of the Middle Ages. The dream of a descent into the gardens of the south always drew German ambitions toward Rome and Sicily. Goethe asks in *Wilhelm Meister* whether we know the land where the lemon trees flower, and the light of the Mediterranean glows through *Torquato Tasso* and the *Roman Elegies*. Goethe believed that the Germanic spirit, with its grave strength but flagrant streaks of brutality and intolerance, should be tempered with the old sensuous wisdom and humanism of the Hellenic. On the narrower ground of poetic form, he felt that in the drama of the future the Greek conception of tragic fate should be joined to the Shakespearean vision of tragic will. The wager between God and Satan brings on the destiny of Faust, but Faust assumes his role voluntarily.

The third Act of *Faust* II is a formal celebration of the union between the Germanic and the classic, between the spirit of Euripides and that of romantic drama. The motif of Faust's love for Helen of Troy goes back to the sources of the Faustian legend. It tells us of the ancient human desire to see the highest wisdom joined to the highest sensual beauty. There can be no greater magic than to wrest from death her in whom the flesh was all, in whom beauty was entirely pure because it was entirely corruptible. It is thus that the brightness of Helen passes through Marlowe's *Faustus*. Goethe used the fable to more elaborate ends. Faust rescuing Helen from Menelaus' vengeance is the genius of renaissance Europe restoring to life the classic tradition. The necromantic change from the palace at Sparta to Faust's Gothic castle directs us to the

aesthetic meaning of the myth—the translation of
antique drama into Shakespearean and romantic
guise.

This translation, or rather the fusion of the two
ideals, creates the *Gesamtkunstwerk*, the "total art
form." This entire section of *Faust* II represents a
search for a synthesis of all previous theatric modes.
It is a weird medley of poetic styles, music, and
ballet. Goethe suggested to Eckermann that the
second half of the Helen Act should be performed
by singers. We are not far from the "totalitarian"
aspirations of Wagner.

Helen and Faust engender a son, Euphorion. He
is emblematic of the supreme beauty and lyric
force which will arise from the union of the classic
and the modern:

HELENA: Liebe, menschlich zu beglücken,
Nähert sie ein edles Zwei;
Doch zu göttlichem Entzücken
Bildet sie ein köstlich Drei.
FAUST: Alles ist sodann gefunden:
Ich bin dein, und du bist mein,
Und so stehen wir verbunden;
Dürft es doch nicht anders sein! [1]

---

[1] HELEN: To enchant with early bliss,
Love conjoins us in a pair;
But for godlike joyousness
Must a third be added there.
FAUST: All is to completion brought:
You are mine and I am yours,
Thus we stand together wrought,
It could not be otherwise!

But like a new Icarus, the godly child plunges swiftly to his ruin. For Euphorion is not only a symbol of the marriage of the Greek and the Germanic. He is Goethe's salute to Byron and to the poet's tragic death on Hellenic soil.

Goethe saw in Byron the foremost talent of the age. He said to Eckermann that the English poet had been neither a classic nor a romantic, but the incarnation of the new harmony between the antique and the modern spirit. Byron's defence of Greek liberty and the sacrifice of his fiery life in that cause were exemplary of the manner in which the strength of northern Europe should bring freedom and rebirth to the classic south. Goethe found in Byron's dramas an attempt to unite the ritual scope of Greek tragedy to the lyricism and characterization of Shakespeare. He discerned in Byron both the Gothic strain of *Manfred* and the luminous sensuality of the isles of Greece. Byron reciprocated Goethe's admiration, seeing in him and in Napoleon his only true peers. It was to "the illustrious Goethe . . . his liege lord, the first of existing writers," that he dedicated *Sardanapalus*.

Today Byron's dramas are hardly ever performed, and they are dismissed by most critics as ambitious failures. Yet they are of the first interest

---

Maddeningly, all attempts to render into English Goethe's gnomic lyricism make the original sound slightly silly. Compare the attempt by Mr. MacNeice. In the German also, the pressure of logic is slight, but the meaning is carried forward by the music of the verse.

to anyone concerned with the idea of tragedy in modern literature. And on returning to them, one recognizes what Goethe meant. The range of technical audacity is extreme. We move from the strict neo-classicism of *Marino Faliero* to the near surrealism of the late mystery plays. Often Byron sought deliberately to surmount the limitations of the traditional stage in order to attain freer, larger forms of symbolic action. Like Aeschylus and Goethe, Byron was prepared to take grave risks, introducing to the theatre religious and philosophic themes. He was the first major English poet since Milton to conceive of Biblical drama. And if Byron's plays are failures, they nevertheless contain within them preliminaries to some of the most radical aspects of modern drama. By comparison Victor Hugo's view of the theatre, and even that of Schiller, strike one as old-fashioned.

Byron started out with the conviction that English tragedy could only regain life if it broke away from its Shakespearean precedent. Referring to *Sardanapalus* and *The Two Foscari* he declared:

You will find all this very *un*like Shakespeare; and so much the better in one sense, for I look upon him to be the *worst* of models, though the most extraordinary of writers.

The romantic imitation of the Elizabethans and Jacobeans seemed to him absurd. He asked that *Marino Faliero* not be judged "by your mad old dramatists . . . those turbid montebanks—always excepting B. Jonson, who was a Scholar and a Classic." We must not, of course, take Byron too literally. Knowing that his contemporaries found in him the very incarnation of the romantic, he enjoyed asserting that he was actually a classic and an Augustan, a craftsman in the tradition of Horace and Pope. He added a postscript to the dedication of *Marino Faliero* in which he suggested that the entire conflict between classic and romantic ideas was merely the invention of a few "scribblers" who abused Pope and Swift because they themselves "did not know how to write either prose or verse." But even if we take into account Byron's delight in bewildering public opinion, it is clear that he was trying to draw English drama away from Shakespeare and toward the classicism of Jonson and Otway. He saw no other means of rousing it from the grave. Writing to Murray in January 1821, Byron expressed the hope that English tragedy might indeed be revived:

I am, however, persuaded, that this is not to be done by following the old dramatists, who are full of gross faults, pardoned only for the beauty of their language; but by writing naturally and *regularly*, and producing *regular* tragedies, like the Greeks; but not in *imitation*, —merely the outline of their conduct, adapted to our own times and circumstances, and of course *no* chorus.

It is this adaptation of the classic form to modern taste which Byron sought to bring about in his two Venetian tragedies and *Sardanapalus*. The true subject of both *Marino Faliero* and *The Two Fos cari* is Venice herself. As Rome was to Corneille, so Venice was to Byron—the place where time and again the great wing-stroke of his imagination came to rest. Venice gave to Byron's sense of history and human conduct a touchstone. As if by virtue of the strong sea-light, men's passions seemed here to have their sharpest edge:

> I loved her from my boyhood; she to me
> Was a fair city of the heart,
> Rising like water-columns from the sea,
> Of joy the sojourn, and of wealth the mart;
> And Otway, Radcliffe, Schiller, Shakespeare's art
> Had stamp'd her image in me, and even so,
> Although I found her thus, we did not part;
> Perchance even dearer in her days of woe,
> Than when she was a boast, a marvel, and a show.

The plot of *Marino Faliero* turns on private affront and public conspiracy. It is not convincing. One finds it hard to accept the idea of a Doge willing to destroy his class and imperil the state in order to avenge a trivial piece of nastiness. But seen as a study of what Henry James called "the sense of place," the manner in which Venice gives to men's lives a special tragic tone, *Marino Faliero* is a moving work. The tension of the play lies in the contrast between its sumptuous, romantic setting and the tough sparsity of the language. Doge Faliero meets with Bertuccio, the chief of the conspirators, on the little square of San Giovanni e San Paolo. Above them towers the monument to Colleoni:

DOGE:	We *are* observed, and have been.
BERTUCCIO:	We observed!
	Let me discover—and this steel—
DOGE:	Put up;
	Here are no human witnesses: look there—
	What see you?
BERTUCCIO:	Only a tall warrior's statue
	Bestriding a proud steed, in the dim light
	Of the dull moon.
DOGE:	That Warrior was the sire
	Of my sire's fathers, and that statue was
	Decreed to him by the twice rescued city:—
	Think you that he looks down on us or no?
BERTUCCIO:	My lord, these are mere fantasies; there are
	No eyes in marble.
DOGE:	But there are in Death.

No one writing drama in English in the early nine-teenth century could have equalled this piece of dialogue or found that Roman epithet "twice res-cued." The cadence is that of Milton, yet it is broken and quickened by a nervousness character-istic of Byron. And around the harsh classic action plays romantic moonlight.

The Two Foscari carries the motif of the city to extremes. Jacopo Foscari would rather perish in a Venetian dungeon than live freely elsewhere:

> I ask no more than a Venetian grave,
> A dungeon, what they will, so it be here.

At certain moments the sheer force of the poetry
makes even this credible:

> Ah! you never yet
> Were far away from Venice, never saw
> Her beautiful towers in the receding distance,
> While every furrow of the vessel's track
> Seemed ploughing deep into your heart; you never
> Saw day go down upon your native spires
> So calmly with its gold and crimson glory,
> And after dreaming a disturbed vision
> Of them and theirs, awoke and found them not.

But as a whole *The Two Foscari* is a convincing example of what Aristotle meant when he advised
dramatists to avoid those occurrences in history
which were more implausible than fiction. Truth
can be absurd.

Realizing that his style of drama could not
achieve success on the contemporary stage—*Marino Faliero* failed totally when it was performed
without the author's consent—Byron withdrew toward what he called "a mental theatre." Thus *Sardanapalus* became a virtuoso exercise in the observance of rigid neo-classic unities. Battles are fought
inside palace halls, and dynastic upheavals tran-
spire in a matter of hours. Yet the play casts a festive light. Nowhere else is Byron more completely
a master of his means. He comes near to writing
the only dramatic blank verse in the English language from which the presence of Shakespeare has

been entirely exorcized. It carries forward from the
best of Ben Jonson:

> Why do I love this man? My country's daughters
> Love none but heroes. But I have no country!
> The slave hath lost all save her bonds. I love him;
> And that's the heaviest link of the long chain—
> To love whom we esteem not. Be it so:
> The hour is coming when he'll need all love,
> And find none.

The plain, rapid monosyllables lay bare the sinews
of the dramatic action. As in much of the finest of
Byron's poetry we are near to a middle ground between verse and an intensely charged prose. One
recognizes the admirer of Horace.

And the Horatian element is strong even where
the play flashes out in brilliant romantic touches.
Sardanapalus asserts that the rays of Myrrha's eyes
are redoubled in

> The tremulous silver of Euphrates' wave,
> As the light breeze of midnight crisps the broad
> And rolling water.

The entire effect depends on the cool sharpness of
the word "crisps." We find it in Ben Jonson, in a
most Latinate conceit, where the wind crisps the
"heads" of rivers. Or take Sardanapalus' proud answer to those who read in the stars portents of his
fall:

> Though they came down
> And marshall'd me the way in all their brightness,
> I would not follow.

It is the sonority of "marshall'd" which gives the romantic boast its persuasion. Could any other English poet since Milton have written that verse? Throughout the entire play the flamboyance of the oriental theme and the exotic, sensual quality of the hero are controlled by the classic tone. *Sardanapalus* resembles a Delacroix—vibrant in colouration, but firm in the drawing.

The two Venetian tragedies and *Sardanapalus* are what the Germans call *Lesedramen*, "dramas to be read," or at most to be recited formally in a style alien to the tradition of the English theatre. They are late and sumptuous examples of that ideal of antique form which began with the Senecan tragedies of the Elizabethan classicists. We find in them a conjunction of classic craftsmanship with the romantic temper. We shall find it again in Alfieri and Kleist. But so far as the actual stage goes, these glittering works are a dead end. They look resolutely to the past.

Byron's "mystery plays," on the contrary, have in them distinct premonitions of the future. There is nothing else in English literature quite like them. *Manfred* is the least original, being a close variation on the theme of Faust and romantic remorse (though Byron does reject the facile, redemptive solution). *Cain, Heaven and Earth,* and *The Deformed Transformed* are a constellation apart. Written under a common impulse in 1821–2, these "sacred dramas" turn their back on realism. They are vast, epic presentations of the mystery of evil.

Behind them lie *Faust*, the *Prometheus*, and Books IX–XII of *Paradise Lost*. They are pageants of the religious imagination. And here Byron is most profoundly non-Shakespearean. For it is one of the root principles of Shakespeare's art that the religious element should be diffuse, provisional, and internal to the poetry, rather than manifest in the plot or the moral. *Lear* is religious tragedy, but from it all assuagements of rite or explicit doctrine are cruelly absent. Byron, on the contrary, rejoins the tradition of the medieval mystery cycle.

But in design, *Cain* and *Heaven and Earth* are futuristic. They require the kind of panoramic stage which Norman Bel-Geddes conceived for a dramatization of Dante's *Inferno*. Concerned only with a theatre of the mind, Byron devised fantastic effects. The encounter between Lucifer and Cain, which is the centre of the play, is set in Hades and "The Abyss of Space." No ordinary stage machinery could create the necessary illusion of stellar and oceanic vastness:

> CAIN: 'Tis like another world; a liquid sun—
> And those inordinate creatures sporting
>   o'er
> Its shining surface?
> LUCIFER: Are its inhabitants,
> The past leviathans.

Heaven and Earth is even further removed from the practical conventions of the theatre. Founded on Genesis and the *Book of Enoch*, it is a kind of dramatic cantata, rather in the manner of Berlioz.

As the Deluge rises to the summits of the Caucasus, Japhet and the Chorus of Mortals intone a *Dies Irae*:

> Some clouds sweep on as vultures for their prey,
> While others, fixed as rocks, await the word
> At which their wrathful vials shall be poured.
> No azure more shall robe the firmament,
> Nor spangled stars be glorious: Death hath risen:
> In the sun's place a pale and ghastly glare
> Hath wound itself around the dying air.

Inevitably, one hears behind the words organ peals and the blast of trumpets. In conversation with Thomas Medwin, Byron indicated how *Heaven and Earth* was to end (what we have is only the first part):

Adah is momentarily in danger of perishing before the eyes of the Arkites. Japhet is in despair. The last wave sweeps her from the rock, and her lifeless corpse floats past in all its beauty, whilst a sea-bird screams over it, and seems to be the spirit of her angel lord.

The tableau is Victorian, like one of those vast, dim canvases by Haydon. But it is also a foreshadowing of Wagnerian opera. The sweep of the waters past the Ark, the beauteous maiden, and the cry of the sea-bird take us directly into the stage world of the Ring. And even further. It is only in the contemporary theatre that such effects have been fully realized. In Claudel's *Cristophe Colomb*, for example, where the resources of the stage are joined to those of the film and the microphone.

The Deformed Transformed shows a tiring of invention. There is in it too much of Goethe's *Faust* and of an obscure Gothic romance, *The Three Brothers*. In writing this curious work Byron played cruelly on his own nerves. The theme of physical deformity obsessed him, and the opening lines embody raw memories of his own childhood:

BERTHA: Out, hunchback!
ARNOLD: I was born so, mother!
BERTHA: Out,
        Thou incubus! Thou nightmare! Of
            seven sons,
        The sole abortion!
ARNOLD: Would that I had been so,
        And never seen the light!
BERTHA: I would so too!

Arnold concludes a Faustian pact and chooses for himself the radiant form of Achilles (it requires no Freudian to note the covert relation between Achilles' heel and Byron's own deformity). The Devil assumes Arnold's discarded shape and takes the name of Caesar. Together they join the armies besieging Rome in May 1527. Historical and fantastic personages mingle. Arnold duels with Cellini and rescues a young woman from the fury of the invading mercenaries. Then the play breaks off, on a pastoral note, at Count Arnold's castle in the Apennines.

But Byron left a sketch of the intended action. The rescued Olimpia is Arnold's bride, but she remains indifferent to him, "a marble maid." She is a modern woman, out of Ibsen or Shaw; she is drawn to the light of intelligence, even where it is devilish, and mere masculine beauty leaves her cold. She is fascinated by the misshapen Caesar, and Arnold grows jealous of his former crippled self. He has given away his hunchback frame at the cost of grace and is now doubly damned in the bargain. There is a hint in Byron's notes that Arnold will try to regain his deformity. It is a startling twist, quite in the manner of Pirandello. And there is a distinctly modern flavour in Caesar's commentary. He surrounds the plot with a Shavian critique. Told by Arnold to hasten to the Colonna palace, the Devil assures him: "Oh! I know My way through Rome."

The mixture of lyric fantasy, wit, and melodrama points directly to *Don Juan*. *The Deformed Transformed* marks a transition in Byron's work from the dramatic to the mock-epic. But one cannot escape the vivid impression that this queer fragment also left a mark on drama; surely it is a kind of prologue to *Peer Gynt*. Both demand from the theatre an enlargement of its conventions and resources. But such enlargement is now possible. Should not these late plays of Byron be given the trial of performance—perhaps, as G. Wilson Knight suggests, on a stage specially designed for them, a Byron *Festspielhaus*?

When wishing to illustrate his own conception of tragedy, Byron said: "Take up a translation of Alfieri." This is not, I suppose, something we do very often. And even in Italy, Alfieri holds a rather remote place; he is esteemed but not much read. Yet he is the most powerful tragic playwright in the language and certainly the only major dramatic talent produced in Italy between Goldoni and Pirandello. He belongs, moreover, to that school of drama which sought to combine classic forms with romantic values. In Alfieri, as in Byron, the neoclassic conventions run directly against the grain of an intensely lyric and romantic temper. This gives to Alfieri's plays their very special quality: they have a kind of fever coldness.

The range of Alfieri's themes is like an index to the romantic imagination. He dramatized the Theban cycle and the *Oresteia*, stressing in both the aspects of horror. The *Agamemnone* shows Aegisthus advancing on the stage, his sword reeking with Agamemnon's blood. In the *Antigone* the body of the heroine is brought on and the final miseries, narrated in Greek tragedy, are here enacted before us. Like Schiller, Alfieri wrote a Don Carlos drama, *Filippo*, and a *Maria Stuarda*. The latter has a special pathos, as the poet was the lover of the Countess of Albany, the much suffering wife of Charles Edward Stuart, the Young Pretender. He turned to renaissance Florence and dramatized the conjuration of the Pazzi against the rule of the Medici. But unlike *Lorenzaccio*, *La Congiura de' Pazzi* adheres pedantically to the unities of time and place. This renders its treatment of a complex and tumultuous political action highly artificial. Alfieri also looked

to the Bible, and here Byron followed his lead. *Saul*
(1782–4) is a beautiful play. Psalms of David are
interwoven into the text, giving to Alfieri's formal
neo-classic style a touch of oriental splendour. The
scene in which David sings, trying to bring light
into the blackness of the King's heart, reminds us
that the romantics saw in Rembrandt one of their
precursors.

Alfieri's masterpiece is *Mirra*, a tragedy written
between 1784 and 1786. Byron ranked the play
above any other modern drama, with the exception
of *Faust*. It is now a museum piece—in part, no
doubt, because of its subject. The theme of incest
haunted the romantic imagination. Incest gave
most drastic expression to certain attitudes which
romanticism exalted: a defiance of social conventions, a pursuit of rare and prohibited experiences,
the desire for a total intimacy and union of souls in
the act of love. It is a favourite motif with Shelley,
Byron, and Wagner. In dramatizing the legend of
Mirra's unavowed love for her father, Alfieri enclosed in a neo-classic style some of the most fervid
and decadent strains of the romantic temper. As in
Athalie, the theatric conventions are themselves expressive of the dramatic meaning. The whole tragedy
turns on Mirra's unwillingness to reveal her hideous
infatuation. It is a study in containment, and all the
neo-classic elements—the formal rhetoric, the sus-
pension of outward action, the brevity of available
time—contribute toward a sense of unendurable

pressure. When Mirra finally hints at the truth the play itself hastens to a grim end:

CINIRO: omai per sempre
      perduto hai tu l'amor del padre.
MIRRA: Oh dura,
      ferra orribil minaccia! . . . Or, nel mio
        estremo
      sospir, che già si appressa, . . . alle tante
        altre
      furie mie l'odio crudo aggiungerassi
      del genitor? . . . Da te morire io lungi?
      Oh madre mia felice! . . . almen con-
        cesso
      a lei sarà . . . di morire . . . al tuo
        fianco . . .[2]

Note how the revelation is ironically prepared for by the cry: "Oh madre mia felice!" The tone is romantic in the extreme, but the actual touch derives from Ovid. Alfieri always tries to give to his stormy feelings a hard classic mould.

It is difficult to imagine *Mirra* being performed in a modern theatre. It requires a style of overacting

[2] CINIRO: now forever
      Hast thou forfeited thy father's love.
MIRRA: Oh harsh,
      Fierce, horrible threat! At my dying gasp,
      Shall there be added to my other pangs . . .
      The cruel hatred of a father?
      Must I die estranged from thee?
      Oh, my fortunate mother! . . . To you, at least,
      It shall be given . . . to die . . . with your
        beloved . . .

which we no longer value. But given the appropriate conventions the play must have been fiercely moving. Byron took from it the name of the heroine in *Sardanapalus,* and once when seeing *Mirra* acted, that strong-nerved man fainted.

In *The Deformed Transformed,* there comes a moment when Olimpia tries to kill herself rather than survive the sack of Rome. Arnold bends anxiously over her seemingly inert body:

ARNOLD: How pale! how beautiful! how lifeless!
Alive or dead, thou essence of all beauty,
I love but thee!
CAESAR: Even so Achilles loved
Penthesilea: with his form it seems
You have his heart, and yet it was no
        soft one.

The Devil's erudition refers us to the most fascinating of all the "romantic classicists" and to his dramatization of the strange, repellent legend of Achilles and the Amazon queen. Kleist's *Penthesilea* is wilder in tone than anything devised by Byron or Alfieri, but it carries to a logical finality the attempt to unite the classic inheritance with the romantic spirit.

Together with Lenz, Büchner, and Hölderlin, Kleist is of that family of hectic genius which German literature brought forth after Goethe and Schiller, like conflagrations after a great noon. These men died early, in madness, or by their own hand. We find in their art an extreme distension, as if they were seeking out the breaking point in the resources of language and poetic form made available to them by Goethe and Schiller. Their talents attained ripeness at a fantastic pace—Büchner was not twenty-one when he wrote *Danton's Tod*—but it was ripeness without completion. Moreover we find in their work that unbalance between energy and repose, between exaltation and forbearance, which was to mark the future course of German affairs. This feverish generation of late romantics brought back into the atmosphere of Europe an edge of hysteria which the renaissance and the secular rationalism of the eighteenth century had kept in check. Given the message of national or racial superiority, these new voices brought madness into European politics. And we cannot but hear them in Kleist's *Die Hermannsschlacht*.

Though he killed himself at thirty-four, Kleist left behind his haunted life seven completed dramas and a number of novellas which are among the masterpieces of that demanding form. All that he wrote, even his essay on the metaphysics of the puppet theatre, betrays an immense inner excitement and exacerbation of sensibility. He saw human affairs in the sharp but unsteady light of the extreme. The sum of Kleist's vision is contained in the famous opening sentence of *The Earthquake in Chili*: we are shown a young Spaniard, about to hang himself in the prison of Santiago, at the very instant of the great earth tremor of 1647. Kleist was a natural dramatist because drama is the formal embodiment of crisis. Even his prose fiction is drama retarded. The style and dramatic technique of Kleist have an unflagging intensity; they are all nervousness. The action proceeds in fitful brightness, as if a torch had suddenly been raised behind the characters and then put out. The romantics had an excessive taste for chiaroscuro; in the dramas of Kleist, as in contemporary engravings, masses of shadow are rent by bolts of light.

By virtue of his extremism Kleist came nearer than either Goethe or Schiller to an uncompromising use of tragic form. *Penthesilea* and the great fragment of *Robert Guiskard* exhibit an archaic sense of how violence and unreason govern man's estate. The plague threatening the Norman army in *Guiskard* has that inhuman, nearly cosmic hideousness which drives the people of Thebes to the palace of Oedipus:

> Wenn er der Pest nicht schleunig uns entreisst,
> Die uns die Hölle grausend zugeschickt,
> So steigt der Leiche seines ganzen Volkes
> Dies Land ein Grabeshügel aus der See!
> Mit weit ausgreifenden Entsetzensschritten
> Geht sie durch die erschrocknen Scharen hin
> Und haucht von den geschwollnen Lippen ihnen
> Des Busens Giftqualm in das Angesicht! [3]

[3] If, swiftly, he cannot deliver us
From pestilence, which Hell has grimly loosed,
This piece of earth shall rear from out the sea
A burial mound unto his fallen host!
With horror's tread, and widely ravening,
The plague is striding through our shaken ranks,

It was this note of pure terror which repelled Goethe. He recognized the parts of savagery and chaos in experience but believed that centuries of rational mediation had thrown a bridge over the abyss. Kleist seemed to be undermining the fragile structure. He represented a nightmarish version of that imaginative unbalance which Goethe had sought to govern in himself and which he had portrayed under the mask of Torquato Tasso. Thus he accorded to the younger poet neither recognition nor good will.

Yet although Kleist brought into German literature a note of absolute tragedy, the originality of his work lies elsewhere. With such dramas as *Das Käthchen von Heilbronn* and the *Prinz von Homburg* the distinction between tragic and comic loses a relevance it had possessed since antiquity. Kleist was the first to establish for the modern theatre its complex terrain of uncertain seriousness. Ambiguity is present in what are called Shakespeare's "dark comedies" or "problem plays." The nature of the plot and the oblique disposal of dramatic conventions gives *Troilus and Cressida* and *Measure for Measure* their sour sweetness. But Kleist goes further. He aims at a polyphony in which irony and commitment, gravity and delight, are

---

And breathes at them out of tumid lips
The poison vapours seething in its breast!

In *Robert Guiskard*, Kleist used German to give effects of weight and solemnity such as we find in Milton. Both poets relished and controlled extreme complications of syntax.

equally implicit. His plots seem to unfold on different levels of reality, and we are left uncertain as to which is at any given moment the "realest." In nearly all of Kleist's dramas there are crucial episodes of sleep or unconsciousness; they represent a transition from one level of reality to another through gates of momentary darkness. With Kleist that characteristically modern insight into the plurality of individual consciousness is given dramatic expression.

The purposeful unsteadiness of Kleist's point of view makes his plays oddly disturbing. *Amphitryon*, *Das Käthchen von Heilbronn*, and the *Prinz von Homburg* end joyously. In each, the final curtain falls on a scene of celebration. But the works leave a wry taste in one's mouth, as if the joy had been too dearly bought. In *Amphitryon* the ancient fable of confused identities is made a symbol of the root mystery of consciousness. The light flickers across this marvellous play leaving us uncertain of the dividing line between the real and the imagined. The scene in which Amphitryon strives to assert his identity against the disguised Jupiter is nearly unbearable. When gods assume the shapes of men, men can reveal themselves only by their weakness. Alkmene knows deep in her aroused blood that she has received immortal visitation. Forced to choose between the rival Amphitryons, she turns to the divine impostor. Then suddenly Jupiter unmasks his immense presence and brings about a reconciliation. But although Amphitryon pays homage to the god and is promised Hercules for a son, he is left cruelly diminished. He has shared his very name, and when Alkmene calls it out, whom is she summoning? The Theban commanders congratulate Amphitryon upon his rare destiny, but their words ring hollow against the truth. Alkmene is scarred with her glory and is no longer at home in the world. The play closes on her inarticulate outcry:

ERSTER FELDHERR:	Fürwahr! Solch ein Triumph—
ZWEITER FELDHERR:	So vieler Ruhm—
ERSTER OBERSTER:	Du siehst durchdrungen uns—
AMPHITRYON:	Alkmene!
ALKMENE:	Ach![4]

It is a strange, bitter joy, and one's uneasiness is increased by Kleist's addition of echoes from the story of Christ to the Greek myth. Jupiter speaks of the coming of Hercules in tones of annunciation. After his fiery death he will receive him as a god. The ironies deepen as does an image in confronted mirrors.

---

[4] FIRST GENERAL: Forsooth! So great a triumph—
SECOND GENERAL: So much glory—
FIRST COMMANDER: You see us overwhelmed—
AMPHITRYON: Alkmene!
ALKMENE: Oh!

Her actual outcry, *Ach!*, is more meaningful than the English counterpart. It conveys both amazement and a momentary stab of regret.

Amphitryon shows that Kleist's sense of the world was far removed from that of Racine or even of Schiller. It is closer, perhaps, to that of Giraudoux. With Kleist a study of the "orthodox" conception of tragic drama could justly conclude.

This is true also in another vital respect. Before Kleist, tragedy embodies the notion of moral responsibility. There is a concordance between the moral character of the tragic personage and his destiny. This concordance is, at times, difficult to make out. The sufferings of Oedipus or Lear are far greater than their vices. But even in these puzzling instances we assume some measure of causal and rational dependence between the character of the man and the quality of the event. The tragic hero is responsible. His downfall is related to the presence in him of moral infirmity or active vice. The agonies of an innocent or virtuous man are, as Aristotle observed, pathetic but not tragic. And Lessing is right when he argues that the Aristotelian conception of tragic responsibility is applicable to Shakespeare, for example to *Othello* and *Macbeth*.

But Kleist departs from this tradition. The Kleistian hero is not directly responsible to the action. The conflict arises from a clash between rival orders of reality. Käthchen von Heilbronn and the Prinz von Homburg are assailed by prophetic dreams. They experience illuminations of consciousness which blind them to the realities of worldly circumstance. The entire drama consists in their stubborn adherence to the truth of vision.

At the last their intense reveries prove stronger than material fact. It is not they who surrender, but the world. Reality comes full turn and enters into the fabric of their dreams. A Kleistian personage is responsible to the disorder of his own consciousness; his heroism is that of the visionary. Not only are the plays themselves rounded with the sleep of the hero, but the plot has the queer abruptness and unlogic of dreams. The dramas of Kleist could have for their motto Keats's lines:

> Was it a vision, or a waking dream?
> Fled is that music:—do I wake or sleep?

The disruption of coherence gives to the art of Kleist its modernity. It explains why a Prussian nationalist poet should play a role in French existentialism, and why there should be essays on "The existential world of *The Prinz von Homburg*." The existentialists recognize in Kleist that discontinuity between moral cause and material effect and that reversal of rational expectations which they call the "absurd." The Prinz von Homburg dreaming his way toward death has become a symbol for the disinherited consciousness of the 1950's.

The dramas of Kleist are dramas not of action but of sufferance. Thus *Käthchen von Heilbronn* is, in part, a study of masochism. It is a powerful yet faintly repellent piece of work in which Kleist uses the fairy tale of the lost princess and her shining knight for his own eccentric purpose. The

Graf vom Strahl (his name signifies "the luminous one") has appeared to Käthchen in an angelic vision. Now the man himself stops at her father's smithy. The girl recognizes the dream figure, and henceforth she follows him like a dog. The Count does everything to rid himself of her abject presence. He spurns her and kicks her out of doors. He nearly resorts to the whip. But Käthchen drinks humiliation as if it were the well of life. She knows her vision will prevail. In the fourth Act, reality turns on its hinges. Vom Strahl realizes that the girl's mad dream matches exactly a vision which he himself experienced during a night of high fever. He acknowledges that some part of his soul has been abroad in fantastic visitation:

> Nun steht mir bei, ihr Götter: ich bin doppelt!
> Ein Geist bin ich und wandele zur Nacht!

It is a terrifying thought and conjures up madness:

> Weh mir! Mein Geist, von Wunderlicht geblen-
> det,
> Schwankt an des Wahnsinns grausem Hang um-
> her! [5]

But the Count makes that choice which is for Kleist the touchstone of heroism: he commits himself to the mysterious intimation rather than the apparent

[5] Now stand beside me, gods, for I am double!
I am a spirit and I roam the night!
. . . .
Woe! My spirit, by enchantment dazzled,
Totters on the grim edge of lunacy!

fact. Vom Strahl becomes the girl's champion and suffers ordeals by mockery and combat until she is recognized to be the Emperor's daughter. Life yields to the insistence of the dream. The drama closes as Käthchen descends the castle ramp to join the Count in marriage.

This ramp appears also in the opening and closing scenes of the *Prinz von Homburg*. It is a bridge between the reality of outward circumstance and the greater reality of vision. The plot is pure romance, though there runs through it a harsh streak of Prussian nationalism. Asleep in the palace garden the Prince dreams an intensely vivid dream of glory and royal betrothal. He wakens but his spirit is numbed by the marvels he has dreamt and he fails to attend to the order of battle. In consequence he imperils victory by a splendid but premature attack. Sentenced to death by court-martial he first refuses to accept the reality of his fate and then pleads wildly for his life; being a sleepwalker between worlds the Prince is both a hero and a coward. Finally, he transcends his fear and recognizes the justice of his condemnation. He refuses the chance of pardon and demands that the sentence be carried out as an example to future valour. The Prince is led blindfolded into the garden in which he had his first vision. He waits for execution as the drums beat out a funeral march. But at that moment the Elector of Brandenburg enters on the terrace above with his courtiers and the Princess Natalie. Bearing a laurel crown, she advances to-

ward her condemned lover. When the blindfold
is removed from his eyes, the Prince sees before
him the exact rendition of his dream and falls unconscious. He is roused to life by martial music
and the thunder of cannon, and the curtain descends on the promise of victorious war.

No summary can convey the curious magic of
the scene. As in *Amphitryon* it derives in part from
hints of a more lofty meaning. The *Prinz von
Homburg* is a parable of resurrection. In the dream
garden the Prince partakes both of the fall of man
and of his redemption. After the momentary death
of unconsciousness he rises to glory in the presence
of him who is to be his father. Indeed, he touches
the bright edge of immortality:

> Nun, o Unsterblichkeit, bist du ganz mein!
> Du strahlst mir, durch die Binde meiner Augen,
> Mit Glanz der tausendfachen Sonne zu!
> Es wachsen Flügel mir an beiden Schultern,
> Durch stille Ätherräume schwingt mein Geist;
> Und wie ein Schiff, vom Hauch des Winds ent-
>   führt,
> Die muntre Hafenstadt versinken sieht,
> So geht mir dämmernd alles Leben unter.[6]

[6] Now thou art mine, O immortality!
Your fiery blaze, as from a thousand suns,
Pierces this blindfold with its radiance!
And now from both my shoulders wings arise,
My spirit wafts through still ethereal space;
And like a ship, led softly by the wind,
That sees the merry harbour fade from sight,
I feel my life sink down into a gloaming.

But the theological motifs are woven tightly into the special fabric of the play. The dominant theme is the equivocation on reality. In the dramas of Kleist, men waken not from sleep but from wakeness. They are most awake when they enter the solid stuff of dreams. From the *Prinz von Homburg* there is only a short step to Pirandello.

Penthesilea is earlier than either of the dream plays and has nothing of their ambiguity. Kleist's treatment of the myth is arch-romantic. The warrior queen sets eyes on Achilles and is infatuated to the pitch of madness. Her desire transcends the erotic. It is an obsession with the absolute such as we find in the narratives of Poe and Balzac. Between the two lovers stands the fact of war, and Kleist plays brilliantly on the nearness in the soul of total lust and total hatred. He knew before Strindberg that sexual passion and armed combat are related modes of encounter. The play is built like a sword dance. Achilles and the Amazon advance and retreat in murderous courtship. Finally Penthesilea's maddened appetites flare out in literal cannibalism. The style of the work precisely mirrors the cruel formality of the action. The verse has a fierce, cold brilliance. Yeats, that master of formal violence, might have written *Penthesilea* had he commanded the necessary breadth of design.

But the play has the vices of its great power. It cries havoc so relentlessly that it turns into an exalted piece of *grand guignol*. Like much of Ger-

man romantic art, it carries too far the conceit that
love and death are kindred. And the notorious
climax—Penthesilea tearing with her teeth at the
fallen Achilles—is one to make the imagination
shudder away in disbelief. Goethe was undeniably
right when he observed in *Penthesilea* signs of
decadence. The tragedy reflects the strain of hysteria and sadism which runs just beneath the surface of romanticism, from the age of the Gothic
novel to that of Flaubert and Oscar Wilde's *Sa-
lomé*.

Yet for all its sombre extravagance, the work
remains of great interest. Kleist goes even further
than Alfieri in using classic mythology for his
private and eccentric purpose. He is a direct pre-
cursor of those modern dramatists who pour into
the old bottles of Greek legend the new wines of
Freudian psychology or contemporary politics. Increasingly unable to create for itself a relevant body
of myth, the modern imagination will ransack the
treasure house of the classic.

Penthesilea was published in 1808. In 1821 Grillparzer completed his trilogy, *The Golden Fleece*.
Byron knew the poet's name and prophesied that
it would achieve wide renown. This has not been
the case, but Grillparzer is a playwright of the first
rank. He does not have Kleist's incandescence and
the dry bitterness of his work mirrors the conditions of intellectual life under Metternich. But unlike Kleist, Grillparzer was in full control of his

means, and his treatment of the Medea legend has a tough-minded dignity which rivals Euripides. Grillparzer develops two principal motifs. Medea is the outsider, the alien torn up by the roots. She stains the light of the Greek setting by her mere presence, for she carries with her the gloom of exile. Moreover, she has committed numerous crimes on Jason's behalf, and for that very reason he no longer trusts her. Having betrayed a father and a brother in order to follow a Greek pirate, Medea may in turn betray the Greek. Jason is repelled by the primitive ferocity of Medea's love. He is no longer the fiery captain of the Argonauts, but a tired, suspicious man in search of anchorage. These elements are present in the myth and in Euripides' version. But by concentrating on them, Grillparzer gives to the tragedy an ironic, modern focus.

Grillparzer is not readily quotable, for he has a characteristic Austrian musicality; the successive moments in his dramas are tightly joined. But in the third Act of *Medea* occurs a piece of dialogue in which Grillparzer's principal virtues are clearly visible:

MEDEA: Du hast zu Liebe mich verlockt, und
        fliehst mich?
JASON: Ich muss!
MEDEA: Du hast den Vater mir geraubt,
        Und raubst mir den Gemahl?
JASON: Gezwungen nur!

MEDEA: Mein Bruder fiel durch dich, du nahmst
    mir ihn,
    Und fliehst mich?
JASON: Wie er fiel, gleich unverschuldet.
MEDEA: Mein Vaterland verliess ich, dir zu
    folgen.
JASON: Dem eignen Willen folgtest du, nicht
    mir.
    Hätts dich gereut, gern liess ich dich
    zurück!
MEDEA: Die Welt verflucht um deinetwillen
    mich,
    Ich selber hasse mich um deinetwillen,
    Und du verlässt mich?
JASON: Ich verlass dich nicht,
    Ein höhrer Spruch treibt mich von dir
    hinweg.
    Hast du dein Glück verloren, wo ist
    meins?
    Nimm als Ersatz mein Elend für das
    deine!
MEDEA: Jason!
JASON: Was ist? Was willst du weiter?
MEDEA: Nichts!
    Es ist vorbei! [7]

[7] MEDEA: You lured me into love, and flee from me?
JASON: I must!
MEDEA: You robbed me of a father,
    And rob me of a husband?
JASON: Only perforce!
MEDEA: You caused my brother's fall, you took him from
    me,
    And now you flee?
JASON: Even as he fell, in equal innocence.
MEDEA: I left my fatherland to follow you.

This is, in its manner, finer than Kleist. It is clearer and sticks more grimly to the point. The prosody is masterful. Grillparzer is able to produce major effects without forcing the tone. He has a faultless ear and uses it to lighten the natural weight of German syntax. The argument is bent to the swift, subtle shape of the verse. The virtuosity of metric invention and the manner in which the stress shifts between the two voices reminds one of the best of Tennyson. Like Tennyson, Grillparzer brought to his own language the resources of Latin versification.

Because the dialogue is so lucid, so unencumbered with mythological ornaments or old-style rhetoric, it has a sharp modernity. It could be contemporaneous with Anouilh's *Médée*:

Où veux-tu que j'aille? Où me renvoies-tu? Gagnerai-je le Phase, la Colchide, le royaume paternel, les champs baignés de sang de mon frère? Tu me chasses. Quelles terres m'ordonnes-tu de gagner sans toi? Quelles mers

---

JASON: You did not follow me but your own will.
   Had you repented, I'd have left you there!
MEDEA: The world heaps curses on me for your sake,
   And for your sake I come to hate myself,
   And you abandon me?
JASON: No, not abandon;
   A higher voice decrees that we must part.
   Your happiness is lost, but where is mine?
   Accept my anguish in exchange of yours!
MEDEA: Jason!
JASON: What is it? What more do you wish?
MEDEA: Nothing!
   'Tis past!

libres? Les détroits du Pont où je suis passée derrière
toi, trichant, mentant, volant pour toi; Lemnos où on
n'a pas du m'oublier; la Thessalie où ils m'attendent
pour venger leur père, tué pour toi? Tous les chemins
que je t'ai ouverts, je me les suis fermés. Je suis Médée
chargée d'horreur et de crimes.[8]

The tone and direction of argument are precisely
the same.

Kleist and Grillparzer were dramatists of transition. They sought to combine the Greek and the
Shakespearean legacy into a form of tragic drama
appropriate to the modern theatre. Their use of
Greek mythology and classic modes was, therefore,
experimental. They stand on the modern side of
the line which divides Racine's view of the antique
from that of Hofmannsthal or Anouilh. But one
should not close a discussion of romantic Hellenism
without referring to those two plays which, together with *Samson Agonistes*, come nearest in
European literature to a reincarnation of the Greek
ideal.

As early as the 1780's, Schiller was determined
to write a play which would embody not only the

[8] Where would you have me go? To where are you sending me
back? Should I proceed to Phasis, to Colchis, my father's realm,
its fields drenched with my brother's blood? You hound me
away. To what lands do you bid me go without you? To what
open seas? The Pontic straits, which I passed through at your
heels, cheating, lying, robbing for you; Lemnos, where they have
surely not forgotten me; Thessaly, where they await my return to
avenge their father whom I slew for your sake? All the roads I
opened for you I closed to myself. I am Medea laden with
abominations and crimes.

concept of Greek tragedy but the actual technical forms. After his Shakespearean period—*Wallenstein, Maria Stuart, Die Jungfrau von Orleans*—he resolved to give to the German theatre an example of Sophoclean drama. This meant the adaptation of a chorus to the modern stage. In the Preface to the *Braut von Messina*, Schiller gives a lucid analysis of the role of the chorus. He regards it as an instrument of necessary unreality. A poetic drama presents an action which is at the same time real and illusory, or rather, which is real only within the special fiction of theatrical performance. By surrounding the action with a wall of formal speech and ceremonious motion, the chorus enforces on the spectator the necessary sense of distance. It makes the real imaginary. Schiller's argument here anticipates Brecht's concept of "estrangement" between the audience and the play. Secondly, Schiller sees in the presence of a chorus a sumptuous "lyric tapestry" (*lyrisches Prachtgewebe*). Against this background, the action can unfold with proper majesty. Choral recitation lifts the dramatic event above the plane of ordinary speech. Finally, Schiller believes that a chorus brings into tragic drama an element of relief. It rounds off the sharp corners of violence and thus enables the mind to witness tragic horrors without falling into despair. The chorus survives the ruin of Agamemnon or Oedipus and can draw a moral which transcends the immediate disaster. Thus it contributes toward Schiller's ideal of a tragedy of reconciliation.

The *Braut von Messina* is not an attractive play. Inspired by the legend of the rivalry and death of the sons of Oedipus, Schiller constructed a tightly symmetrical plot. To make doom inescapable, events have to interlock with maddening coincidence. Though the play is severely classical in form, it is in fact built around a series of melodramatic hazards. It depends entirely on chance encounters, sudden disappearances, and delayed recognitions. If there is such a thing as Sophoclean melodrama, we find it here. And the tragic close is unconvincing. Don Caesar is determined to kill himself in order to restore a precise balance of justice. He carries out his resolve although he knows that only his survival could mend the havoc he and his fierce brother have caused. The doomed puppet begins gesturing stiffly behind the human mask. Moreover, as Schiller himself realized, the chorus departs from its formal and contemplative role. Divided into rival factions, it intervenes in the murderous intrigue.

And yet there are moments in the *Braut von Messina* to match Sophocles. The chorus uses both rhyme and blank verse of varying measure. Certain passages come closer than anything else written in a modern tongue to our conjectures of what the Greek chorus must have sounded like:

> Aber das Ungeheure auch
> Lerne erwarten im irdischen Leben!
> Mit gewaltsamer Hand
> Löset der Mord auch das heiligste Band,

In sein stygisches Boot
Raffet der Tod
Auch der Jugend blühendes Leben!
Wenn die Wolken getürmt den Himmel schwär-
zen,
Wenn dumpftosend der Donner hallt,
Da, da fühlen sich alle Herzen
In des furchtbaren Schicksals Gewalt.[9]

Beneath the words resounds the tread of the dance. Schiller conceived of the recitation as half-sung, and demonstrated that given sufficient poetic skill, choral drama remained a vital possibility. The *Braut von Messina* is the keystone in the long arch that reaches from *Samson Agonistes* to *Murder in the Cathedral*.

There is no chorus in the successive, fragmentary versions of Hölderlin's *Empedokles* (though the outline for *Empedokles auf dem Ätna* calls for

[9] What is appalling—that also
Learn to expect in mortal life!
With violent hand
Murder loosens the holiest bond,
To its Stygian ferry
Death does carry
Those also who die in the spring of life!
When towering clouds blacken the sky
And sullen thunders roll,
Then every heart must feel
The power of dreadful destiny.

The crux is *das Ungeheure*. It means that which is terrible through its strangeness and immensity. It is "the inhuman," being exterior to man and greater than he. Some such paraphrase as "the strangely terrible" might come closest. But the beat calls for a single, emphatic term.

one). But Hölderlin's dramatic poem is the summit
of romantic Hellenism. It was never intended for
the actual stage and remains a series of great fragments over whose incompletion falls the shadow
of the poet's insanity. But it tells us how far it has
been possible for a modern poet to adopt the tone
and vision of the Greek tragic theatre. Hölderlin,
moreover, chose the most remote and difficult
version of the classic spirit. The indebtedness of
neo-classic and modern drama is mainly to Sophocles and Euripides. Hölderlin goes back to Aeschylus and to those predramatic forms of enacted
lament or incantation which we discern dimly at
the threshold of Aeschylean tragedy. Not since the
Prometheus had drama known such austere passion.
Der Tod des Empedokles and the three completed
scenes of *Empedokles auf dem Ätna* are among
the mountain tops of literature—cold, difficult of
access, and incomparably noble:

> Ha! Jupiter, Befreier! näher tritt
> Und näher meine Stund' und vom Geklüfte
> Kommt schon der traute Bote meiner Nacht,
> Der Abendwind zu mir, der Liebesbote.
> Es wird! gereift ists! o nun schlage, Herz,
> Und rege deine Wellen, ist der Geist
> Doch über dir, wie leuchtendes Gestirn,
> Indes des Himmels heimatlos Gewölk
> Das immerflüchtige, vorüberwandelt.
>
> . . . .
> Zufrieden bin ich, suche nun nichts mehr
> Denn meine Opferstätte. Wohl ist mir.
> O Iris' Bogen! über stürzenden

Gewässern, wenn die Wog' in Silberwolken
Auffliegt, wie du bist, so ist meine Freude! [1]

Drama has never again approximated so closely the Greek ideal. *Empedokles* seems to stand furthest of any European tragedy from the spell of Shakespeare. But neither the *Braut von Messina* nor *Empedokles* could contribute to the life of the practical theatre; their splendour lay too high. For that life to continue, the imagination had to descend to the plains.

[1] Ha! Jupiter, liberator! nearer draws
And nearer my hour, and from the chasm
There comes already the true messenger
Of night, the evening wind, bearer of love.
It comes to being! It is ripe! Oh heart,
Beat now, and rouse your inward surge; the Spirit
Is above you like a cluster of bright stars,
While through the heavens, homeless evermore,
The rack of clouds goes past in constant flight.
. . . .
I am content; some place in which to offer
Sacrifice is all I further crave. I feel
Heart's ease. O bow of Iris, as you are,
When the wave leaps in clouds of silver spray
Above downrushing waters, so is my joy!

I have tried to translate as closely, as literally, as possible to get the meaning right. The concise, strange beauty of Hölderlin's style is unrecapturable. By *Geist* (Spirit), Hölderlin presumably means the Greek Ψυχή.

VII

ALL THE PLAYS we have considered so far are written in verse. This has its reasons. For more than two thousand years the notion of verse was nearly inseparable from that of tragic drama. The idea of "prose tragedy" is singularly modern, and to many poets and critics it remains paradoxical. There are historical reasons for this and reasons of literary technique. But there are also causes deeply rooted in our common understanding of the quality of language. I say verse and not poetry, for poetry can be a virtue of prose, of mathematics, or any action of the mind that tends toward shape. The poetic is an attribute; verse is a technical form.

In literature, verse precedes prose. Literature is a setting apart of language from the requirements of immediate utility and communication. It raises discourse above common speech for purposes of invocation, adornment, or remembrance. The natural means of such elevation are rhythm and explicit prosody. By not being prose, by having metre or rhyme or a pattern of formal recurrence, language imposes on the mind a sense of special occasion and preserves its shape in the memory. It becomes verse. The notion of literary prose is highly sophisticated. I wonder whether it has any relevance before the orations recorded or contrived by Thucydides in his account of the Peloponnesian Wars and before the Dialogues of Plato. It is in these works that we first encounter the feeling that prose could aspire to the dignity and "apartness" of literature. But Thucydides and Plato come late in the evolution of Greek letters, and neither was concerned with drama.

It is certain that Greek tragedy was, from the outset, written in verse. It sprang from archaic rituals of celebration or lament and was inseparable from the use of language in a heightened lyric mode. Attic drama represents a convergence of speech, music, and dance. In all three, rhythm is the vital centre, and when language is in a state of rhythm (words in the condition of ordered motion), it is verse. In the *Oresteia* no less than in the *Bacchae*, perhaps the last of the great feats of the Greek tragic imagination, the action of the drama and the moral experience of the characters are wholly united to the metric form. Greek tragedy is sung, danced, and declaimed. Prose has no place in it.

Very early, moreover, the mind perceived a relation between poetic forms and those categories of truth which are not directly verifiable. We speak still of "poetic truth" when signifying that a statement may be false or meaningless by the test of empiric proof, yet possesses at the same time an important, undeniable verity in a moral, psychological, or formal domain. Now the truths of mythology and religious experience are largely of this order. Prose submits its own statements to criteria of verification which are, in fact, irrelevant or inapplicable to the realities of myth. And it is on these that Greek tragedy is founded. The matter of tragic legend, whether it invokes Agamemnon, Oedipus, or Alcestis torn from the dead, cannot be held liable to prosaic inquisition. As Robert Graves says, the imagination has extra-territorial rights, and these are guarded by poetry.

Poetry also has its criteria of truth. Indeed, they are more severe than those of prose, but they are different. The criterion of poetic truth is one of internal consistency and psychological conviction. Where the pressure of imagination is sufficiently sustained, we allow poetry the most ample liberties. In that sense, we may say that verse is the pure mathematics of language. It is more exact than prose, more self-contained, and more capable of constructing theoretic forms independent of material basis. It can "lie" creatively. The worlds of poetic myth, like those of non-Euclidean geometry, are persuasive of truth so long as they adhere to their own imaginative premises. Prose, on the contrary, is applied mathematics. Somewhere along the line the assertions it makes must correspond to our sensual perceptions. The houses described in prose must stand on solid foundations. Prose measures, records, and anticipates the realities of practical life. It is the garb of the mind doing its daily job of work.

This is no longer entirely the case. Modern literature has developed the concept of "poetic prose," of a prose liberated from verifiability and the jurisdiction of logic as it is embodied in common syntax. There are prophetic traces of this idea in Rabelais and Sterne. But it does not really assume importance before Rimbaud, Lautréamont, and Joyce. Until their time the distinctions between the role of verse and that of prose were firm.

Verse is not only the special guardian of poetic truth against the critique of empiricism. It is the prime divider between the world of high tragedy and that of ordinary existence. Kings, prophets, and heroes speak in verse, thus showing that the exemplary personages in the commonwealth communicate in a manner nobler and more ancient than that reserved to common men. There is nothing democratic in the vision of tragedy. The royal and heroic characters whom the gods honour with their vengeance are set higher than we are in the chain of being, and their style of utterance must reflect this elevation. Common men are prosaic, and revolutionaries write their manifestoes in prose.

Kings answer in verse. Shakespeare knew this well. *Richard II* is a drama of languages which fail to communicate with each other. Richard goes to ruin because he seeks to enforce the criteria of poetic truth on the gross, mutinous claims of political reality. He is a royal poet defeated by a rebellion of prose.

Like music, moreover, verse sets a barrier between the tragic action and the audience. Even where there is no longer a chorus it creates that necessary sense of distance and strangeness to which Schiller referred. The difference of languages between the stage and the pit alters the perspective and gives to the characters and their actions a special magnitude. And by compelling the mind to surmount a momentary barrier of formality, verse arrests and ripens our emotions. We can identify ourselves with Agamemnon, Macbeth, or Phèdre, but only partially, and after preliminary effort. Their use of a language shaped more nobly and intricately than our own imposes on us a respectful distance. We cannot leap into their skins as we are invited to do in naturalistic drama. Thus verse prevents our sympathies from growing too familiar. At the courts of great monarchs, lesser nobility and the third estate were not allowed too near the royal person. But prose is a leveller and gets very close to its object.

Verse at once simplifies and complicates the portrayal of human conduct. That is the crucial point. It simplifies because it strips away from life the encumbrances of material contingency. Where men speak verse, they are not prone to catching colds or suffering from indigestion. They do not concern themselves with the next meal or train time-tables. I have cited earlier the opening line of Victor Hugo's *Cromwell*. It infuriated contemporary critics because it used an *alexandrin*, the very mark of high and timeless life, for a precise temporal statement. It drew tragic verse down to the gross world of clocks and calendars. Like wealth, in the poetics of Henry James and Proust, verse relieves the personages of tragic drama from the complications of material and physical need. It is because all material exactions are met by the assumption of financial ease that Jamesian and Proustian characters are at liberty to live in full the life of feeling and intelligence. So it is in tragedy. In a very real sense, the tragic hero lets his servants live for him. It is they who assume the corrupting burdens of hunger, sleep, and ailment. This is one of the decisive differences between the world of the novel, which is that of prose, and the world of the tragic theatre, which is that of verse. In prose fiction, as D. H. Lawrence remarked, "you know there is a watercloset on the premises." We are not called upon to envisage such facilities at Mycenae and Elsinore. If there are bathrooms in the houses of tragedy, they are for Agamemnon to be murdered in.

It is this distinction which lies behind the neoclassic belief that verse should not be made to

243

express menial facts. Since Wordsworth and the romantics, we no longer accept this convention. From the time of the *Lyrical Ballads* to that of *Prufrock*, poetry has appropriated to itself all domains, however sordid or familiar. It is held that all manner of reality can be given suitable poetic form. I wonder whether this is really so. Dryden conceded that verse might be made to say "close the door," but was dubious whether it should. For in performing such tasks it descends into the chaos of material objects and bodily functions where prose is master. Certain styles of action are more appropriate to poetic incarnation than others. Because we have denied the fact, so much of what passes for modern poetry is merely inflated or bewildered prose. In contemporary verse drama, we see repeated failures to distinguish between proper and improper uses of poetic form. The recent plays of T. S. Eliot give clear proof of what happens when blank verse is asked to carry out domestic functions. It rebels.

But if verse simplifies our account of reality by eliminating life below the stairs, it also immensely complicates the range and values of the behaviour of the mind. By virtue of elision, concentration, obliqueness, and its capacity to sustain a plurality of meanings, poetry gives an image of life which is far denser and more complex than that of prose. The natural shape of prose is linear; it proceeds by consequent statement. It qualifies or contradicts by what comes after. Poetry can advance discordant

persuasions simultaneously. Metaphors, imagery,
and the tropes of verse rhetoric can be charged with
simultaneous yet disparate meanings, even as music
can convey at the same moment contrasting energies of motion. The syntax of prose embodies the
central role which causal relations and temporal
logic play in the proceedings of ordinary thought.
The syntax of verse is, in part, liberated from cau-
sality and time. It can put cause before effect and
allow to argument a progress more adventurous
than the marching order of traditional logic. That
is why good verse is untranslatable into prose. Consider an example from *Coriolanus* (a play in which
Shakespeare's purpose depends heavily on the prerogatives of poetic form):

No take more!
What may be sworn by, both divine and human,
Seal what I end withal! This double worship—
Where one part does disdain with cause, the other
Insult without all reason; where gentry, title, wis-
    dom
Cannot conclude but by the yea and no
Of general ignorance—it must omit
Real necessities, and give way the while
To unstable slightness. Purpose so barr'd, it fol-
    lows
Nothing is done to purpose. Therefore, beseech
    you—
You that will be less fearful than discreet;
That love the fundamental part of state
More than you doubt the change on't; that prefer

A noble life before a long, and wish
To jump a body with a dangerous physic
That's sure of death without it—at once pluck out
The multitudinous tongue; let them not lick
The sweet which is their poison.

No prose paraphrase can give a fair equivalent. Nor can we "translate" downward Hamlet's soliloquies, Macbeth's meditation on death, or Cleopatra's lament over her fallen lover.

As mathematics recedes from the obvious, it becomes less translatable into anything but itself. As poetry moves further from the prosaic, as it gains in subtlety and concentration, it becomes irreducible to any other medium. Bad verse, verse which is not strictly necessary to the purpose, profits from good paraphrase or even from translation into another language. Witness how much finer Poe sounds in French. But good verse, that is to say poetry, is all but lost.

So far, therefore, as tragic drama is an exaltation of action above the flux of disorder and compromise prevalent in habitual life, it requires the shape of verse. The stylization and simplification which that shape imposes on the outward aspects of conduct make possible the moral, intellectual, and emotional complications of high drama. Poetic conventions clear the ground for the free play of moral forces. The tragic actors in the Greek theatre stood on lofty wooden shoes and spoke through great masks, thus living higher and louder than life. Verse provides a similar altitude and resonance.

This is not to deny that prose has its own tragic register. One would not wish Tacitus to have written in verse, and Keats's letters attain depths of feeling even greater than those of his poetry. But the two spheres are different, and the decision of certain playwrights to carry tragedy from the realm of verse into that of prose is one of the decisive occurrences in the history of western drama.

Traditionally the frontier between verse and prose corresponds to that which separates the tragic from the comic. What has come down to us of Greek and Latin comedy is in verse. Many of the same metres are used both by the tragedians and by Aristophanes, and this is true also of Plautus and Terence. But most probably there flourished below the level of literary drama traditions of folk comedy and farce presented in prose. That no texts have survived points to the larger fact that prose had not yet been accorded the dignity of belles-lettres. It was improvised and transmitted by word of mouth, if at all. But there can be no doubt that the association between comedy and prose is a very ancient and natural one. Verse and tragedy belong together in the domain of aristocratic life. Comedy is the art of the lesser orders of men. It tends to dramatize those material circumstances and bodily functions which are banished from the tragic stage. The comic personage does not transcend the flesh; he is engrossed in it. There are no lavatories in tragic palaces, but from its very dawn, comedy has had use for chamber pots. In tragedy, we do not observe men eating, nor do we hear them snore. But the nightcap and the cooking ladle flourish in the art of Aristophanes and Menander. And they thrust us downward, to the world of prose.

Medieval literature had its rich comic undergrowth. Nonliterary forms of dramatic entertainment, compounded of mime, jugglery, and broad horseplay, were widely popular. They enter the mystery cycles in the guise of comic interludes. The substitution of a sheep for the Child Jesus in the Shepherd's Play is a notorious instance. No doubt there lies behind it a long tradition of dramatic farce. Vernacular prose, moreover, was gaining in strength and resource. With the renaissance, it was ready to assume the full rights of literature. It did so in Rojas's *Celestina* (1499), a work part novel and part drama, and in Machiavelli's *Mandragola* (1522), the first great modern comedy. From the *Mandragola* the way lies open to the comic prose of Molière and Congreve.

The traditional association between the comic genre and the prose form is implicit throughout Elizabethan drama. Often the double plot of an Elizabethan or Jacobean play is divided between prose comedy and verse tragedy. Clowns, fools, menials, and rustics speak prose in the very same scenes in which their masters speak in iambic verse. Such separation according to social rank and dramatic mood is frequent in Shakespeare. In *A Midsummer Night's Dream*, Theseus and his courtiers use verse. So do the fairies in whom all language bursts into the flame of poetry. Peter Quince and his crew, on the other hand, express themselves in gnarled, clotted prose. Much of our pleasure springs from the counterpoint. When the rustics act their play before him, Theseus does them the courtesy of descending into prose (how else should they understand his thanks?). But it is a prose shot through with the cadence of his natural poetic style: "The best in this kind are but shadows; and the worst are no worse, if imagination amend them." The fun of *Love's Labour's Lost* arises in part from Armado's fantastical prose. He speaks "not like a man of God's making" because he torments prose into the florid shapes of the poetical. In the late Shakespeare, distinctions between verse and prose are attenuated by the search for an inclusive form, instantaneously responsive to the conditions of dramatic action and feeling. Yet even here we perceive the old usage. The comedy and the prose belong to low life, the grief and the poetry to high. In the last Act of *Cymbeline*, the caustic, sententious prose of the jailer falls across the way of some of the most melodious verse Shakespeare ever wrote. In *The Winter's Tale* the use of prose precisely marks the limits of the pastoral. The clown, the servant, and the shepherds speak in prose though poetry knocks at every door. In *The Tempest* this ancient division is most clear. The isle is full of rarest music, but the low creatures on it—Caliban, Trinculo, and Stephano—riot and conspire in rank prose. Caliban, who has in him a kind of angry poetry, turns prosaic under the influence of Stephano's bottle. Yet none of these instances is conclusive. Cloten, in *Cymbeline*, nearly always uses prose as if to show that, although a royal personage, he is base and misshapen. *The Winter's Tale* opens with a scene in which two courtiers converse in prose. And the castaway lords in *The Tempest* sometimes fall out of verse.

The subject of Shakespeare's alternate use of verse and prose is complex and fascinating. Despite the great mass of Shakespearean criticism, it has received no thorough treatment. There is a technical difficulty. The distribution between blank verse and prose sometimes depends on the vagaries of the printer and the loose habits of Elizabethan punctuation rather than on the intentions of the poet. In certain plays such as *As You Like It* and *Coriolanus*, the printer seems to have gone particularly astray, making prose paragraphs of iambic pentameter or hypermetric lines of what was meant to be prose. Moreover, there is the fact that Elizabethan and Jacobean prose has a tendency to fall into the gait of blank verse.

But these accidents have been overstressed. In most cases, Shakespeare knew precisely what he was about when he changed from verse to prose or back again. He modulated the expressive form according to the requirements of character, mood, and dramatic circumstance. It is a matter of poetic tact, of an instrument played incomparably by ear. Both modes were equally pliant to his touch. Shakespeare was fully aware of the dramatic possibilities inherent in the shift from one to the other. He knew what effects of irony or contrast could be derived from a sudden confrontation of the poetic and the prosaic voice. And he was beginning to explore, in such plays as *Lear* and *Coriolanus*, those special resources of prose which are not available to poetry even where it is most complex.

The function of contrast is beautifully shown in *Much Ado About Nothing*. Nearly the entire play is written in prose. The few passages of verse are only a kind of shorthand to quicken matters. Indeed, with this play English prose established a firm claim to the comedy of intellect. Congreve, Oscar Wilde, and Shaw are direct heirs to Shakespeare's presentation of Beatrice and Benedick. Verse would mar the stringent, bracing quality of their love. They are lovers in the middle range of passion, enamoured neither of the flesh nor altogether of the heart, but caught in the enchantment of each other's wit. Their bright encounters show how intelligence gives to prose its real music. But in the last Act, poetry makes a memorable entrance. The setting is Hero's false tomb. Claudio, Don Pedro, and their musicians come to do it sorrowful honour. They sing a mournful lyric: "Pardon, goddess of the night." Then the prince turns to the players:

> Good morrow, masters, put your torches out.
> The wolves have prey'd, and look, the gentle day,
> Before the wheels of Phoebus, round about
> Dapples the drowsy east with spots of grey.

The lines cast a healing spell. They brush away the squalid machinations of the plot. At the touch of poetry, the entire play moves into a more luminous key. We know that disclosure is imminent and that the affair will end happily. This salutation to the morning, moreover, delivers a gentle rebuke to Beatrice and Benedick. Don Pedro invokes the pastoral and mythological order of the world. It has none of the sophistication of the lovers' prose. But it is more enduring.

Another example of intended contrast is that of the rival funeral orations in *Julius Caesar*. Brutus speaks in prose:

Had you rather Caesar were living, and die all slaves, than that Caesar were dead, to live all freemen? As Caesar love'd me, I weep for him; as he was fortunate, I rejoice at it; as he was valiant, I honour him; but— as he was ambitious, I slew him. There is tears for his love; joy for his fortune; honour for his valour; and death for his ambition.

A moment later, Mark Anthony launches into verse rhetoric of matchless cunning. We are meant to observe the full force of the contrast. Brutus' style is dry and noble, as from a book of law. It proceeds in the vein of reason and solicits the mind. Anthony throws fire into the blood. He uses every licence of poetic form to lash the mob into a frenzy. He tells us: "I am no orator, as Brutus is." True; he is a word-conjurer and poet. Like all men to whom prose is the natural voice of public affairs, Brutus fails to realize how much there is in politics of eloquent unreason. Even before Anthony has ceased, Brutus and Cassius have to "ride like madmen through the gates of Rome." A fierce poetry is at their heels.

Sometimes Shakespeare uses the collision between verse and prose to articulate the principal meaning of a play. In *Henry IV* there is a manifold dialectic: nobility against crown; north against south; the life of the court against that of the tavern. Embracing all, is the clash between the chivalric ideal of conduct, already tainted with decay, and the new mercantile empiricism foreshadowed in Falstaff. Hotspur, Northumberland, and the King use high-flown verse, rich with the allegoric devices of feudal rhetoric. Falstaff speaks shrewd, carnal prose. We hear in it the voice of Elizabethan London. The two languages are constantly set against each other. Hotspur invariably strikes the medieval chord:

> Now, Esperance! Percy! and set on.
> Sound all the lofty instruments of war,
> And by that music let us all embrace;
> For, heaven to earth, some of us never shall
> A second time do such a courtesy.

The Gallic battle cry and the archaic sense of "courtesy" (*courtoisie*) make the style as medieval as full armour. Falstaff gives the answer of the modern common man:

Can honour set a leg? No. Or an arm? No. Or take away the grief of a wound? No. Honour hath no skill in surgery then? No. What is honour? A word. What is that word honour? Air. A trim reckoning!

The counting-house note in "reckoning" is deliberate. This is already the voice of Sancho Panza and the Good Soldier Schweik. It gives the lie to the heroic ideal. It is right that it should be Falstaff who claims victory over Hotspur and carries his body off the field. The Hotspurs are out of date.

Prince Hal moves between verse and prose with a cool sense of occasion. That is his special strength. He can use both the courtly and the tavern worlds toward his own ambitions. He has seen through their rival pretensions and is servant to neither. In the early part of the drama, the Prince allows Falstaff to set the tone. When they meet during the battle of Shrewsbury, Hal enters in the style of Hotspur:

> Many a nobleman lies stark and stiff
> Under the hoofs of vaunting enemies,
> Whose deaths are yet unreveng'd. I prithee
> Lend me thy sword.

But Falstaff is immune to chivalry. He answers in prose: "take my pistol, if thou wilt." Prose and firearms go together. They are distinctly of the modern world. In Part II, on the contrary, the encounter between verse and prose ends with the necessary triumph of the poetic:

> When thou dost hear I am as I have been,
> Approach me, and thou shalt be as thou wast,
> The tutor and the feeder of my riots.

254

> Till then I banish thee, on pain of death,
> As I have done the rest of my misleaders,
> Not to come near our person by ten mile.

The verse beats like a stick across the old carouser's back. But with his superb sense of controlled complication, Shakespeare allows Falstaff a parting word: "Master Shallow, I owe you a thousand pound." The line is prose and the matter is money. It speaks of modern life, whereas there shines on Henry V, as he sets off to France and the last of medieval wars, the glory of a passing age.

In *Troilus and Cressida* the clash between the heroic ideal and prosaic realism occurs on more narrow and acrimonious ground. The mirror which Thersites holds up to the chivalric action is clouded and distorting. But there is a certain base truth in the image. Thersites is, perhaps, the first of those whom Dostoevsky calls "the men from the underground"; he reviles society for being hypocritical in its professed ideals and pours over others the dregs of his self-contempt. Thersites does more than speak prose; he is the incarnation of the antipoetic. His prose flourishes on the refuse of language. It is rank with gall and seeks to strip away the ornamental and discretionary conventions of the courtly style. In Act V, the two visions of life are confronted. The scene is a marvel of precise intonation. Troilus has observed Cressida's falsehood and is about to be escorted from the Greek camp (this interlude in the midst of war is itself a convention of chivalry). He speaks in the elaborate style of

courtly love and bids Diomed defiance in terms
which bring vividly to mind feudal warfare and
heraldic usage. But Thersites has been listening in
the dark. As the noble lords withdraw, he pro-
nounces a gross epitaph on the entire tradition of
heroic romance. In a single moment, the wheel of
language is brought full circle:

TROILUS: Have with you, Prince. My courteous
           lord, adieu.
           Farewell, revolted fair! and, Diomed,
           Stand fast and wear a castle on thy
           head!
ULYSSES: I'll bring you to the gates.
TROILUS: Accept distracted thanks.
THERSITES: Would I could meet that rogue
           Diomed! I would croak like a raven; I
           would bode, I would bode. Patroclus
           will give me anything for the intelli-
           gence of this whore. The parrot will
           not do more for an almond than he
           for a commodious drab. Lechery, lech-
           ery! still wars and lechery! Nothing
           else holds fashion. A burning devil
           take them!

To the prose in *King Lear*, the rest of Shakespearean prose, and the style of Thersites in particular, seem preliminary. The functions of ironic contrast and social distinction are now surpassed and
we find, for the first time in drama, a dissociation
of tragedy from poetic form. The prose in *Lear* is
a complete tragic medium and lies at the centre of
the play. It shows virtues which differ from those of

dramatic blank verse not in degree but in essence. This was Shakespeare's radical insight. It made accessible a notion which the tragic theatre since Aeschylus had left unexamined: that of prose tragedy. And being the most comprehensive image of man's estate in Shakespeare's entire work, *King Lear* seems to marshal all the resources of language. The two voices of poetry and prose are heard in their full range.

The prose of *Lear* is charged with many tasks. It serves the considered malice of Edmund, the inspired gibberish of the Fool, the feigned distraction of Edgar, and Lear's true madness. There is superb poetry in the play. The little that Cordelia says is marked by the concise music of Shakespeare's late poetic manner. But the weight of suffering lies with the prose. This is true particularly of the scenes on the heath and during the storm. There nature herself has broken the mould of order, and so far as verse is order, it would do the occasion and the setting unmerited grace. Robbed of the honours, comforts, and powers of kingship, Lear discards the dignities of verse. His maddened spirit cries out in a prose which strains at the bonds of reason and syntax:

Thou ow'st the worm no silk, the beast no hide, the sheep no wool, the cat no perfume. Ha! Here's three on's are sophisticated! Thou art the thing itself; unaccommodated man is no more but such a poor, bare, forked animal as thou art. Off, off you lendings! Come, unbutton here.

He has learnt that in the mouths of a Regan and a Goneril words can be made the mask of pure falsehood. In his agony, therefore, he uses them with a kind of lavish hatred. Having been unutterably wronged by fair but treacherous speech, Lear seeks to degrade language by steeping it in grossness and cruelty:

Behold yond simp'ring dame, whose face between her forks presages snow; that minces virtue, and do's shake the head to hear of pleasure's name. The fitchew nor the soiled horse goes to't with a more riotous appetite. Down from the waist they are Centaurs, though women all above; but to the girdle do the gods inherit, beneath is all the fiend's. There's hell, there's darkness, there's the sulphurous pit; burning, scalding, stench, consumption.

This passage is often printed in irregular verse. But one's ear supports the reading of the First Quarto. The horror of the play has been gathering toward some expression of ultimate loathing and the comeliness of poetic form, however momentary, would diminish the monstrous sense of Lear's assertion. These scenes on the heath draw the imagination to what Coleridge termed a "world's convention of agonies." In that last blackness, Shakespeare found prose to be the more just conveyor.

But this enrichment of the formal resources of tragic drama went largely unobserved. Neither during the eighteenth century, nor in the romantic period, did criticism concern itself with Shakespearean prose. Editors took it for granted or sought to rearrange it into blank verse. In his commentary on *Lear*, Coleridge never stops to note the special character of the expressive means. He points out that Lear's madness is like "an eddy without progression," yet fails to remark how closely the effect of static frenzy depends on the quality of the prose. This omission is characteristic. Shakespeare anchored in the minds of later English poets a firm association between tragedy and verse. His own blank verse seemed to control the shape of the language. To write tragedy at all, was to write verse drama. The neglect of Shakespearean prose is understandable, but it proved costly to the future of the English theatre.

The conception of prose tragedy was first argued in France. During the quarrel between ancients and moderns, Fontenelle and La Motte protested against the tyranny of verse. In 1722 La Motte began writing prose tragedies on Biblical and classical themes; his prose *Oedipus* appeared in 1730. He lacked the talent necessary to show the strength of his idea. But although verse tragedy continued to be the dominant genre, opposition to it never ceased. In the 1820's Stendhal declared repeatedly that tragedy would survive in modern literature only if it were written in prose. He could have argued from historical precedent, for the French language had already crossed the psychological and conventional barriers between prose and tragic drama in the late seventeenth century.

The decisive advance occurs in Molière's *Don*

Juan (1665). The play is a tragedy neither according to the canons of Molière's own time nor, I
suppose, by any larger definition. It presumes that
damnation is real, but the action is viewed from an
angle which is not wholly serious. The mastery of
the play, its capacity to delight and disquiet at the
same time, lies precisely in this slight distortion of
perspective. The plot is grim, yet the actual events
provoke a persistent drollery. And the reason is that
we do not see them in the round. They are shown
to us with a deliberate flatness. Don Juan is not
a complete dramatic character. He can neither
change nor mature. His responses are utterly pre-
dictable, and there is about him something of an
eloquent, vivacious marionette. Few dramatic personages of comparable fascination show so little
trace of any life outside their stage presence. He
lives only in the theatrical moment, as does even
the most brilliant of puppets. *Don Juan* represents
a final heightening of that element of farce which
is always latent in Molière. It translates into rhetorical and psychological terms the strong but
somewhat shallow vitality of slapstick.

But even if it is something less than tragedy,
Don Juan has an undeniable, grim force. And the
nature of that force depends closely on Molière's
handling of dramatic prose. Some of the most striking effects are of a kind which verse might render
in its own way, but it would, I think, be less natural
and direct. Consider the famous scene (long sup-

pressed for its libertine cruelty) in which Don Juan
seeks to tempt a starving hermit into committing
blasphemy:

DON JUAN: Tu n'as qu'à voir si tu veux gagner
            un louis d'or, ou non; en voici un
            que je te donne, si tu jures. Tiens,
            il faut jurer.
LE PAUVRE: Monsieur . . .
DON JUAN: A moins de cela, tu ne l'auras pas.
SCANARELLE: Va, va, jure un peu; il n'y a pas de
            mal.
DON JUAN: Prends, le voilà, prends, te dis-je;
            mais jure donc.
LE PAUVRE: Non monsieur, j'aime mieux mourir
            de faim.
DON JUAN: Va, va, je te le donne pour l'amour
            de l'humanité.[1]

The tone is one of delicate balance between the
savage and the frivolous; verse would bend it to
either side. In the last moments of the play, the

---

[1] DON JUAN: You have only to decide whether you
                    want to earn a gold sovereign or not;
                    here is one that I shall give you, if you
                    will say an oath. Come, you must swear.
THE POOR MAN: Sir . . .
DON JUAN: Short of that, you shan't have it.
SCANARELLE: Go on, go on, swear a little; there's no
                    harm in it.
DON JUAN: Take it, here it is, take it, I say; but
                    swear.
THE POOR MAN: No, sir, I had rather die of hunger.
DON JUAN: Come, come, I give it to you for love of
                    humanity.

advantages of prose are again apparent. Don Juan is dragged to the flames of hell. His servant crawls out of the smoke and débris shouting for his wages:

> SGANARELLE: Ah! mes gages! mes gages! Voilà, par sa mort, un chacun satisfait. Ciel offensé, lois violées, filles séduites, familles déshonorées, parents outragés, femmes mises à mal, maris poussés à bout, tout le monde est content; il n'y a que moi seul de malheureux. Mes gages, mes gages, mes gages! [2]

Two of the most delightful traits in this passage derive from the tactics of rhetoric: the diminuendo of outrage which begins in heaven and ends with the cuckolds, and the double reference of the terms with which Sganarelle enumerates Don Juan's victims. Each applies to its particular domain but carries at the same time a sexual connotation (*violées, séduites, déshonorées, outragés*). Thus the "violation" of the law at once evokes that of women, and the entire conceit is wound up in the *double-entendre* of *poussés à bout*.

But the dramatic value of Sganarelle's outburst does not lie primarily in these rhetorical devices. What matters is the inappropriateness of Sgana-

---

[2] Ah! my wages! my wages! Here, at one stroke, his death has satisfied everyone. The offended heavens, the ravished laws, the seduced girls, the dishonoured families, the outraged parents, the women marred, the husbands thrust to the wall—all the world is content; I alone am wretched. My wages, my wages, my wages!

relle's feelings, his gross insensibility to the surrounding circumstance. This can best be rendered in prose. It is the indifference of the servant which makes explicit the damnation of the master. Having expended his vitality on empty lust, Don Juan has come to signify nothing even to his closest companion. He is a wildly animate shadow, snuffed out on the instant. His perdition and the eternity of his future torment leave Sganarelle unmoved. All he cares about are his unpaid wages, and his outcry for them is Don Juan's sole epitaph.

It is no accident that both the scenes I have quoted from should involve money. The world of prose is that in which money counts, and the ascendancy of prose in western literature coincides with the development during the sixteenth century of modern economic relations. Like British reigning monarchs, the noble characters of tragedy carry no purse. We do not see Hamlet worrying about how to pay the players or Phèdre pondering her household accounts. It is only base creatures, such as Roderigo, who are shown putting money in their purse. But once economic factors have become dominant in society, the notion of the tragic will broaden to include financial ruin and the money-hatreds of the middle class. Molière was among the first to grasp the immense role which monetary relations assume in modern life. In Shakespeare, these relations retain an archaic innocence. One must possess money, as in The Merchant of Venice, for the stylish pursuit of love or to content one's friends. But it comes from far places on sudden argosies. In Shakespearean drama, money is not an abstract counter of exchange whose only value derives from a fiction of reason; it is the daemon gold. Timon scatters it in compulsive waste and then finds it again, buried mysteriously on the edge of the sea. Of the Elizabethans, Ben Jonson had the truest insight into the mercantile temper. But even in *Volpone*, that great comedy of low finance, money has an irrational aura. It is a golden, sensuous god entering like fire into men's veins. We are not shown how it is really earned, and the use of it is magic rather than economic.

Here again, the late seventeenth century marks the great division of sensibility, separating the world of Shakespeare from that of Voltaire and Adam Smith. It is in the late seventeenth century that literature begins taking a realistic view of money. Molière and Defoe realize that most of it comes neither from the fabled east nor out of the alchemist's crucible. In *Moll Flanders* we glimpse the nervous and cerebral excitement of financial dealings. Swift went further. He had a sardonic insight into the unconscious roots of economic desire and played knowingly on the scatological aspects of avarice. The novels of Smollett show money being made and lost in rational and technical ways, and in the gambling scenes of *Manon Lescaut* there are intimations of that poetry of money which plays so large a part in Balzac, Ibsen, and Zola. But the poetry of money is prose.

The modern novel is a direct response to this turn of consciousness toward economic and bourgeois life. But this turn, which is one of the foremost occurrences in the entire history of the imagination, also affected drama. We can trace it back to George Lillo and the grimly prosaic plays that he wrote during the 1730's. His influence outside England was immense, and drama went middle-class with a vengeance. These "sentimental comedies" or, more aptly, *comédies larmoyantes* of the eighteenth century have not worn well. Their moralizing and pathos are so insistent as to become intolerable. We would have our feelings acted upon, not taken by the throat. Nevertheless, such plays as Lessing's *Miss Sara Sampson* and Diderot's *Le Fils naturel* are of great historical interest. They lowered the range of drama so as to bring it into focus with the new realities of middle-class feeling. They are distant outriders to Ibsen. These parables of bourgeois life and suffering were written in prose. Lessing and Diderot sought to restore to the theatre the efficacy of current speech. For it was this that was entirely lacking in eighteenth-century tragedy. Yet the tragic poets, still in the grip of neo-classic conventions, would countenance no descent to the prosaic. Hence even their noblest efforts, Addison's *Cato* and Samuel Johnson's *Irene*, are cold, lifeless stuff. By refusing to avail itself of the reach of prose, tragedy veered away from the possibilities opened to it in *Don Juan*. The gap between tragic drama and the vital centres of imaginative concern wid-

ened and was never again completely bridged. And
the formation of a dramatic prose appropriate to
the conveyance of complex tragic emotions was delayed for perhaps a century.

The next step toward such a prose was taken by
Goethe. In the initial, fragmentary version of *Faust*,
the *Urfaust*, two scenes are in prose. One of these,
Margarete in prison, Goethe changed to verse. But
the encounter between Faust and Mephistopheles,
which immediately precedes it, remained essentially intact throughout the sixty years during
which Goethe worked on the Faust saga. It stands
like an erratic bloc in the midst of poetry. But this
scene, marked *Trüber Tag. Feld.*, is notable not
only for the singularity of its form, but also because
it is probably the earliest in date of composition. It
may go back as far as 1772, when the poet was under the impact of the trial and execution of a young
woman who had murdered her illegitimate child.
The dialogue seems to have been given to Goethe's
imagination whole and at white heat. The fact that
he left it unaltered during the long years of revision
affirms its inspired quality. The virtues of the prose
are sparseness and accumulated stress. To show
this, I must quote at some length:

> FAUST: Im Elend! Verzweifelnd! Erbärmlich auf
> der Erde lange verirrt und nun gefangen!
> Als Missetäterin im Kerker zu entsetzli-
> chen Qualen eingesperrt, das holde, unse-
> lige Geschöpf! Bis dahin! dahin!—Ver-

räterischer, nichtswürdiger Geist, und das
hast du mir verheimlicht! Steh nur, steh!
Wälze die teuflischen Augen ingrimmend
im Kopf herum! Steh und trutze mir
durch deine unerträgliche Gegenwart!—
Gefangen! Im unwiederbringlichen
Elend! Bösen Geistern übergeben und
der richtenden, gefühllosen Menschheit!
Und mich wiegst du indes in abge-
schmackten Zerstreuungen, verbirgst mir
ihren wachsenden Jammer und lässest sie
hilflos verderben!

MEPHISTOPHELES: Sie ist die erste nicht!

FAUST: Hund! abscheuliches Untier!—Wandle
ihn, du unendlicher Geist! wandle den
Wurm wieder in seine Hundsgestalt, wie
er sich oft nächtlicherweile gefiel, vor
mir herzutrotten, dem harmlosen Wan-
drer vor die Füsse zu kollern und sich
dem niederstürzenden auf die Schultern
zu hängen. Wandl' ihn wieder in seine
Lieblingsbildung, dass er vor mir im Sand
auf dem Bauch krieche, ich ihn mit Füs-
sen trete, den Verworfnen!—Die erste
nicht! Jammer! Jammer![3]

---

[3] FAUST: In misery! Despairing! Long and piteously lost
on earth, and now a prisoner! The comely, hapless
creature, a criminal thrown in a dungeon for horrible torments! Driven to that! To that!—Traitor-
ous, vile spirit—and this you have concealed from
me! Stand fast, stand! Roll your devilish eyes in a
rage! Stand and beard me with your unbearable
presence!—A prisoner! In irreparable misery! Delivered up to evil spirits and to harsh judging,

In part, the fierceness of the scene derives from the contrast between the prose and the surrounding poetry. Just before Faust breaks out in rage and grief, the vision of the *Walpurgisnacht* has faded away on a note of pure enchantment. The last quatrain sung by the receding spirits is marked *pianissimo*. The descent into prose is as sudden and violent as the change of setting from Oberon's palace to the dreary day on the open field. But the tragic weight lies mainly in the occasion. Faust now recognizes the absolute vileness of Mephisto, the sheer nastiness of evil. His pact with the night has lost its grandeur. Faust is aware that his own consciousness is being drawn into the mire. He is no longer a Promethean rebel, but an adventurer engaged in a vile, petty piece of seduction. Evil can diminish the boundaries of the soul. Mephisto, who perceives in Faust's outrage the glimmerings of his

---

unfeeling men!—And in the meantime you lull me with stale pastimes, hide from me her growing wretchedness, and would let her go helpless to perdition!

MEPHISTOPHELES: She is not the first!

FAUST: Dog! loathsome beast!—Change him, thou boundless Spirit! Change the reptile back into his dog's shape in which, at nighttime, he often delighted to frisk before me, rolling at the feet of the harmless wanderer, and having tripped him, fanging at his back! Change him back to his favourite shape so he may fawn on his belly in the sand in front of me, so I can tread on him with my feet, the damnable one!—"Not the first!" The pity of it! The pity!

future subjection, rubs in the sense of nastiness and banality: Margarete is not the first girl thus seduced. Faust cries back at his tormentor: "Dog! loathsome beast!" His reference is exact: it is in the shape of a fawning poodle that evil first approached him. The poodle fawns, and the hounds of hell follow.

The scene closes on a rush of action:

> MEPHISTOPHELES: Ich führe dich, und was ich tun
> kann, höre! Habe ich alle Macht im Him-
> mel und auf Erden? Des Türners Sinne
> will ich umnebeln; bemächtige dich der
> Schlüssel und führe sie heraus mit Men-
> schenhand! Ich wache! die Zauberpferde
> sind bereit, ich entführe euch. Das vermag
> ich.
> FAUST: Auf und davon! [4]

Prose is performing certain tasks here which verse would, I think, perform with less stringency. Metrically, the staccato of the successive statements, the rapid fire of assertions, would yield a halting and unnatural line. It is the jaggedness of the prose and the disruption of natural cadence, which account for its unrelenting pressure. The ironies, moreover, are of a kind which is nearly too drastic for verse.

---

[4] MEPHISTOPHELES: I will lead you, and hear what I *can* do! Am I omnipotent in heaven and earth? I will fog the jailer's senses; get hold of the keys and lead her out with human hands! I will keep a lookout! The magic steeds are ready; I carry you off. That much I can do.
FAUST: Up and away!

I mean that verse, being necessarily adornment, would round the edges of savagery. Margarete is to be led from her dungeon "by a human hand," but it is, in fact, the Devil's claw that shall open the gates. *Ich entführe euch*, promises Mephisto: "I shall lead you away." The phrase is apposite, for it signifies also "to elope" and "to abduct."

This grim debate calls to mind the thought of what *Faust* might have been had Goethe written all of it, or a major part, in such prose. The actual language would, in that case, have conspired against the evasion of tragedy. As it stands, this scene invokes tragic emotions more naked than any we find elsewhere in the play. Once Goethe had written it, there was no further need in German literature for a dissociation between prose and tragedy. Nearly at one stroke, German prose had ripened to the highest dramatic purpose.

That purpose was, in part, fulfilled by Georg Büchner. In part only, because Büchner died at twenty-three. Throughout this book, I have to consider dramatists who failed because they lacked talent, because their natural bent lay in poetry or fiction rather than in drama, or because they could not reconcile their ideal vision of the theatre with the requirements of the actual stage. To Büchner these causes of defeat are not applicable. Had he lived, the history of European drama would probably have been different. His absurdly premature death is a symbol of waste more absolute than that of either of the two instances so often quoted in indictment of mortality, the deaths of Mozart and Keats. Not that one can usefully set Büchner's work beside theirs; but because the promise of genius in his writings is so large and explicit that what we have is like a mockery of that which was to come. There is some flagging in Keats's late poetry. Büchner was cut down in full and mounting career. One can scarcely foresee the directions in which might have matured a young boy who had already written *Dantons Tod, Leonce und Lena, Woyzeck,* and that massive torso of prose narrative, *Lenz.* At a comparable age, Shakespeare may have been the author of a few amorous lyrics.

Büchner's instantaneous ripeness staggers belief. The mastery is there from the outset. There is hardly an early letter or piece of political pamphleteering which does not bear the mark of originality and stylistic control. If we make exception of Rimbaud, there is no other writer who was so completely himself at so early an age. Usually passion or eloquence come long before style; in Büchner they were at once united. One marvels also at Büchner's range. In Marlowe, for example, there is a voice prematurely silenced, but already having defined its particular timbre. Büchner commits his powers to many different directions; all in his work is both accomplishment and experiment. *Dantons Tod* renews the possibilities of political drama. *Leonce und Lena* is a dream-play, a fusion of irony and heart's abandon that is still in advance of the modern theatre. *Woyzeck* is not only the historical source of "expressionism"; it poses in a new way the entire problem of modern tragedy. *Lenz* carries the devices of narrative to the verge of surrealism. I am mainly concerned with Büchner's dramatic prose and with his radical extension of the compass of tragedy. But every aspect of his genius reminds one that the progress of moral and aesthetic awareness often turns on the precarious pivot of a single life.

It turns also on trivial accidents. The manuscript of *Woyzeck* vanished from sight immediately after the death of Büchner in 1837. The faded, nearly illegible text was rediscovered and published in 1879, and it was not until the first World War and the 1920's that Büchner's dramas became widely known. They then exercised a tremendous influence on expressionist art and literature. Without Büchner there might have been no Brecht. But the long, fortuitous gap between the work and its recognition poses one of the most tantalizing questions in the history of drama. What would have happened in the theatre if *Woyzeck* had been recognized earlier for the revolutionary masterpiece it is? Would Ibsen and Strindberg have laboured over their unwieldy historical dramas if they had known *Dantons Tod?* In the late nineteenth century only Wedekind, that erratic, wildly gifted figure from the underworld of the legitimate theatre, knew and profited from Büchner's example. And had it not been for a minor Austrian novelist, Karl Emil Franzos, who rescued the manuscript, the very existence of *Woyzeck* might now be a disputed footnote to literary history.

Büchner knew the prose scene in *Faust* and cites one of Mephisto's derisive retorts in *Leonce und Lena*. He was familiar, also, with the energetic, though rather crude, uses of prose in Schiller's *Die Räuber*. But the style of *Woyzeck* is nearly autonomous; it is one of those rare feats whereby a writer adds a new voice to the means of language. Van Gogh has taught the eye to see the flame within the tree, and Schoenberg has brought to the ear new areas of possible delight. Büchner's work is of this order of enrichment. He revolutionized the language of the theatre and challenged definitions of tragedy which had been in force since Aeschylus. By one of those fortunate hazards which sometimes occur in the history of art, Büchner came at the right moment. There was crucial need of a new conception of tragic form, as neither the antique nor the Shakespearean seemed to accord with the great changes in modern outlook and social circumstance. *Woyzeck* filled that need. But it surpassed the historical occasion, and much of what it revealed is as yet unexplored. The most exact parallel is that of a contemporary of Büchner, the mathematician Galois. On the eve of his death in a ridiculous duel at the age of twenty, Galois laid down the foundations of topology. His fragmentary statements and proofs, great leaps beyond the bounds of classic theory, are still to be reckoned with in the vanguard of modern mathematics. Galois's notations, moreover, were preserved nearly by accident. So it is with *Woyzeck*; the play is incomplete and was nearly lost. Yet we know now that it is one of the hinges on which drama turned toward the future.

Woyzeck is the first real tragedy of low life. It repudiates an assumption implicit in Greek, Elizabethan, and neo-classic drama: the assumption that tragic suffering is the sombre privilege of those who are in high places. Ancient tragedy had touched the lower orders, but only in passing, as if a spark had been thrown off from the great conflagrations inside the royal palace. Into the dependent griefs of the menial classes, moreover, the tragic poets introduced a grotesque or comic note. The watchman in *Agamemnon* and the messenger in *Antigone* are lit by the fire of the tragic action, but they are meant to be laughed at. Indeed, the touch of comedy derives from the fact that they are inadequate, by virtue of social rank or understanding, to the great occasions on which they briefly perform. Shakespeare surrounds his principals with a rich following of lesser men. But their own griefs are merely a loyal echo to those of kings, as with the gardeners in *Richard II*, or a pause for humour, as in the Porter's scene in *Macbeth*. Only in *Lear* is the sense of tragic desolation so universal as to encompass all social conditions (and it is to *Lear* that *Woyzeck* is, in certain respects, indebted). Lillo, Lessing, and Diderot widened the notion of dramatic seriousness to include the fortunes of the middle

274

class. But their plays are sentimental homilies in which there lurks the ancient aristocratic presumption that the miseries of servants are, at bottom, comical. Diderot, in particular, was that characteristic figure, the radical snob.

Büchner was the first who brought to bear on the lowest order of men the solemnity and compassion of tragedy. He has had successors: Tolstoy, Gorky, Synge, and Brecht. But none has equalled the nightmarish force of *Woyzeck*. Drama is language under such high pressure of feeling that the words carry a necessary and immediate connotation of gesture. It is in mounting this pressure that Büchner excels. He shaped a style more graphic than any since *Lear* and saw, as had Shakespeare, that in the extremity of suffering, the mind seeks to loosen the bonds of rational syntax. Woyzeck's powers of speech fall drastically short of the depth of his anguish. That is the crux of the play. Whereas so many personages in classic and Shakespearean tragedy seem to speak far better than they know, borne aloft by verse and rhetoric, Woyzeck's agonized spirit hammers in vain on the doors of language. The fluency of his tormentors, the Doctor and the Captain, is the more horrible because what they have to say should not be dignified with literate speech. Alban Berg's operatic version of *Woyzeck* is superb, both as music and drama. But it distorts Büchner's principal device. The music makes Woyzeck eloquent; a cunning orchestration gives speech to his soul. In the play, that soul is nearly mute and it is the lameness of Woyzeck's words which conveys his suffering. Yet the style has a fierce clarity. How is this achieved? By uses of prose which are undeniably related to *King Lear*. Set side by side, the two tragedies illuminate each other:

GLOUCESTER: These late eclipses in the sun and moon portend no good to us. Though the wisdom of nature can reason it thus and thus, yet nature finds itself scourg'd by the sequent effects. Love cools, friendship falls off, brothers divide. In cities, mutinies; in countries, discord; in palaces, treason; and the bond crack'd twixt son and father. This villain of mine comes under the prediction; there's son against father; the King falls from bias of nature; there's father against child. We have seen the best of our time.
(I, ii)

WOYZECK: Aber mit der Natur ist's was anders, sehn Sie; mit der Natur das is so was, wie soll ich doch sagen, zum Beispiel. . . .
. . . .
Herr Doktor, haben Sie schon was von der doppelten Natur gesehn? Wenn die Sonn in Mittag steht und es ist, als ging' die Welt in Feuer auf, hat schon eine fürchterliche Stimme zu mir geredt!
. . . .

Die Schwämme, Herr Doktor, da,
da steckt's. Haben Sie schon gesehn,
in was für Figuren die Schwämme
auf dem Boden wachsen? Wer das
leṣen könnt!

("Beim Doktor")

LEAR: Down from the waist they are Centaurs, though women all above; but
to the girdle do the gods inherit, beneath in all the fiend's. There's hell,
there's darkness, there's the sulphurous pit; burning, scalding, stench,
consumption. Fie, fie, fie! pah, pah!

(IV, v)

WOYZECK: Immer zu—immer zu! Immer zu,
immer zu! Dreht euch, wälzt euch!
Warum bläst Gott nicht die Sonn
aus, dass alles in Unzucht sich übe-
reinander wälzt, Mann und Weib,
Mensch und Vieh?! Tut's am hellen
Tag, tut's einem auf den Händen
wie die Mücken!—Weib! Das Weib
is heiss, heiss! Immer zu, immer zu!

("Wirtshaus")

LEAR: And when I have stolne upon these
son in lawes,
Then kill, kill, kill, kill, kill, kill!

(IV, v)

WOYZECK: Hör ich's da auch?—Sagt's der
Wind auch?—Hör ich's immer, immer zu: stich tot, tot!

("Freies Feld") [5]

[5] WOYZECK: But with Nature, you see, it's something else
again; with Nature it's like this, how shall I
say, like. . . .

. . . .

277

There are direct echoes. Lear calls upon the elements to "crack nature's mould" at the sight of man's ingratitude; Woyzeck wonders why God does not snuff out the sun. Both Lear and Woyzeck are maddened with sexual loathing. Before their very eyes, men assume the shapes of lecherous beasts: the polecat and the rutting horse in *Lear*; the gnats coupling in broad daylight in *Woyzeck*. The mere thought of woman touches their nerves like a hot iron: "there's the sulphurous pit; burning, scalding"; "Das Weib is heiss, heiss!" A sense of all-pervading sexual corruption goads the old mad king and the illiterate soldier to the same murderous frenzy: "kill, kill"; "stich tot, tot!"

Herr Doktor, have you ever seen anything of compound Nature? When the sun is at midday and it feels as though the world might go up in flame, then a terrible voice has spoken to me!

. . . .

In toadstools, Herr Doktor, there, there's where it lurks. Have you already observed in what configurations toadstools grow along the ground? He that could riddle that!

* * * * * * *

Ever and ever and ever and ever! Whirl around, wind around! Why does God not blow out the sun so that all may pile on top of one another in lechery, man upon woman, human upon beast?! They do it in broad daylight, they do it on your hands like gnats! Woman! Woman's hot, hot! Ever and ever!

* * * * * * *

Do I hear it here also?—Does the wind say it also?—Shall I hear it ever and ever: stick her dead, dead!

But it is in their use of prose that the two plays stand nearest to each other. Büchner is plainly in Shakespeare's debt. Prose style is notoriously difficult to analyse, and there is a great and obvious distance between post-romantic German and Elizabethan English. Yet when we place the passages side by side, the ear seizes on undeniable similarities. Words are organized in the same abrupt manner, and the underlying beat works toward a comparable stress and release of feeling. Read aloud, the prose in *Lear* and in *Woyzeck* carries with it the same shortness of breath and unflagging drive. The "shape" of the sentences is remarkably similar. In the rhymed couplets of Racine there is a quality of poise and roundedness nearly visible to the eye. But in the prose of *Lear* as in *Woyzeck*, the impression is one of broken lines and rough-edged groupings. Or, to paraphrase a conceit in *Timon of Athens*, the words "ache at us."

Yet the psychological facts with which Shakespeare and Büchner deal are diametrically opposed. The style of Lear's agony marks a ruinous fall; that of Woyzeck, a desperate upward surge. Lear crumbles into prose, and fearing a total eclipse of reason, he seeks to preserve within reach of his anguish the fragments of his former understanding. His prose is made up of such fragments arrayed in some rough semblance of order. In place of rational connection, there is now a binding hatred of the world. Woyzeck, on the contrary, is driven by his torment toward an articulateness which is not native to him.

He tries to break out of silence and is continually drawn back because the words at his command are inadequate to the pressure and savagery of his feeling. The result is a kind of terrible simplicity. Each word is used as if it had just been given to human speech. It is new and full of uncontrollable meaning. That is the way children use words, holding them at arm's length because they have a natural apprehension of their power to build or destroy. And it is precisely this childishness in Woyzeck which is relevant to Lear, for in his decline of reason Lear returns to a child's innocence and ferocity. In both texts, moreover, one important rhetorical device is that of a child—repetition: "kill, kill, kill"; "never, never, never"; "immer zu, immer zu!"; "stich tot, tot!" as if saying a thing over and over could make it come true.

Compulsive repetition and discontinuity belong not only to the language of children, but also to that of nightmares. It is the effect of nightmare which Büchner strives for. Woyzeck's anguish crowds to the surface of speech, and there it is somehow arrested; only nervous, strident flashes break through. So in black dreams the shout is turned back in our throats. The words that would save us remain just beyond our grasp. That is Woyzeck's tragedy, and it was an audacious thought to make a spoken drama of it. It is as if a man had composed a great opera on the theme of deafness.

One of the earliest and most enduring laments

over the tragic condition of man is Cassandra's outcry in the courtyard of the house of Atreus. In the
final, fragmentary scene of *Woyzeck* there are implications of grief no less universal. Woyzeck has
committed murder and staggers about in a trance.
He meets an idiot and a child:

> WOYZECK: Christianchen, du bekommst ein Reu-
> ter, sa, sa: da, kauf dem Bub ein Reu-
> ter! Hop, hop! Ross!
> KARL: Hop, hop! Ross! Ross! [6]

In both instances, language seems to revert to a
communication of terror older than literate speech.
Cassandra's cry is like that of a sea bird, wild and
without meaning. Woyzeck throws words away like
broken toys; they have betrayed him.

Büchner's was the most radical break with the
linguistic and social conventions of poetic tragedy.
But these conventions were losing their grip
throughout the European theatre. Musset had
neither the originality of Büchner nor his imaginative force. But he rebelled against the autocracy
of verse in French serious drama. In his rebellion,
unfortunately, as in much else in his life and art,
Musset lacked conviction. He was reluctant to con-
fide the responsibility for full-scale dramatic emotion even to a prose as resourceful as his own.

[6] WOYZECK: Christianchen, you'll get a gee-gee, ho, ho:
there, buy the lad a gee-gee! Giddy-up, giddy-
up, horsey!
KARL: Giddy-up, giddy-up! Horsey! Horsey!

Hence the deliberate slightness, the brittle charm, of the *Comédies et proverbes*. Musset stayed the distance only once, in *Lorenzaccio*.

In many respects, the play is typical of romantic historical melodrama. The evasive hero is compounded of Hamlet and autobiography. The republican conspirators are modelled on Schiller's *Fiesco*, and there are touches derived from that arch-romantic, Jean Paul Richter. But the language is new. *Lorenzaccio* is written in a sinuous prose, full of darting motion, and able to make explicit those nuances of feeling which characterize the romantic view of man. The prose is all action. Musset took over into dramatic dialogue the sparseness and clarity achieved by the novelists and *philosophes* of the preceding age. The melodramas of Victor Hugo are written as if neither Voltaire nor Laclos had used the French language. The style of *Lorenzaccio*, on the contrary, stems directly from the sharpening of prose which occurred during the eighteenth century. Lorenzaccio's extended dialogue with Philippe Strozzi in the third Act rivals Stendhal; it has the same outward economy and richness of interior life:

Il est trop tard—je me suis fait à mon métier. Le vice a été pour moi un vêtement, maintenant il est collé à ma peau. Je suis vraiment un ruffian, et quand je plaisante sur mes pareils, je me sens sérieux comme la Mort au milieu de ma gaieté. Brutus a fait le fou pour tuer Tarquin, et ce qui m'étonne en lui, c'est qu'il n'y ait pas laissé sa raison. Profite de moi, Philippe, voilà ce que j'ai à te dire—ne travaille pas pour ta patrie.[7]

But this intriguing play had little influence. It did not free French romantic tragedy from the rule of bombast and hollow verse. For all its virtues, *Lorenzaccio* lacks weight. The structure is too random for so delicate and swift-moving a style. The dramatic tension lies in the detail rather than in the general design. Like the rest of Musset's plays, therefore, it is more alive on the page than in performance. Yet, in breaking with the precedent of heroic verse Musset took a large step toward modernity. Stendhal's plea for a tragic drama written in the language of the living is as implicit in *Lorenzaccio* as it is in *Woyzeck*.

[7] It is too late—I have cast myself into the mould. I wore vice like a garment, now it is stuck to my skin. I am truly a ruffian, and when I joke about my own kind, I feel serious as Death amidst my gaiety. To kill Tarquin, Brutus played the madman, and what surprises me about him is that he did not lose his reason at that game. Profit by my example, Philip, here is what I have to say to you—don't work for your country.

VIII

THE IDEAL of tragedy in the classic or Shakespearean tradition was challenged not only by the spread of realistic prose, but also by music. In the second half of the nineteenth century, opera puts forward a serious claim to the legacy of tragic drama.

This claim is inherent in all grand opera, but it is rarely sustained. The great majority of operas are libretti set to music, words accompanied or embellished by voice and orchestral sound. The relation between word and music is one of formal concordance, and the development of dramatic action depends on elaborate and implausible conventions whereby speech is sung rather than spoken. The music surrounds the text with a code of emphasis or appropriate mood; it does not fuse with language to create a complete dramatic form. The first to achieve a complete articulation of dramatic feeling through musical means was Gluck, in his *Orfeo*. He was followed by Mozart, whose *Don Giovanni* plays in the history of music-drama a role comparable to that of Molière's *Don Juan* in the history of the spoken theatre. Both widen the limits of dramatic form. Mozart had a total command of the dramatic resources of music, and his operas suggest that only music could animate the conventions of tragic myth and tragic conduct which had lapsed from the theatre after the seventeenth century.

But Mozart had no immediate successors. The operatic genre seemed incapable of seizing upon the possibilities opened to it by the decline of tragedy. Beethoven concentrated his tremendous dramatic powers in chamber music and in the orchestral drama of the symphony. *Fidelio*, in fact, marks a retreat from the ideal of coherent operatic form. And thus it was not until the late romantic period that opera came into its full tragic inheritance. Verdi and Wagner are the principal tragedians of their age, and Wagner in particular is a dominant figure in any history of tragic form. He had a genius for posing decisive questions: could music-drama restore to life those habits of imagination and symbolic recognition which are essential to a tragic theatre but which rationalism and the era of prose had banished from western consciousness? Could opera achieve the long-sought fusion of classic and Shakespearean drama by creating a total dramatic genre, the *Gesamtkunstwerk?* Wagner was not alone in pursuing this dream of unity.

Berlioz's career shows a constant swing of the pendulum between the Shakespearean mood, as in *The Damnation of Faust*, and the classic, Virgilian conception of *Les Troyens*. But Wagner went much further. He accepted Shelley's axiom that the health of drama is inseparable from that of society at large. Thus he set out not only to create a new art form, but also a new audience. Bayreuth represents far more than the technical devising of a novel stage and acoustical space. It aims to revolutionize the character of the public and, by inference, that of society. The use to which the Nazis put Wagner was an abject perversion; but there is no doubt that his image of the theatre had drastic social implications. It sought to evoke from a modern society the kind of unified and disciplined response of feeling which made possible the Greek and, to a lesser degree, the Elizabethan drama.

But in Wagner's complex genius there was a streak of shrewd rationalism. He knew that the organic world-image of Sophoclean and Shakespearean tragedy could not be revived even by musical hypnosis. He determined, therefore, to construct a new mythology. What came of his attempt is a strange witches' brew of Victorian aesthetics, late romantic Christianity, and the venom of nationalism which had been pouring into the bloodstream of Europe. The sheer beauty and cunning of Wagnerian music gives to this mythology a monumental coherence. Drawn into the tonal web of *Parsifal*, the listener is led toward a direct sensuous experience of the mystical beliefs incarnate in the legend. And this was Wagner's intent. Music would rebuild the bridges between intellect and faith torn down by the shallow vehemence of post-Newtonian rationalism. The Wagnerian mythology of redemption through love would serve as a school to the imagination, and the *Festspielhaus* being both temple and place of learning, would once again be at the nerve centre of society.

Spurred on by Nietzsche, Wagner confidently invoked for his own vision the precedent of the antique theatre. He argued, as did Nietzsche, that tragedy had been born of music and dance. Spoken drama had been a long detour; by returning to music, the tragic play would, in fact, be returning to its true nature. Moreover, as it bore the stamp of Socratic and Voltaireian scepticism, modern speech unaided by music could no longer release in men the dark springs of mythical awareness.

Yet although he argued for the primacy of total musical form, Wagner was a master of language and a skilful contriver of melodrama. As a manipulator of dramatic shock, he was no loftier than Sardou. *Tristan und Isolde* is a drawing-room triangle on a cosmic scale, and there are as many implausible coincidences and startling revelations in the *Ring* as in any well-made play. It is this adroit but somewhat meretricious treatment of theatric form which betrayed the Wagnerian ideal. Wagner undoubtedly holds a massive and lasting place in the operatic repertoire. But his achievement marks the end of the romantic and Victorian tradition of drama. If we except Richard Strauss, modern opera has not followed on Wagner but turned against him. Despite strenuous attempts at modernistic productions, Bayreuth is today an antiquarian shrine. With his rare nervous acuity, Nietzsche from the very start caught the scent of decay. He detected in Wagner the part of the charlatan and found at Bayreuth not the cold sea air of the Greek tragic spirit but a hothouse of romantic religiosity. Nietzsche's later tracts against Wagner are unjust and sour with admiration gone bad. But he was right when he characterized Wagner as a master showman addressing himself less to the virtues or intelligence of the age than to its jaded nerves. There is much in Wagnerian drama which is closer to Sardou and Dumas fils than to either Sophocles or Shakespeare. Nevertheless, and this is what Nietzsche failed to realize, *Tristan und Isolde* is nearer to complete tragedy than anything else produced during the slack of drama which separates Goethe from Ibsen. And nearly as much may be asserted of two other operas of the late nineteenth century, Mussorgsky's *Boris Godunov* and Verdi's *Otello*.

In the twentieth century, opera has further strengthened its claim to the tragic succession. There is little in the prose theatre or in the revival of verse drama to match the coherence and eloquence of tragic emotion which we find in the operas of Janáček and Alban Berg. It may be that the shaping powers of the modern imagination are committed to the symbolic languages of the sciences and to the notations of music rather than to the word. It is not a play but an opera that now holds out the most distinct promise of a future for tragedy.

Schoenberg did not complete *Moses und Aron*. But in the two acts that he composed he gave to the coexistence of word and music a logic and expressive conviction as great, I think, as any achieved hitherto. Both the word and the musical sound retain their specific authority, but Schoenberg establishes between them, or rather in their interaction, a middle ground of intense dramatic meaning. The word sings, and the music speaks. Neither fiction nor the spoken theatre have until now, found an adequate response to the monstrous sufferings inflicted upon men during the immediate past, and most of our poetry has remained private and silent. *Moses und Aron* was conceived on the eve of the catastrophe, in the early 1930's, but the statements which it makes about the necessary absence of God and the madness of the human will proved grimly pertinent to the condition of politics. Great tragedy is at all times timely.

With the development during the nineteenth century of a mature dramatic prose and of operatic forms able to convey complicated and serious action, our main theme is ended. After *Woyzeck* and *Tristan und Isolde* the old definitions of the tragic genre are no longer relevant, and the road lies open

to Ibsen, Strindberg, and Chekhov. These playwrights did not ask themselves whether they were
writing tragedies in any formal or traditional sense.
Their work has no bearing on the conflict of ideals
which had dominated the poetics of tragedy since
the late seventeenth century. Their plays belong
neither to the classic nor to the Shakespearean tradition and make no attempt to unite them in some
artificial synthesis of total form.

With Ibsen, the history of drama begins anew.
This alone makes of him the most important playwright after Shakespeare and Racine. The modern
theatre can be dated from *Pillars of Society* (1877).
But like most great artists, Ibsen worked from
within the available conventions. The four plays of
his early maturity—*Pillars of Society, A Doll's
House, Ghosts,* and *An Enemy of the People*—are
marvels of construction in the prevailing manner
of the late nineteenth-century drawing-room play.
The joints are as closely fitted as in the domestic
melodramas of Augier and Dumas. What is revolutionary is the orientation of such shopworn devices
as the hidden past, the purloined letter, or the
deathbed disclosure toward social problems of urgent seriousness. The elements of melodrama are
made responsible to a deliberate, intellectual purpose. These are the plays in which Ibsen is the
dramatist Shaw tried to make of him: the pedagogue
and the reformer. No theatre has ever had behind it
a stronger impulse of will and explicit social philosophy.

But these tracts, enduring as they may prove to be by virtue of their theatrical vigour, are not tragedies. In tragedy, there are no temporal remedies. The point cannot be stressed too often. Tragedy speaks not of secular dilemmas which may be resolved by rational innovation, but of the unaltering bias toward inhumanity and destruction in the drift of the world. But in these plays of Ibsen's radical period, such is not the issue. There are specific remedies to the disasters which befall the characters, and it is Ibsen's purpose to make us see these remedies and bring them about. *A Doll's House* and *Ghosts* are founded on the belief that society can move toward a sane, adult conception of sexual life and that woman can and must be raised to the dignity of man. *Pillars of Society* and *An Enemy of the People* are denunciations of the hypocrisies and oppressions concealed behind the mask of middle-class gentility. They tell us of the way in which money interests poison the springs of emotional life and intellectual integrity. They cry out for explicit radicalism and reform. As Shaw rightly says: "No more tragedy for the sake of tears." Indeed, no tragedy at all, but dramatic rhetoric summoning us to action in the conviction that truth of conduct can be defined and that it will liberate society.

These programmatic aims extend into Ibsen's middle period. But with *The Wild Duck* (1884), the dramatic form deepens. The limitations of the well-made play and its deliberate flatness of perspective began crowding in on Ibsen. While retaining the prose form and outward conventions of realism, he went back to the lyric voice and allegoric means of his early experimental plays, *Brand* and *Peer Gynt*. With the toy forest and imaginary hunt of old Ekdal in *The Wild Duck*, drama returns to a use of effective myth and symbolic action which had disappeared from the theatre since the late plays of Shakespeare. In *Rosmersholm, The Lady from the Sea*, and *Hedda Gabler*, Ibsen succeeded in doing what every major playwright had attempted after the end of the seventeenth century and what even Goethe and Wagner had not wholly accomplished: he created a new mythology and the theatrical conventions with which to express it. That is the foremost achievement of Ibsen's genius, and it is, as yet, not fully understood.

As we have seen, the decline of tragedy is inseparably related to the decline of the organic world view and of its attendant context of mythological, symbolic, and ritual reference. It was on this context that Greek drama was founded, and the Elizabethans were still able to give it imaginative adherence. This ordered and stylized vision of life, with its bent toward allegory and emblematic action, was already in decline at the time of Racine. But by strenuous observance of neo-classic conventions, Racine succeeded in giving to the old mythology, now emptied of belief, the vitality of living form. His was a brilliant rear-guard action. But after Racine the ancient habits of awareness and immediate recognition which gave to tragic drama its frame of reference were no longer prevalent. Ibsen, therefore, faced a real vacuum. He had to create for his plays a context of ideological meaning (an effective mythology), and he had to devise the symbols and theatrical conventions whereby to communicate his meaning to an audience corrupted by the easy virtues of the realistic stage. He was in the position of a writer who invents a new language and must then teach it to his readers.

Being a consummate fighter, Ibsen turned his deprivations to advantage. He made the precariousness of modern beliefs and the absence of an imaginative world order his starting point. Man moves naked in a world bereft of explanatory or conciliating myth. Ibsen's dramas presuppose the withdrawal of God from human affairs, and that withdrawal has left the door open to cold gusts blowing in from a malevolent though inanimate creation. But the most dangerous assaults upon reason and life come not from without, as they do in Greek and Elizabethan tragedy. They arise in the unstable soul. Ibsen proceeds from the modern awareness that there is rivalry and unbalance in the individual psyche. The ghosts that haunt his characters are not the palpable heralds of damnation whom we find in *Hamlet* and *Macbeth*. They are forces of disruption that have broken loose from the core of the spirit. Or, more precisely, they are cancers growing in the soul. In Ibsen's vocabulary, the most deadly of these cancers is "idealism," the mask of hypocrisy and self-deception with which men seek to guard against the realities of social and personal life. When "ideals" seize upon an Ibsen character, they drive him to psychological and material ruin as the Weird Sisters drive Macbeth. Once the mask has grown close to the skin, it can be removed only at suicidal cost. When Rosmer and Rebecca West have attained the ability to confront life, they are on the verge of death. When the mask no longer shields her against the light, Hedda Gabler kills herself.

To articulate this vision of a God-abandoned world and of man's splintered and vulnerable consciousness, Ibsen contrived an astounding series of symbols and figurative gestures. Like most creators of a coherent mythology, moreover, he determined early on his objective incarnations. The meanings assumed by the sea, the fjord, the avalanches, and the spectral bird in *Brand* carry over to Ibsen's very last play, *When We Dead Awaken*. The new church in *Brand* brings on the moment of disaster, as does the new steeple in *The Master Builder*. The white stallion of Peer Gynt foreshadows the ghost-chargers at Rosmersholm. From the start, Ibsen uses certain material objects to concentrate symbolic values (the wild duck, General Gabler's pistols, the flagpole standing in front of the house in *The Lady from the Sea*). And it is the association of an explicit, responsible image of life with the material setting and objects best able to denote and dramatize this image that is the source of Ibsen's power. It allows him to organize his plays into shapes of action richer and more expressive than any the theatre had known since Shakespeare. Consider the stress of dramatic feeling and the complexity of meaning conveyed by the tarantella which Nora dances in A *Doll's House*; by Hedda Gabler's proposal to crown Lövborg with vine leaves; or by the venture into high narrow places that occurs in *Rosmersholm*, *The Master Builder*, and *When We Dead Awaken*. Each is in itself a coherent episode in the play, yet it is at the same time a symbolic act which argues a specific vision of life. Ibsen arrived at this vision, and he devised the stylistic and theatrical means that give it dramatic life. This is his rare achievement.

Ibsen's late plays represent the kind of inward motion that we find also in the late plays of Shakespeare. *Cymbeline*, *The Winter's Tale*, and *The Tempest* retain the conventions of Jacobean tragicomedy. But these conventions act as signposts pointing toward interior meanings. The storms, the music, the allegoric masques have implications which belong less to the common imaginative repertoire than they do to a most private understanding of the world. The current theatrical forms are a mere scaffold to the inner shape. That is exactly the case in *The Master Builder*, *Little Eyolf*, *John Gabriel Borkman*, and *When We Dead Awaken*. These dramas give an appearance of belonging to the realistic tradition and of observing the conventions of the three-walled stage. But, in fact, this is not so. The setting is thinned out so as to become bleakly transparent, and it leads into a strange landscape appropriate to Ibsen's mythology of death and resurrection.

It is in these four plays—and they are among the summits of drama—that Ibsen comes nearest tragedy. But it is tragedy of a peculiar, limited order. These are fables of the dead, set in a cold purgatory. Halvard Solness is dead long before he ascends the tower of his new villa. Allmers and Rita are dead to each other in the suffocation of their marriage. Borkman is an enraged ghost pacing up and down in a coffin that has the semblance of a house. In *When We Dead Awaken*, the purgatorial theme is explicit. In the mad egotism of his art, Rubeck has trampled on the quick of life. He has destroyed Irene by refusing to treat her as a living being. But in such destruction there is always a part of suicide, and the great sculptor—the shaper of life—has withered to a grotesque shadow. Yet there remains a chance of miracle; in sharing mortal danger, the dead may awaken. And so Rubeck and Irene press on, up the storm-swept mountain.

There are in these fierce parables occasional resonances from classic and Shakespearean tragedy. We do, I think, experience a related sense of tragic form when Agamemnon strides across the purple carpet and Solness mounts to his tower. But the focus is utterly different. Ibsen starts where earlier tragedies end, and his plots are epilogues to previous disaster. Suppose Shakespeare had written a play showing Macbeth and Lady Macbeth living out their black lives in exile after they had been defeated by their avenging enemies. We might then have the angle of vision that we find in *John Gabriel Borkman*. These are dramas of afterlife, engaging vivid shadows such as animate the lower regions of the *Purgatorio*. But even in these late works, there is a purpose which goes beyond tragedy. Ibsen is telling us that one need not live in premature burial. He is reading the lesson of meaningful life. The Allmers and the Rubecks of the world can waken from their living death if they establish among themselves relations of honesty and sacrifice. There is a way out, even if it leads up to the glaciers. There is no such way for Agamemnon or Hamlet or Phèdre. In the gloom of the late Ibsen the core of militant hope is intact.

Why is it that this magnificent body of drama has not exercised a greater or more liberating influence on the modern theatre? Such playwrights as Arthur Miller stand toward Ibsen rather as Dryden stood toward Shakespeare. They have observed the technical means of the Ibsen play and adopted some of its conventions and defining gestures. But the rich and complex critique of life implicit in Ibsen, and the transparency of his realistic settings to the light of symbolism, are absent. Where Ibsen has been influential, as in the case of Shaw, it is the programmatic plays that have counted, not the harrowing dramas of his maturity. Why should this be? In part, the answer is that Ibsen did his work too well. Many of the hypocrisies that he strove against have loosened their grip on the mind. Many of the spectres of middle-class oppression have been exorcized. The triumph of the reformer has obscured the greatness of the poet. In part, there is the barrier of language. Those who read Norwegian tell one that Ibsen's mature prose is as tightly wrought in cadence and inner poise as is good verse. As in poetry, moreover, the force and direction of meaning often hinge on the particular inflections and array of sounds. These resist translation. And so there is in the versions of Ibsen's plays available to most readers a prosaic flatness entirely inappropriate to the symbolic design and lyricism of the late dramas. In short, that which translates best in Ibsen is perhaps the least notable. Thus we do not yet have the Ibsen playhouse for which Shaw pleaded at the turn of the century.

If Ibsen falls outside the scope of classic or Shakespearean tragedy, the same is true to an even greater extent of Strindberg and Chekhov.

In the plays of Strindberg we find some of the radical conventions of the late Ibsen, without the sustaining fabric of a responsible vision of life. The symbolism has a wild, arresting brilliance, but there is behind it no controlling mythology. The conception of the world implicit in Strindberg's plays is hysterical and fragmentary. No playwright ever made of so public a form as drama a more private expression. Strindberg's characters are emanations from his own tormented psyche and his harrowed

life. Gradually, they lose all connection to a governing centre and are like fragments scattered from
some great burst of secret energy. In *The Spook
Sonata* and *A Dream Play*, the personages seem to
collide at random in a kind of empty space. Hence
the conventions of irreality and the allegory of the
spectre and the dream. These dramas belong to a
theatre of the mind and work inside us like re-
membered music. But what Strindberg achieved in
depth, he lost in theatrical coherence. These ghost-
plays are shadows of drama.

This queer perspective, as if all things were seen
through mist and in broken lines, extends even to
the historical plays. Strindberg's treatment of
Charles XII diminishes the scale of politics to that
of a puppet theatre full of strange, nervous mario-
nettes. It is over the short run that Strindberg suc-
ceeds. *Miss Julie* and *Creditors* are masterpieces.
The high pitch of feeling and nervous susceptibility
on which they rely can be enforced over a single,
brief action. Miss Julie's final exit is like the receding terror of a nightmare. We wake from it drugged
and appalled. But over the longer or more elaborate
course, the tension breaks, and we get the kind of
flaccid obscurity that disfigures *To Damascus* and
even the finest of Strindberg's surrealistic plays, *The
Dance of Death*.

Strindberg is neither in the dominant tradition
of the tragic theatre nor does he build forward from
Ibsen. He stands with Kleist and Wedekind on that
eccentric verge where drama is not primarily an

imitation of life, but rather a mirror to the private
soul. And the expressive means of his art, influential
as they have been on certain experimental movements in modern drama, belong less to the playhouse than they do to the distorting and halluci-
natory modes of the film.

In Strindberg's late style, the conflicts of ideology
and character from which drama normally proceeds are eroded. Instead, we find the creation of
a special mood or atmosphere in which the shape
of action becomes fluid and musical. Sometimes,
Strindberg uses actual music to establish or modu-
late the tone of feeling. The theatre of Chekhov
always tends toward the condition of music. A
Chekhov play is not directed primarily toward a
representation of conflict or argument. It seeks to
exteriorize, to make sensuously perceptible, certain
crises of interior life. The characters move in an
atmosphere receptive to the slightest shift in intonation. As if passing through a magnetic field,
their every word and gesture provokes a complex
disturbance and regrouping of psychological forces.
This kind of drama is immensely difficult to produce because the means of realization are very close
to music. A Chekhovian dialogue is a musical score
set for speaking voice. It alternates between ac-
celeration and retardment. Pitch and timbre are
often as meaningful as the explicit sense. The design of the plot, moreover, is polyphonic. Several
distinct actions and levels of consciousness are developed at the same time. The characteristic gather-

ings—the theatrical *soirée* in *The Sea-Gull*, the party at the house of the three sisters, the outing in *The Cherry Orchard*—are ensembles in which the various melodies combine or clash in dissonance. In the second Act of *The Cherry Orchard*, the voices of Madame Ranevsky, Lopakhin, Gayev, Trofimov, and Anya perform a quintet. The melodic lines move in isolation and seeming incongruence. Suddenly a mysterious sound is heard in the evening sky, "the sound of a snapped string." It changes the key of the entire play. The brittle weariness in the different voices now swells to a great sombre chord. "Well, good people, let us go," says Madame Ranevsky, "it's getting dark."

But it is as difficult for the language of criticism to deal with the art of Chekhov as it is for any language to deal with music. All I would stress here is the fact that Chekhov lies outside a consideration of tragedy. He himself insisted that his plays were comedies, and so they are regarded on native ground. It is when travelling west that the wine has darkened. To us, these grave, lyric portrayals of the failure of human beings to master their condition or communicate with each other, convey an unutterable sadness. But perhaps we are reading into them too much lastingness. Chekhov's dramas are rooted in a specific historical circumstance and contain a strong element of political irony and social satire. These bruised, exquisite beings in their genteel poverty are doomed, and their pretensions are ridiculous. The axe must ring out in the cherry orchard if there is to be new life in the world. Lopakhin is a vulgar brute; but vulgarity is health, and it will build houses for the living on the fallow estates of the dead. Chekhov was a physician, and medicine knows grief and even despair in the particular instance, but not tragedy.

Or perhaps one should approach these elusive plays by discarding all traditions of dramatic genre. At the close of the *Symposium*, Socrates compelled his listeners to agree that the genius of comedy was the same as that of tragedy. Being drowsy with wine, they were unable to follow his argument. One after another, they fell asleep around the master; he alone remained serene and lucid till break of dawn. Even Aristophanes could not stay awake to discover in what manner he might be regarded as a tragedian. Thus the Socratic demonstration of the ultimate unity of tragic and comic drama is forever lost. But the proof is in the art of Chekhov.

IX

IBSEN AND CHEKHOV were revolutionaries whose
achievement should have made impossible a return
to the chimeras of the past. They had shown that
prose and the economy of realism—the daylit, secular furnishings of common experience—could produce theatrical conventions relevant to the modern
world, yet as rich and persuasive as those of verse
tragedy. Ibsen constructed dramatic forms suitable
to the lack of a central mythology and to the nervous isolation of the modern temper. Chekhov was
the explorer of an inner space, of an area of social
and psychological turbulence midway between the
ancient poles of the tragic and the comic. It is subtle
ground, and mastery of it demands delicacy of
spirit, but it is the terrain most appropriate to the
dry and private character of modern suffering. The
agonies of reason require neither palace nor city

square; they are acted out in private drawing-rooms. The ghosts that scar the secular mind do not fear electric light. Both playwrights, moreover, brought to the instrument of prose the dramatic resources that Berlioz, Wagner, and Richard Strauss brought to the modern orchestra. After *John Gabriel Borkman* and *The Cherry Orchard*, drama should have risen from the dead.

But the ash was too thick in its mouth. As we enter the twentieth century, the old shadows and stale ideals again crowd upon us. The modern pursuit of tragedy is marred by a great failure of nerve. The tragic poets of our own time are graverobbers and conjurers of ghosts out of ancient glory. With Yeats, Hofmannsthal, Cocteau, and T. S. Eliot, we are back where we started. We are back amid the conflicts of purpose and tradition which beset Dryden. Arguments over the nature of tragedy, rivalries between verse and prose, between the classic and the open form—the entire baggage of dusty theory is again invoked, long after Ibsen and Chekhov have shown that it is irrelevant to the modern spirit. The idols overthrown after the bankruptcy of romantic drama are again in the market place. It is a strange and exasperating reversion. The image of the theatre implicit in *Elektra, La Machine infernale,* and *The Family Reunion* is a noble phantom. It haunts the modern poet as it haunted Dryden and Goethe. But it should never have been summoned back to the electric light, where it stands naked and inept. The verse tragedies produced by

304

modern European and American poets are exercises in archaeology and attempts to blow fire into cold ash. It cannot be done.

What drove the theatre back to the old dead gods? Had Ibsen and Chekhov written in languages more immediately accessible to other playwrights, had they worked nearer the geographical centres of taste—in Paris, say, or London or Vienna—the entire course of modern drama might have been different. Their accomplishment could then have acted with the sustaining force of example. But those who came after them saw their works through a veil of translation and cultural remoteness. They discerned in the two masters skilful artisans of realism, not the great creators of myth and symbolic form which they in fact were. They observed the scaffolding of realistic conventions and drawing-room scenes, yet were blind to the poetic life within. The realism of Ibsen and Chekhov is a discipline of unfolding insight whose authority leads from the real of the letter to the more real of the spirit. The walls of the drawing room in an Ibsen play are transparent to the radiance or blackness of the controlling symbolic vision. A deep and shadowy tide of meaning seems to rise to the verge of Chekhov's gardens and villas. The realism of the commercial theatre is something grotesquely different. It is mere *reportage*, telling us what daily life looks and smells and sounds like in this tenement or along that wharf. The perspective of commercial realistic drama is blind as a camera and leads each year nearer the heart of drabness. There is no place in it for the inward stress and resonance that give to the art of Ibsen and Chekhov its marvellous plurality.

Yet modern poets have confused the two modes. T. S. Eliot notes that Ibsen and Chekhov have achieved in prose certain effects of which he had thought that only poetry was capable. But the manner of his concession implies that these are momentary strokes of good fortune or individual talent. He does not realize that there lies behind them a revolutionary and coherent poetic of drama. This failure of judgement has had wide implications. It has led the poet-dramatists in our time to turn their backs on prose and on the future of the living theatre. Yeats, Hofmannsthal, and Eliot were perfectly justified in rejecting the flat, cabbage-smell realism which governs the aesthetics of the commercial stage. But they rejected also the imaginative richness and relevance to modern life of the dramatic tradition that leads from Büchner to Strindberg. And in doing so, they turned back to a ghostly past.

Verse drama, however, reacts not only against the gross limitations of "social realism." In attempting to recapture the nobility of the tragic style, the dramatic poet is trying to meet the challenge of the novel. A writer who turns toward serious drama in the twentieth century has before him the fact that prose fiction is the most vital and dominant form of literary statement. More than any rival genre, it sustains the habit of stylistic awareness and organizes, by virtue of its own profuse life, the general defence of the imagination. In the renaissance and the neo-classic period, it is the dramatist who is emblematic of literature; during romanticism, it is the lyric poet. But since the time of the industrial revolution, the writer in essence, the man who typifies even at first glance the profession of letters, is the novelist.

The sphere of the novel is prose, and modern fiction has greatly enlarged its compass. The decline of tragedy and narrative verse—of which the failure of the epic after Milton is striking proof—restored to the common of language domains of rhetoric and invention once reserved to the drama-tist and the poet. Flaubert seized hold of the new ground; he wrote prose as burnished, as intricate, and as ceremonious as poetry in the grand manner. The modern novel has followed in his acquisitive path. It is in prose fiction that we find the commit-ment of language to the widest range of possible meaning. Joyce was a poet, a maker of words to match the rush and twist of feeling as it throngs at us out of the wide-flung gates of the unconscious. He quarried out of language metals new to the tongue, some acrid and impure, but others spun through with ancient gold. *Ulysses* adds to the scope of possible experience in the measure that it adds to the trove of language. Proust instilled into prose the simultaneity and interior motion of music. Like the melodic phrase, Proustian syntax levies equally on recollection and expectation, surrounding the present fact with the structure of governed time. In the novels of Hermann Broch, German achieves one of its rare flights from the temptations of systematic assertion. In *Der Tod des Vergil*, this language, so bone-stiff with abstraction, assumes a subtle, electric vitality and moves like a bright tracer across the shadow line of the unconscious. That is a domain of which lyric verse was traditionally the guardian. But from Flaubert to Broch, the adventurers of the word have been the novelists.

Every art form seeks to define its own idiom, either by enhancement of the available modes, or by reaction against them. Yeats, Claudel, and their successors have returned to the tradition of dramatic verse in order to distinguish their art from the flattened, tawdry prose of the commercial playhouse and from the medium of prose itself, which carries upon it the stamp of the novel. As he often does, T. S. Eliot spoke for many when he defined his goal:

I have before my eyes a kind of mirage of the perfection of verse drama, such as to present at once the two aspects of dramatic and of musical order. . . . To go as far in this direction as it is possible to go, without losing that contact with the ordinary everyday world with which drama must come to terms, seems to me the proper aim of dramatic poetry.

The words are not the same as those used by Dryden. But the ideal described by Eliot and the practical difficulties that lie in the way are precisely those that concern Dryden and all English tragedy

after the seventeenth century. But to turn the
mirage into reality is now far more difficult than
it was in the time of *All for Love*.

The contact between verse of a dramatic and
musical order and the everyday world has grown
ever more precarious and infrequent. The process
is not easy to describe, but it represents one of the
principal changes in western sensibility. Verse no
longer stands at the centre of communicative discourse. It is no longer, as it was from Homer to
Milton, the natural repository of knowledge and
traditional sentiment. It no longer gives to society
its main record of past grandeur or its natural setting for prophecy, as it did in Virgil and Dante.
Verse has grown private. It is a special language
which the individual poet insinuates, by force of
personal genius, into the awareness of his contemporaries, persuading them to learn and perhaps
hand on his own uses of words. Poetry has become essentially lyric—that is to say, it is poetry of
private vision rather than of public or of national
occasion. The epic of Russian national consciousness is *War and Peace*, not a poem in the heroic
style. The chronicle of the modern soul's descent
into hell is no *Divina Commedia*, but the prose fiction of Dostoevsky and Kafka. The natural language
of statement, justification, and recorded experience
is now prose. This does not signify that modern
poetry is any the less compelling or important to
the survival of literacy and sensuous apprehension.

But it does mean that the distance between verse and the realities of common action with which drama must deal is greater than ever before.

And this widening of distance has had a crucial effect on the history of the theatre. In each of the principal modern languages there comes a definite historical moment in which verse drifts away from the living stage. In English, that moment occurs during the first part of the eighteenth century; in the dramatic verse of Addison and Johnson there is already the coldness of decay. Despite the virtuosity of Rostand, the authority of direct feeling seems to recede from the *alexandrin* after Vigny. Kleist is the last of the German dramatists who made of the poetic form an essential condition of plot and meaning rather than a secondary ornament. Dramatic verse continues to be written throughout the nineteenth century by notable poets such as Browning and Hebbel. But it is less and less relevant to the actual stage and to the kind of drama produced for a normal audience. And as verse moves further away from the actual practise of the theatre, there arises what Eric Bentley has defined as the crisis of modern drama: the divorce between literature and the playhouse.

Sophocles, Shakespeare, and Racine were dramatists working toward the kind of theatrical performance normal and central to their respective societies. *Lear* was destined for the Broadway of its day. Goethe and Schiller were intimately concerned, on the financial and technical level, with the life of the Weimar stage. The heroic melodramas of Victor Hugo and Vigny still belong to the sphere of commercial production. After that the chasm widens. The late nineteenth and the early twentieth centuries are the classic era of the coterie play intended for performance before a special audience and in a special theatre. It is the age of the *atelier*, of the dramatic studio or workshop, of the reading-performance and the experimental stage. Yeats wrote his dramas for a kind of Japanese dance-theatre whose conventions of mask and music are calculated to achieve the furthest possible distance from those of the commercial playhouse. Strindberg, Maeterlinck, and Cocteau worked with troupes of actors specially drilled to achieve esoteric effects. Even where it looks to the larger audience, modern poetic drama is often related to a ceremonious and non-theatrical setting: Eliot wrote *Murder in the Cathedral* for a pageant at Canterbury, and Hofmannsthal conceived *Jedermann* for ritual performance before the cathedral doors in Salzburg. Literature moves out of the theatre as poetry withdraws from the centre of moral and intellectual activity.

There are bridges across the intervening gap. Certain plays at first intended for esoteric performance later gain access to the living repertoire. Shaw straddles with majestic ease the two worlds of serious drama and commercial entertainment. But the special quality of his plays, that which at the beginning made of them a minority art, lies in their radical doctrine, not in their language or conventions. Believing that dramatic verse was no longer appropriate to modern ideology and modern experience, Shaw wrote superbly articulate prose. He beat the West End at its own game, producing plays wittier and more vivacious than those of his commercial rivals. But precisely because they address themselves so brilliantly to the topics of the moment, these comedies of argument are already dated. Perhaps Shaw would have wished this to be the case. He was not concerned with the ideal pursued by Yeats and Eliot. It appeared to Shaw to be a snobbish and antiquarian fancy. He called *The Doctor's Dilemma* a tragedy, but attached to the word neither stylistic nor metaphysical implications. *Saint Joan* comes nearer to a tragic ordering of life, and it is a magnificent play. Yet one cannot help feeling that it falls short of the first rank by some small, obstinate margin. And defenders of verse drama would say that it is precisely that margin which divides the best of prose from poetry.

Verse drama itself has rarely crossed over from literature to Broadway. Or it has done so at the cost of cheapening and self-denial. The costume tragedies of Maxwell Anderson are written in a style never spoken by any living creature (at the moment of parting, characters say to each other: "We two must twain"). They belong to the dust and tinsel-world of the Victorian charade. The recent plays of Eliot, which represent the most urbane assault of the poetic on the commercial, are drawing-room parables in flaccid blank verse. They have little resemblance to the pattern of tragedy Eliot had before him when first he turned to drama. The distance between the poetic mode and the commercial playhouse seems to be too great. The voice of poetry has become too intimate to impose itself in that most public of places—a modern theatre.

But the plain fact that most modern poetry is too private for effective use on a commercial stage is only one aspect of the dilemma. The condition of language itself in our time may be such as to render nearly impossible a renascence of dramatic verse. This is a vast, intricate subject. I have touched on it elsewhere and will give only a summary indication of what I mean.

We cannot be certain that there is either in language or in the forms of art, a law of the conservation of energy. On the contrary, there is evidence to show that reserves of feeling can be depleted, that particular kinds of intellectual and psychological awareness can go brittle or unreal. There is a hardening in the arteries of the spirit as in those of the flesh. It is at least plausible that the complex of Hellenic and Christian values which is mirrored in tragic drama, and which has tempered the life of the western mind over the past two thousand years, is now in sharp decline. The history of modern Europe—the deportation, murder, or death in battle of some seventy million men, women, and children between 1914 and 1947—suggests that the reflexes by which a civilization alters its habits in order to survive mortal danger are no longer as swift or realistic as they once were.

In language this stiffening of the bone is, I submit, clearly discernible. Many of the habits of language in our culture are no longer fresh or creative responses to reality, but stylized gestures which the intellect still performs efficiently, but with a diminishing return of new insight and new feeling. Our words seem tired and shopworn. They are no longer charged with their original innocence or with the power of revelation (think of what light and fire the word *amor* could still cast into the soul as late as the thirteenth century). And because they are weary, words no longer seem prepared to assume the burden of new meaning and plurality which Dante, Montaigne, Shakespeare, and Luther placed upon them. We add to our technological vocabulary by joining together used scraps, like a reclaimer of old metals. We no longer fuse the raw materials of speech into new glory as did the compilers of the King James Bible. The curve of invention points downward. Compare the gray jargon of the contemporary economist to the style of Montesquieu. Set the counting-house prose of the modern historian next to that of Gibbon, Macauley, or Michelet. Where the modern scholar cites from a classic text, the quotation seems to burn a hole in his own drab page. Sociologists, mass-media experts, the writers of soap operas and politicians' speeches, and teachers of "creative writing" are the gravediggers of the word. But languages only let themselves be buried when something inside them has, in fact, died.

The political inhumanity of our time, moreover, has demeaned and brutalized language beyond any precedent. Words have been used to justify political falsehood, massive distortions of history, and the bestialities of the totalitarian state. It is conceivable that something of the lies and the savagery has crept into their marrow. Because they have been used to such base ends, words no longer give their full yield of meaning. And because they assail us in such vast, strident numbers, we no longer give them careful hearing. Each day we sup our fill of horrors—in the newspaper, on the television screen, or the radio— and thus we grow insensible to fresh outrage. This numbness has a crucial bearing on the possibility of tragic style. That which began in the romantic period, the inrush of current political and historical emotions on daily life, has become a dominant fact of our own experience. Compared with the realities of war and oppression that surround us, the gravest imaginings of the poets are diminished to a scale of private or artificial terror. In *The Trojan Women*, Euripides had the poetic authority to convey to the Athenian audience the injustice and reproach of the sack of Melos. Cruelty was still commensurate to the scope or response of the imagination.

I wonder whether this is still the case. What work of art could give adequate expression to our immediate past? The last war has had neither its *Iliad* nor its *War and Peace*. None who have dealt with it have matched the control of remembrance achieved by Robert Graves or Sassoon in their accounts of 1914–18. Language seems to choke on the facts. The only array of words still able to get near the quick of feeling is the kind of naked and prosaic record set down in *The Diary of Anne Frank*.

Given the abuses of language by political terror and by the illiteracy of mass consumption, can we look to a return of that mystery in words which lies at the source of tragic poetry? Can the *newspeak* of George Orwell's *1984* (and that year is already upon us) serve the needs of tragic drama? I think not, and this is why T. S. Eliot is so right when he describes the ideal of modern dramatic verse as "a mirage."

Naturally such judgement can only be provisional. A master of verse tragedy may arrive on the scene tomorrow. The acclaim given to Archibald MacLeish's *JB* shows that hopes remain high. In English, moreover, there is at least one group of modern verse plays that comes very close to solving the problem of tragic style. Already in *The Countess Cathleen*, Yeats went further than any poet since Dryden in restoring to blank verse the sinews of action:

THE ANGEL: The Light of Lights
Looks always on the motive, not the deed,
The Shadow of Shadows on the deed alone.

OONA: Tell them who walk upon the floor
  of peace
That I would die and go to her I
  love;
The years like great black oxen tread
  the world,
And God the herdsman goads them
  on behind,
And I am broken by their passing
  feet.

In *Purgatory*, the mirage of the perfection of dramatic verse is within grasp. Nowhere in the entire play is there a single stopgap or looseness. Every line is held taut, and the cold, luminous power is that of language which has passed through the schooling of the great centuries of prose:

        Study that tree.
It stands there like a purified soul,
All cold, sweet, glistening light.
Dear mother, the window is dark again,
But you are in the light because
I finished all that consequence.
I killed that lad because had he grown up
He would have struck a woman's fancy,
Begot, and passed pollution on.
I am a wretched foul old man
And therefore harmless.

But *Purgatory* is a feat which is only briefly sustained, over a single scene involving two voices. Being a vision of an intermediary moment in the proceedings of the soul—a moment between damnation and the greater trial of grace—it is sufficient unto itself. But it offers no solution toward the problem of full-scale drama. And this is true of all of Yeats's best plays. They are glowing embers, as if the virtues of their poetry were too fragile and instantaneous to support the fabric of intrigue and argument required of the normal theatre. *The Dreaming of the Bones* and *Purgatory* are prolegomena to a future drama. Their limitation tells us that a renascence of poetic tragedy demands more than the attainment of style.

It demands that that style be brought into contact with the ordinary everyday world. Such contact does not depend on the degree of realism or modernity which the poet is prepared to allow. The work of art can cross the barriers that surround all private vision—it can make a window of the poet's mirror—only if there is some context of belief and convention which the artist shares with his audience; in short, only if there is in live force what I have called a mythology. Yeats's attempt to create such a mythology is notorious, but inconclusive. The body of myth which he devised for his poems and plays is full of vivid imaginings. In the good poems it shimmers in the far background with a hint of proximate revelation. But often it obtrudes between the reader and the text like stained glass. In reading a poem, there is time and incentive to acquire the esoteric knowledge needed for comprehension; the eye grows used to the darkness and flicker of private meaning. But not in the theatre;

our understanding of a stage play must carry instantaneous conviction.

Yeats's failure to construct a mythology for the age is part of that larger failure or withdrawal from imaginative commitment which occurs after the seventeenth century. Greek tragedy moved against a background of rich, explicit myth. The landscape of terror was entirely familiar to the audience, and this familiarity was both a spur and a limit to the poet's personal invention. It was a net to guard from ruin the acrobatics of his fancy. The mythology at work in Shakespearean drama is less formal, being construed of a close yet liberal conjunction of the antique and the Christian world view. But it still gave to reality shape and order. The Elizabethan stage had behind it an edifice of religious and temporal values on whose façade men had their assigned place as in the ranked sculpture of a Gothic portal. The tracery of literal meaning and allegoric inference extended from brute matter to the angelic spheres. The alphabet of tragic drama —such concepts as grace and damnation, purgation and relapse, innocence and corruption through daemonic power—retained a clear and present meaning. There plays around the thoughts and statements of the individual characters in Elizabethan tragedy a light of larger reference. And in varying degrees of immediacy, this light was perceptible to the theatrical audience. No footnote was required to convey the nature of the devilish temptation which ensnares Macbeth; Hamlet's appeal to ministers of grace could strike home without a theological gloss. The playwright depended on the existence of a common ground; a kind of preliminary pact of understanding had been drawn up between himself and his society. Shakespearean drama relies on a community of expectation even as classical music relies on an acceptance of the conventions of interval in the tempered scale.

But the pact was broken during the splintering of the ancient hierarchic world image. Milton was the last major poet to assume the total relevance of classic and Christian mythology. His refusal in *Paradise Lost* to choose between the Ptolemaic and the Copernican accounts of celestial motion is a gesture both serene and sorrowful; serene, because it regards the proposals of natural science as less urgent or assured than those of poetic tradition; sorrowful, because it marks the historical moment in which the forms of the cosmos recede from the authority of humanistic judgement. Henceforth the stars burn out of reach. After Milton the mythology of animate creation and the nearly tangible awareness of a continuity between the human and the divine order—that sense of a relationship between the rim of private experience and the hub of the great wheel of being—lose their hold over intellectual life. Wallace Stevens wrote of "the gods that Boucher killed." Rococo painting and the court ballet did worse than kill; they diminished the ancient mysteries and their emblems to ornate trivia. An eighteenth-century pastoral in mythological costume is more than a refusal of myth; it is a parody.

The myths which have prevailed since Descartes and Newton are myths of reason, no truer perhaps than those which preceded them, but less responsive to the claims of art. Yet when it is torn loose from the moorings of myth, art tends toward anarchy. It becomes the outward leap of the impassioned but private imagination into a void of meaning. The artist is Icarus looking for safe ground, and the unsustained solitude of his flight communicates to his work that touch of vertigo which is characteristic of romanticism no less than of modern abstract art. Secure inside the citadel of his persuasions, Chesterton observed how the modern artist lives either by the rags and leavings of old, worn-out mythologies, or seeks to create new ones in their stead. The nineteenth and twentieth centuries have been a classic period for the artist as reviver or maker of myth. *Faust* II is an attempt to fuse Hellenic, Christian, and gnostic elements into a coherent design. Tolstoy and Proust elaborated mythologies of time and of time's governance over man. Zola fell prey to a mystique of the literal fact, constructing his works as do certain modern sculptors when they weld together scrap iron. D. H. Lawrence worshipped the dark gods and the fire in the blood. Yeats strove to persuade himself and his readers (thus making them accomplices to his own doubt) of a mythology of lunar phases and communion with the dead. Blake and Rilke peopled their solitude with angelic hosts.

But where the artist must be the architect of his own mythology, time is against him. He cannot live long enough to impose his special vision and the symbols which he has devised for it on the habits of language and feeling in his society. The Christian mythology in Dante had behind it centuries of elaboration and precedent to which the reader could naturally refer when placing the particular approach of the poet. The cabalistic system invoked by Blake and the moon-magic of Yeats have only a private or occult tradition. There is outside the poem no stable edifice built on authorities or conventions independent of the poet's assertion (it was the genius of Joyce to observe the need for exterior corroboration when he anchored *Ulysses* to the *Odyssey*). The idiosyncratic world image, without an orthodox or public fabric to support it, is kept in focus only by virtue of the poet's present talent. It does not take root in the common soil.

This is true even in the case of Wagner, although he came closer than anyone else to transforming a private revelation into a public creed. By the enormous strength of his personality and by his cunning rhetoric, he nearly instilled his concocted mythology into the general mind. The Wagnerian note sounded throughout social and political life and had its mad echoes in the ruin of modern Europe. But it is now rapidly fading. Wagnerian symbolism has receded into the limits of the operatic and no longer plays a significant role in the repertoire of feeling.

What I am trying to make clear is a fact which is simple yet decisive toward an understanding of the crisis of modern tragedy. The mythologies that have centred the imaginative habits and practices of western civilization, that have organized the inner landscape, were not the product of individual genius. A mythology crystallizes sediments accumulated over great stretches of time. It gathers into conventional form the primal memories and historical experience of the race. Being the speech of the mind when it is in a state of wonder or perception, the great myths are elaborated as slowly as is language itself. More than a thousand years of reality lay behind the fables of Homer and Aeschylus. The Christian image of the pilgrimage of the soul was ancient before Dante and Milton made use of it. Like a stone that has lain in live water, it had become firm and lustrous to the touch of the poet. When the classic and the Christian world order entered into decline, the consequent void could not be filled by acts of private invention.

Or so it would have seemed until the twentieth century. For we have before us now the startling fact of a mythology created at a specific time by a particular group of men, yet imposed upon the lives of millions. It is that explicit myth of the human condition and of the goals of history which we call Marxism. Marxism is the third principal mythology to have taken root in western consciousness.

How long or how deeply it will scar the course of moral and intellectual experience remains uncertain. Perhaps the roots are shallow precisely because the Marxist world view came into being through political fiat rather than by the ripening of collective emotion. Perhaps it is being maintained only by material power and will prove incapable of inward growth. But at present it is as articulate and comprehensive as any mythology ever devised to order the complex chaos of reality. It has its heroes and sacred legends, its shrines and emblems of terror, its rites of purgation and anathema. It stands as one of the three major configurations of belief and symbolic form available to the poet when he seeks a public context for his art.

But of the three, there is none that is naturally suitable to a revival of tragic drama. The classic leads to a dead past. The metaphysics of Christianity and Marxism are anti-tragic. That, in essence, is the dilemma of modern tragedy.

Modern literary drama has turned to antique mythology on a massive scale. Any record of the contemporary tragic theatre reads like a primer of Greek myths: *Antigone, Medea, Electre, Oedipus und die Sphinx, Orphée, Oedipe Roi, Mourning Becomes Electra, La Guerre de Troie n'aura pas lieu*. Often the new title merely disguises the ancient theme: *La Machine infernale* is a version of the Oedipus catastrophe; Eliot's *The Family Re-*

union and Sartre's *Les Mouches* are variations
on the *Oresteia*. The modern playwright is frequently a translator of the Greek text: Claudel
turned *The Libation Bearers* into his own loose and
sumptuous style; Yeats and Ezra Pound have rendered Sophocles into their distinct idiom. Robinson
Jeffers's *Medea* and the *Elektra* of Hofmannsthal
stand midway between direct translation and re-
invention. Like Cocteau, Gide uses the classic fable
in the manner of parody or critique (*Ajax*, *Philoc-
tète*). One could continue this enumeration; it includes every major figure in modern poetic drama,
with the striking exception of Brecht.

Underlying this attempt to slip into the old
masks is the awareness that no mythology created
in the age of rational empiricism matches the antique in tragic power or theatrical form. But the
contemporary dramatist turns to Orpheus, Agamemnon, or Oedipus in a special way. He seeks to
enhance the old, stolen bottles with new wine. The
vintage is part Freud and part Frazer. It has been
one of the notable discoveries of the modern temper that the ancient fables can be read in the light
of psychoanalysis and anthropology. By manipulat-
ing the values of myths one can bring out from
within their archaic lineaments shadows of psychic
repression and blood ritual. It is a fascinating game
and no doubt legitimate within certain bounds of
integrity. So far as they have roots in the primal
remembrance of man, and so far as they record, in
a code of fantasy, certain very old and cruel prac-

tices, the Greek myths may justly document the speculations of psychology and. *The Golden Bough*. Had these legends not sprung from the very sources of our being, they could not cast their enduring spell. But the use of the classic fable toward the modern ideology requires an acute awareness of the great changes in meaning and intonation. It is this awareness which is so often lacking in the modern play.

O'Neill, Giraudoux, Hofmannsthal, Cocteau, and the lesser men often proceed with wanton artifice. They would have it both ways, combining the resonance of the classic theme with the savour of the new. By invoking the names of Medea, Agamemnon or Antigone, the playwright sets an ambush for the imagination. He knows that these high shadows will rise in our minds with an attendant train of association. They pluck the chords of memory and set off majestic echoes. The antique legend, moreover, is like gold hammered fine and pliant by previous art. Half the work is done for the poet before the curtain rises. The audience are familiar with the story, and there is no need for him to construct a plausible intrigue. He can proceed to devise sinister or mocking variations on themes already at hand, whose mere presence sounds the tragic note. The result can be momentarily arresting; it can solace or excite our fretted nerves. But it cannot escape the staleness which falls upon any fancy-dress party at the break of day.

In trying to give the classic fable a novel twist,

the modern play tends to destroy its meaning. The
fortunes of Oedipus on the contemporary stage are
an indictment of the frivolity and perversion of our
fancies. Gide makes of him a petulant little man
who arrives at the extraordinary insight that his
marriage to Jocasta was evil because it drew him
back to his childhood and thus prevented the free
development of his personality (one recognizes in
this farrago the Gidean motif of the prodigal son).
Hofmannsthal and Cocteau leap like shortsighted
harpies on those two episodes in the legend which
Greek drama had the moral reticence and technical
sophistication to leave intact: the encounter between Oedipus and the Sphinx and the wooing of
Jocasta. Cocteau ascends to the pinnacle of bad
taste. *La Machine infernale* closes in the bridal
chamber. Oedipus lies sleeping on his nuptial bed,
his arm resting on the cradle of Jocasta's lost child,
while the noble lady daubs cold cream on her face
in a frenzied attempt to make herself look younger
and more desirable. Under such blunt hammers the
tragic nobility of the action crumbles. We are left
with a strident *jeu d'esprit*. O'Neill commits inner
vandalism by sheer inadequacy of style. In the mo-
rass of his language the high griefs of the house of
Atreus dwindle to a case of adultery and murder in
some provincial rathole.

But the poverty of these stuffed ghosts can be
seen even where the poet approaches his material
with tact and formal skill. In *The Family Reunion*,
Eliot makes wary use of the *Oresteia*. He keeps

327

poised in our minds the near presence of the Aeschylean tragedy. This presence glows and darkens
behind the frail structure of the modern work. For
a time the dual focus is effective. We do seem to
hear above the nerve-tight cadence of genteel
speech the overtones of ancient disaster. But at the
crowning moment of the play the device fails drastically. Harry tells how he is pursued by the avenging Furies, "the sleepless hunters that will not let
me sleep." The window curtains part "revealing the
Eumenides." Mary does not see them but Harry
assures us that "They are here." Later they are seen
by other characters, and the butler recognizes in
them the touch of future mercy. As in the *Oresteia*,
the hell-hounds will change to guardian spirits.

What, in fact, has Eliot done? Unable to bring
the rational, drawing-room version of the myth to a
sufficient pitch of terror, he has drawn the curtains
of the modern window to show beyond it the ancient daughters of the night. He performs a sleight-
of-hand, shifting from one convention to another,
in the hope of creating by association the tragic
shock which he could not elicit from his own play.
But the problem is not merely one of contrivance
or "unfairness" of means. The trick simply does not
come off on the actual stage. The Furies stand
there either as pasteboard phantoms or as realities
so intense that they bring the entire fabric of the
play tumbling down around them. A poet borrows
at his peril. The neighbourhood of greatness, as of

fire, can consume. Eliot has been his own most lucid critic:

I should either have stuck closer to Aeschylus or else taken a great deal more liberty with his myth. One evidence of this is the appearance of those ill-fated figures, the Furies. They must, in future, be omitted from the cast, and be understood to be visible only to certain of my characters, and not to the audience. We tried every possible manner of presenting them. We put them on the stage, and they looked like uninvited guests who had strayed in from a fancy dress ball. We concealed them behind gauze, and they suggested a still out of a Walt Disney film. We made them dimmer, and they looked like shrubbery just outside the window. I have seen other expedients tried: I have seen them signalling from across the garden, or swarming on the stage like a football team, and they are never right. They never succeed in being either Greek goddesses or modern spooks. But their failure is merely a symptom of the failure to adjust the ancient with the modern.

That failure goes far beyond technical repair. No amount of theatrical ingenuity will make the Furies look natural in the sharp, thin light of the modern world. The ancient is not a glove into which the modern can slip at will. The mythology of Greek drama was the expression of a complete and traditional image of life. The poet could achieve with his audience an immediate contact of terror or delight because both shared the same habits of belief. When these habits are no longer current, the corresponding mythology goes dead or spurious.

Racine was still able to use the myths of classic drama because their symbolism and conventions of meaning retained a certain vitality. The seventeenth-century spectator did not literally believe that Phèdre was a descendant of the sun, but the implications of magic and daemonic chaos in the blood which such a legend conveys were still acceptable. It was one of those miracles of afterlife which sometimes occur in art. But today the context is so totally altered that the ancient myths appear in the modern playhouse either as a travesty or as an antiquarian charade. Eliot's circumvention is preferable to Cocteau's tomfoolery. But neither makes for a living play.

There is, perhaps, one exception. Anouilh's *Antigone* does adjust the ancient with the modern, illuminating both. But the case is a special one. Political fact gave to the legend a grim relevance. The clash between the morality of protest and the morality of order had so direct a bearing on the condition of the audience in occupied France that Anouilh could preserve intact the meaning of the Sophoclean play. His translation of Greek values was literal in the sense of being a translation into present anguish. Moreover, Anouilh had to produce the work in the face of the enemy; he presented an *Antigone* at the court of Creon. Thus he had every right to use the code of myth. Had he chosen a contemporaneous episode, the play could not have been performed. Thus the antique mask served as a true visage of the times. But *Antigone* remains an achievement apart. Elsewhere, variations on classic themes have yielded eccentric and often ignoble results. Where the dead gods have been summoned back to the modern footlights, they have brought with them the odour of decay.

In the age of Dante, the mind moved in the world as in a drama of Christ's being. That being and the miracle of its incarnation gave to reality its design and purpose. It shone through the trembling of the leaf and the falling of the star, soliciting the soul to a pilgrimage of grace. All matter and degrees of experience, all observed fact and conjectured cause, were comprehended in the "true mythology" of the church and in its conventions of rite and sacrament. This mythology, spanning life like the high-flung arch of a Gothic nave, is no longer the only or even the principal configuration of western thought. Here and there it is already in ruin. The saints no longer set their fiery feet on the high places. Rites have become ceremonies empty of belief and the lips intone to mask the silence in the heart. Nevertheless, Christian symbolism and the context of Christian meaning still temper the climate of western life. The modern Christian poet stands nearer to Dante than Racine stood to Euripides.

But the problem of Christian tragedy is not one of historical distance or of a mythology gone stale. There has been no specifically Christian mode of tragic drama even in the noontime of the faith. Christianity is an anti-tragic vision of the world.

This is as true today as it was when Dante entitled his poem a *commedia* or Corneille wrestled with the paradox of sainthood in *Polyeucte*. Christianity offers to man an assurance of final certitude and repose in God. It leads the soul toward justice and resurrection. The Passion of Christ is an event of unutterable grief, but it is also a cipher through which is revealed the love of God for man. In the dark light of Christ's suffering, original sin is shown to have been a joyous error (*felix culpa*). Through it humanity shall be restored to a condition far more exalted than was Adam's innocence. In the drama of Christian life, the arrow beats against the wind but points upward. Being a threshold to the eternal, the death of a Christian hero can be an occasion for sorrow but not for tragedy. We are rightly admonished in *Samson Agonistes:* "Come, come, no time for lamentation now." Real tragedy can occur only where the tormented soul believes that there is no time left for God's forgiveness. "And now 'tis too late," says Faustus in the one play that comes nearest to resolving the inherent contradiction of Christian tragedy. But he is in error. It is never too late to repent, and romantic melodrama is sound theology when it shows the soul being snatched back from the very verge of damnation.

The Christian view knows only partial or episodic tragedy. Within its essential optimism there are moments of despair; cruel setbacks can occur during the ascent toward grace. But, as a Portuguese proverb has it, *Deus escreve direito por linhas tortas*. It is precisely this proverb which the master of Catholic drama has chosen for a motto, to which he adds two words from St. Augustine: *Etiam peccata*.

Claudel is a maddening writer: he is pompous, intolerant, rhetorical, amateurish, prolix—what you will. Many of his plays are fantastically turgid, and there are in all of them patches of arid vehemence. He stomps through the theatre like an incensed bull, goring and tossing and finally running into the wall with a great crack of horns. But no matter. There is enough grandeur left, enough sheer power of invention, to make of Claudel one of the two great lyric playwrights of the century. With Claudel there returns to the theatre the fantasy, the spaciousness, the blaze of rhetoric which had lain dormant since Shakespeare and Calderón. His manner is baroque; it conjoins in wild profusion the tragic and the comic, the solemn and the farcical, the sacred and the profane. Where the classic poet works by privation, Claudel gives to his style a wilful enormity. It breaks like a tall wave, sending words and glittering images hurtling toward us. Often they run to shallow disorder. But at times these high tides of language have the persuasion of music.

The dramas of Claudel do violence to the logic of time and space. Claudel bends back the arc of time to produce confrontations of characters and events which are, in historical fact, half a century apart. *Partage de Midi* and *Le Soulier de satin*

encompass both hemispheres. Claudel's favourite
images are the island-studded, inconstant sea, har-
bouring its armadas of whales, or the tropic sky
with its far legions of fire. As in medieval mystery
plays, the scale is the world. England becomes a
dovecot surrounded by the flutter of white sea
foam; Africa is a red flame burning in the loins of
the earth. Poised in Darien, Don Rodrigue compares himself to a man astride two vast steeds, the
Atlantic and the secret Pacific, *cette Mer séques-
trée*. His shadow, thrown against the Zodiac, seems
to touch both poles.

Yet in all this loose immensity there are principles of dramatic structure. They are difficult to
analyse, as they pertain more to music than to the
spoken word. Claudel has learnt from Wagner.
The flow of argument moves through his plays
gathering to climaxes of lyric incantation. All of
Claudel's stylistic and technical experiments are
intended to give to drama the directed energy and
freedom of musical form. In *Le Livre de Christophe
Colomb* and *Jeanne d'Arc au bûcher*, Claudel uses
the orchestra, the film, and the mechanical enlargement of the human voice to break the bounds of
the traditional stage. For Claudel, as for Greek
tragedy and Wagnerian opera, language is only one
of the carriers of meaning. Ideally, all modes of dramatic presentation—discourse, gesture, music, the
image on the screen—should collaborate toward a
kind of orchestral completion.

Being a dramatist with a bias toward the tragic

and also a devout Catholic committed to a view of the world's reality in Christ, Claudel had to meet head on the paradox of Christian tragedy. He resolved it in a manner both trenchant and naïve, as was his nature. Claudel's characters experience destinies which are tragic because they are detours or deflections from the meridians of God's purpose. Looking back, they know that they have wrought useless havoc, and this knowledge brings with it a recognition of tragic waste. Ysé and Mesa meet on the rim of death (Claudel always chose names which surround his personages with a penumbra of strangeness, which convey that they are beings set apart for the grace of exceptional suffering). The lovers join in an act of ecstatic contrition, for behind them lie ruin and evil which might have been avoided even as the cruel chaos of human history might have been avoided. But it is precisely the measure of man's guilt which makes the coming of Christ a necessary miracle. Claudelian drama is set in the hour before day when the eye looks at once on the receding night and on the morning star.

This design is beautifully sustained in *Le Soulier de satin*, one of the few plays in modern literature that comes near to being great tragedy. God uses crooked lines (*linhas tortas*) to write straight. The lives of Don Rodrigue and Dona Prouhèze are enmeshed. But if they were to be prematurely unravelled, God's purpose would be marred, for on the map of the soul's journey there are no short cuts. These two superb beings, larger than life in their

torment no less than in their valour, deny themselves the fulfilment of love. They put oceans between them and the blade of the will. One last
time, the conquistador and the exiled, ravaged
woman face each other in the flesh. But each is already turning away from life so that their souls may
be freed to meet again in ultimate and enduring
nakedness. Through the grave cadence of their parting we seem to hear the echo of an ancient heresy:
the supposition that the souls of the blessed may be
joined after death in an embrace ardent beyond the
fiercest imaginings of the flesh. If there can be sensual desire in Paradise, Don Rodrigue and Dona
Prouhèze shall burn with it. Their last encounter
in the world is among the glories of drama:

DONA PROUHÈZE: Qu'ai-je voulu que te donner la
joie! ne rien garder! être en-
tièrement
cette suavité! cesser d'être moi-
même
pour que tu aies tout!
Là où il y a le plus de joie, com-
ment
croire que je suis absente? là
où il
y a le plus de joie, c'est là qu'il y
a le plus Prouhèze!
Je veux être avec toi dans le
principe! Je veux
épouser ta cause! je veux appren-
dre avec Dieu à ne

rien réserver, à être cette chose
toute bonne et toute
donnée qui ne réserve rien et à
qui l'on prend tout!
Prends, Rodrigue, prends, mon
coeur, prends, mon
amour, prends ce Dieu qui me
remplit!
La force par laquelle je t'aime
n'est pas différte
de celle par laquelle tu existes.
Je suis unie pour toujours à cette
chose qui te donne la vie
éternelle!
Le sang n'est pas plus uni à la
chair que Dieu ne
me fait sentir chaque battement
de ce coeur dans ta
poitrine qui à chaque seconde
de la bienheureuse éternité
S'unit et se resépare.

LE VICE-ROI: Paroles au delà de la Mort et
que je comprends à
peine! Je te regarde et cela me
suffit! O Prouhèze,
ne t'en va pas de moi, reste
vivante!

D. PROUHÈZE: Il me faut partir.

LE VICE-ROI: Si tu t'en vas, il n'y a plus
d'étoile pour me
guider, je suis seul!

D. PROUHÈZE: Non pas seul.

LE VICE-ROI: A force de ne plus la voir au
ciel je l'oublierai.

Qui te donne cette assurance
  que je ne puisse cesser
de t'aimer?

D. PROUHÈZE: Tant que j'existe et moi je sais
  que tu existes avec moi.

LE VICE-ROI: Fais-moi seulement cette pro-
  messe et moi je
garderai la mienne.

D. PROUHÈZE: Je ne suis pas capable de pro-
  messe.

LE VICE-ROI: Je suis le maître encore! Si je
  veux, je peux
t'empêcher de partir.

D. PROUHÈZE: Est-ce que tu crois vraiment
  que tu peux m'empêcher de
partir?

LE VICE-ROI: Oui, je peux t'empêcher de partir.

D. PROUHÈZE: Tu le crois? eh bien, dis seulement un mot et
je reste. Je le jure, dis seulement un mot, je
reste. Il n'y a pas besoin de violence.
Un mot, et je reste avec toi. Un
  seul mot,
est-il si difficile à dire? Un seul
  mot et je reste avec toi.
(*Silence. Le Vice-Roi baisse la
  tête et pleure. Dona Prouhèze
s'est voilée de la tête aux
  pieds.*) [1]

---

[1] DONA PROUHÈZE: What have I willed but to give you joy!
  to withhold nothing! to be utter de-

Don Rodrigue cannot say that one, simple, little word. It would break the spell of honour and of God's design. But in the darkness of the hour there is also light. Dona Prouhèze leaves behind her young daughter, and it is she whose voice we shall hear in the last moments of the play signifying the triumph of the Catholic fleets at Lepanto.

---

light for you! to cease to be myself so that you shall have all!

How should I believe that I am absent where there is most joy? Where there is most joy, that is where Prouhèze abounds!

I want to be with you at the core! I want to espouse your cause! I want to learn with God how to keep nothing back, how to be that which is wholly good and wholly given, which holds nothing back and from which one takes all!

Take, Rodrigue, take, my heart's beloved, take, my love, take the God who fills me!

The strength by which I love you does not differ from the strength by which you exist.

I am forever united to that which gives you life everlasting!

Blood is no nearer to flesh than God has set me next to your heartbeat in your breast which at every second of blessed eternity

Folds and unfolds.

THE VICEROY: Words beyond Death and which I scarcely comprehend! I look upon you and that suffices! O Prouhèze, do not go from me, stay alive!

D. PROUHÈZE: I must go.

339

But one cannot conclude from Claudel's bizarre and private genius that the Christian world view is about to produce a body of tragic drama. Claudel was less a Christian than a special and somewhat terrifying kind of Roman Catholic. He was of the age of Gregory rather than of the modern church.

THE VICEROY:	If you go, there is no star left to guide me, I am alone!
D. PROUHÈZE:	Not alone.
THE VICEROY:	By virtue of seeing it no longer in the sky I shall forget it. Who gives you the certainty that I cannot cease loving you?
D. PROUHÈZE:	So long as I am and know that you exist with me.
THE VICEROY:	Make me that promise only and I will keep mine.
D. PROUHÈZE:	I am not capable of making promises.
THE VICEROY:	I am the master still! If I will, I can prevent you from leaving.
D. PROUHÈZE:	Do you really believe that you can prevent me from leaving?
THE VICEROY:	Yes, I can prevent you from leaving.
D. PROUHÈZE:	You believe so? very well, say but one word and I stay. I swear it, say but one word, I stay. There is no need of coercion.
	One word, and I stay with you. One single word, is it so difficult to say? One single word and I stay with you. *(Silence. The Viceroy bows his head and weeps. Dona Prouhèze has veiled herself from head to foot.)*

I don't fully understand some of Dona Prouhèze's words, particularly the close of her offertory, her self-giving to Rodrigue. But Rodrigue's answer suggests that we are not meant to grasp her entire meaning. These are words "beyond Death." I have, so far as possible, retained Claudel's subtle, deliberate punctua-

The glow of hell-fire seemed to evoke in him a stern approval, nearly a delight in the vengeful grandeur of God's ways. There are pages in his dramas and scriptural commentaries which read as if they had been discovered in a monastic library and were the labour of some tyrannic abbot looking out upon the corruptions of man. Few of Claudel's plays, moreover, were intended for practical performance. Several can be produced at all only in shortened or simplified versions. The essential device in *Le Soulier de satin* is the instantaneous transition from the real, in a visual and normal sense, to the purely imaginary. In the actual theatre these transitions pose problems of extreme difficulty. In short, there is in Claudel's art more of the dramatic than of drama. And above all, neither Claudel's singular venture nor such instances as Eliot's *Murder in the Cathedral* can alter the fact that the Christian vision of man leads to a denial of tragedy. An actor who has often played the role of Becket put the matter succinctly: "I know I am being murdered on stage, but not once have I really felt dead."

The notion of partial tragedy implicit in Claudel, the conception of tragedy as waste rather than predestined or inevitable disaster, is central to the art of Brecht. This was bound to be the case. The

---

tion'. Like Whitman, he uses punctuation or the absence of it to order the motion of his loose, tidal stanza. Note how the dropping of a comma in Dona Prouhèze's final statement gives it an urgency which the same words, used earlier, had not quite attained.

Marxist world view, even more explicitly than the Christian, admits of error, anguish, and temporary defeat, but not of ultimate tragedy. Despair is a mortal sin against Marxism no less than against Christ. Lunacharsky, the first Soviet commissar of education, proclaimed that one of the defining qualities of a communist society would be the absence of tragic drama. Convinced that the powers of reason can master the natural world and give to human life a complete dignity and purpose, a communist can no longer recognize the meaning of tragedy. Or he will see in tragedy a relic in the museum of the moral past. The tragic theatre is an expression of the pre-rational phase in history; it is founded on the assumption that there are in nature and in the psyche occult, uncontrollable forces able to madden or destroy the mind. The Marxist knows that such forces have no real existence; they are metaphors of ancient ignorance or phantasms with which to frighten children in the dark. He knows that there is no such thing as *Anangké*, the blind necessity which overwhelms Oedipus. "Necessity is blind," said Marx and Engels, "only where it is not understood." Tragedy can occur only where reality has not been harnessed by reason and social consciousness. When the new man of the communist society comes to a crossing of three roads, he will encounter a factory or a hall of culture, not enraged Laius in his cart.

Moreover, the Marxist creed is immensely, perhaps naïvely optimistic. Like the medieval visionary with his absolute faith in the advent of the Kingdom of God, the communist is certain that the kingdom of justice is nearing on earth. The Marxist conception of history is a secular *commedia*. Mankind is advancing toward the justice, equality, and leisure of the classless society. When capitalist exploitation shall have ended and the state withered away, war and poverty will vanish into a nightmare of dim remembrance, and the world will once again be a garden for man. There are catastrophes along the road. The condemned *bourgeoisie* fights for its life with savage cunning and, over the short run, can achieve political or military success. There are premature risings, such as the Commune and the insurrection of 1905, in which the blood of the labouring classes is spilled toward no apparent end. There can be detours of heresy and schism within the socialist camp. But even the grimmest setback gives no ground for tragic despair. The march forward continues, for it has behind it the inexorable laws of history; final victory is as certain as the coming of dawn.

Marxist literature, therefore, is joyous affirmation or a cry to battle. Stalin was perfectly consistent with the aims of a communist society when he demanded that all plays and novels should have a happy ending. Soviet censors were right when they sought to banish Dostoevsky's *Possessed,* that parable of the ultimate ruin of the socialist utopia. In a communist state, tragedy is not only bad art; it is treason calculated to subvert the morale of the front lines. This axiom of necessary joy was made explicit in the title of a play produced in 1934, Vishnievsky's *The Optimistic Tragedy*. It dramatizes the heroic death in battle of a company of Red marines. All perish before our eyes, but we are not meant to regard their sacrifice as tragic, for it contributes to the final victory of the Party and the Soviet Union. Together with the devout Christian, the communist can ask: "Death, where is thy sting?"

It is remarkable that so shrill and naïve a mythology should have served the ends of a dramatist of the stature of Brecht. But Brecht's relations to Marxism were always oblique. Like Claudel, he had that edge of heresy which allows a poet to work against the grain of an orthodox faith. Where Claudel lacked charity, Brecht lacked hope. His poetics were shaped not by the inexorable rise of Soviet power, but by the failure and destruction of the German communist movement. This disastrous episode coloured his entire outlook and threw its shadow against the glare of Stalinist optimism. Brecht neither lived in Russia nor joined the official establishment of Stalinist literature. Nearly to the end, he preferred life in exile. When the weight of military and political success shifted to the Marxist camp, he remained in the aura of previous defeat (Brecht's last play deals with the suppression of the Commune). This refusal to run with the victorious pack gave to Brecht's politics a private, anarchic flavour often irreconcilable with the official "posi-

tive" line. This was true, I think, even of his last
years in East Berlin. He played off his gaunt realism, his satiric bias and unruly wit against the
ideology which he sincerely and openly professed.
Thus there is in his works, as in those of Corneille,
a deliberate clash between the natural quality of
the poet's mind and the outward direction of his
rhetoric. Brecht, moreover, was not greatly concerned with the paradox of "optimistic tragedy."
He was a virtuoso of theatrical styles, equally at
home in music and the film, in lyricism and propa-
ganda. He rarely used the tragic genre for his astute
and radical game. But in the one major instance,
in *Mutter Courage*, Brecht's notion of tragedy is
not far removed from that of a Christian poet.

Brecht believed in the dialectical process of history and in the inevitable accomplishment of the
Marxist ideal. But he kept his cold eye on the present. He was too realistic not to know that the light
on the horizon lay immensely far off and that there
would be terrible suffering along the way. Hosannas shall blow in the kingdom of justice, but not
tomorrow or even the day after. Yet just because
final victory is certain, all the suffering that must
precede it has a quality of weird, inhuman waste. It
is monstrous because it is somehow avoidable.
Claudel's characters entangle themselves in tragedy
because they turn their backs on the redemptive
power of God. Their suffering is real, but metaphys-
ically absurd. So it is with Brecht. A Marxist knows
that it is absurd for a man to strive against the laws

345

of history. If the capitalist class would recognize
that it stands condemned, if it would accept the
manifest truth of the socialist revelation, there
would be no need of further struggle. If the prole-
tariat would understand the nature of the historical
process and turn to the communist vanguard as its
natural leader, the entire fabric of war and mercantile greed would collapse. But men are blind to
their own salvation. Thus innumerable lives are
broken, and broken uselessly.

Mutter Courage is an allegory of pure waste. The
crazy old woman loses her children, one by one, in
the murderous sweep of the Thirty Years' War.
These lives squandered are waste enough. But the
real waste lies inside. Mutter Courage learns nothing from her agony. She refuses to grasp the plain
truth that those who live by selling the sword shall
perish by the sword. She drags her sutler's wagon
from battle to battle. She knows that where men
are wounded they will call for brandy and that
where guns fire there is need of powder. Each time
one of her children is murdered, Mutter Courage
could stop. Instead, she harnesses the survivors to
her wagon and marches on like a vulture hobbling
after carrion. As she draws the wagon, the revolving
stage begins turning, more and more quickly. The
foolish creature thinks she is advancing. In fact, she
is treading a mill of ruin. But she refuses to yield so
long as there is a ducat to be earned somewhere in
the charred landscape between Alsatia and Prague.
She leaves her dead to winter and the wolves, and

presses on. The horrors that befall her are pure
waste, as if lightning struck cold ash. She forces
back her shoulders, gets into harness again, and
sings the songs of war:

> Von Ulm nach Metz, von Metz nach Mähren!
> Mutter Courage ist dabei!
> Der Krieg wird seinen Mann ernähren
> Er braucht nur Pulver zu und Blei.
> Von Blei allein kann er nicht leben
> Von Pulver nicht, er braucht auch Leut!
> Müssts euch zum Regiment begeben
> Sonst steht er um! So kommt noch heut! [2]

Mutter Courage knows that war eats men. She for-
gets that one's own children are devoured first.
Finally her last child, mute Kattrin, is killed. But
even this horror is a dead loss. Courage is now a
scarecrow giving a grotesque semblance of life. But
the scent of war and money draws her still: "I hope
I can pull the wagon by myself. I'll manage. There's
not much in it." A regiment passes in the background, drum and fife playing. She cries to them:
"Take me with you." She straps on her harness and

[2] From Ulm to Prague and back again!
Mother Courage comes along!
War makes a living for its man,
Just add lead and powder on.
It cannot live by lead alone
Nor powder only, it needs chaps!
To the regiment, my son,
Enlist today! Else wars collapse!

"Chaps" is Edwardian and does not translate *Leut*—plain folk.
But Brecht loved and frequently imitated Kipling's ballads; so
I don't think he would have minded.

the stage begins turning again under an empty sky. The marching song tells us that the war will last a hundred years.

And so it shall; and the war after that, two hundred. Is there no end in sight to waste and murder? Not until women refuse to yield their sons for cannon-fodder; not until men cease forging the weapons that kill their own children. There is a streak of dawn on the far horizon of the play. In the dialectic of events, a time shall come when nations lay down their arms by still waters. But Mutter Courage keeps that time from coming nearer. Brecht would have us revile the old harpy for her stupid greed. He would have us understand that waste is neither noble nor tragic, but simply and horribly useless. That is the whole point of the play. Mutter Courage has learnt nothing so that the audience may have learnt something. End of lesson.

But, of course, it doesn't quite work out that way. The moralist must share his platform with the poet. And the poet is skilful. He lets the moralist have his say; he does not deny for a moment that Courage is responsible for her pack of misery. He merely asks us to look at her. She is so enormously alive in each leathery sinew, so rapacious and unconquerable. She is the salt of the earth, destructive yet zestful. We cannot detach ourselves from the play and merely pass cool judgement on her faults. We too are hitched to the wagon, and it is beneath our feet that the stage turns.

Brecht is entirely aware of this, although he pretends to regard any identification of the spectator with the characters as romantic nonsense. In the duel between artist and dialectician, he allows the artist a narrow but constant margin of victory. By that margin, *Mutter Courage* is tragedy; incomplete, perhaps, because of the redemptive politics which surround it, but real and consuming nevertheless. Brecht stands midway between the world of Oedipus and that of Marx. He agreed with Marx that necessity is not blind, but like all true poets, he knew that she often closes her eyes. And when she has closed them, she lies in ambush for the coming of man along the road from Corinth.

I have not dealt, in this essay, with the group of dark plays that has come out of the French theatre since the war. The plays of Sartre, Camus's *Caligula*, and the black fantasies of Samuel Beckett are so close to us in date as to make any judgement precarious. My own feeling is that their importance lies mainly outside the sphere and authority of drama. *Huis Clos, Le Diable et le Bon Dieu,* and *Caligula* are not primarily theatre, but rather uses of the stage. Like Diderot, Sartre and Camus make of dramatic action a parable of philosophic or political argument. The theatrical form is nearly fortuitous; the plays are essays or pamphlets declaimed and underlined by graphic gesture. In these allegories we hear voices, not characters.

The case of Beckett is more intriguing. He has

derived from his personal association with Irish letters a distinct note of comic sadness. There are moments in *Waiting for Godot* that proclaim with painful vividness the infirmity of our moral condition: the incapacity of speech or gesture to countenance the abyss and horror of the times. But again, I wonder whether we are dealing with drama in any genuine sense. Beckett is writing "antidrama"; he is showing, with a kind of queer Irish logic, that one can bar from the stage all forms of mobility and natural communication between characters and yet produce a play. But the result is, I think, crippled and monotonous. At best, we get a metaphysical *guignol*, a puppet show made momentarily fascinating or monstrous by the fact that the puppets insist on behaving as if they were alive.

None of these playwrights has the gift possessed by Claudel and Brecht and without which drama cannot endure: the creation of characters endowed with the miracle of independent life. Bertolt Brecht is dead, and time may deliver us from the nightmare of his politics. But his imagined beings have taken on a tough vitality. When Brecht's name has passed into the burial of literary history, Mutter Courage shall continue to pull her wagon through the winter night.

X

I WANT to end this essay on a note of personal recollection rather than of critical argument. There are no definite solutions to the problems I have touched on. Often allegory will illuminate them more aptly than assertion. Moreover, I believe that literary criticism has about it neither rigour nor proof. Where it is honest, it is passionate, private experience seeking to persuade. The three incidents I shall recount accord with the threefold possibility of our theme: that tragedy is, indeed, dead; that it carries on in its essential tradition despite changes in technical form; or, lastly, that tragic drama might come back to life.

I was taking a train journey through southern Poland not long ago. We passed a gutted ruin on the comb of a hill. One of the Poles in my compartment told me what had taken place there. It had been a monastery, and the Germans had used it as a prison for captured Russian officers. In the last year of the war, when the German armies began receding from the east, no more food reached the prison. The guards pillaged what they could off the land, but soon their police dogs turned dangerous with hunger. After some hesitation, the Germans loosed the dogs on the prisoners, and maddened by hunger, the dogs ate several of them alive. When the garrison fled, they left the survivors locked in the cellar. Two of them managed to keep alive by killing and devouring their companions. Finally, the advancing Soviet army found them. The two men were given a decent meal and then shot lest the soldiers see to what abjection their former officers had been reduced. After that, the monastery was burnt to the ground.

The other travellers in our compartment had listened, and now each in turn recounted some incident comparable or worse. One woman told of what had been done to her sister in the death-camp at Matthausen. I will not set it down here, for it is the kind of thing under which language breaks. We were all silent for a time, and then an older man said that he knew a medieval parable which might help one understand how such events had come to pass:

In some obscure village in central Poland, there was a small synagogue. One night, when making his rounds, the Rabbi entered and saw God sitting in a dark corner. He fell upon his face and cried out: "Lord God, what art Thou doing here?" God answered him neither in thunder nor out of a whirlwind, but with a small voice: "I am tired, Rabbi, I am tired unto death."

The bearing of this parable on our theme, I take it, is this: God grew weary of the savagery of man. Perhaps He was no longer able to control it and could no longer recognize His image in the mirror of creation. He has left the world to its own inhuman devices and dwells now in some other corner of the universe so remote that His messengers cannot even reach us. I would suppose that He turned away during the seventeenth century, a time which has been the constant dividing line in our argument. In the nineteenth century, Laplace announced that God was a hypothesis of which the rational mind had no further need; God took the great astronomer at his word. But tragedy is that form of art which requires the intolerable burden of God's presence. It is now dead because His shadow no longer falls upon us as it fell on Agamemnon or Macbeth or Athalie.

Or, perhaps, tragedy has merely altered in style and convention. There comes a moment in *Mutter Courage* when the soldiers carry in the dead body of Schweizerkas. They suspect that he is the son of Courage but are not quite certain. She must be forced to identify him. I saw Helene Weigel act the scene with the East Berlin ensemble, though acting is a paltry word for the marvel of her incarnation. As the body of her son was laid before her, she merely shook her head in mute denial. The soldiers compelled her to look again. Again she gave no sign of recognition, only a dead stare. As the body was carried off, Weigel looked the other way and tore her mouth wide open. The shape of the gesture was that of the screaming horse in Picasso's *Guernica*. The sound that came out was raw and terrible beyond any description I could give of it. But, in fact, there was no sound. Nothing. The sound was total silence. It was silence which screamed and screamed through the whole theatre so that the audience lowered its head as before a gust of wind. And that scream inside the silence seemed to me to be the same as Cassandra's when she divines the reek of blood in the house of Atreus. It was the same wild cry with which the tragic imagination first marked our sense of life. The same wild and pure lament over man's inhumanity and waste of man. The curve of tragedy is, perhaps, unbroken.

Finally, there should be present to our minds the possibility—though I judge it remote—that the tragic theatre may have before it a new life and future. I have seen a documentary film showing the activities of a Chinese agricultural commune. At one point, the workers streamed in from the fields, laid down their mattocks, and gathered on the barrack square. They formed into a large chorus and began chanting a song of hatred against China's foes. Then a group leader leapt from the ranks and performed a kind of violent, intricate dance. He was acting out in pantomime the struggle against the imperialist bandits and their defeat by the peasant armies. The ceremony closed with a recital of the heroic death of one of the founders of the local Communist Party. He had been killed by the Japanese and was buried near by.

Is it not, I wonder, in some comparable rite of defiance and honour to the dead that tragedy began, three thousand years ago, on the plains of Argos?

INDEX

Index

Index

INDEX

Pembroke, Mary Herbert,
    Countess of, 27
Picasso, Pablo,
    Guernica, 354
Pickersgill, Joshua,
    Three Brothers, The, 211
Pico della Mirandola, Giovanni, 16
Pirandello, Luigi, 38, 124, 212,
    213, 227
Plato,
    Dialogues of, 239
    Symposium, 302
Plautus, 247
Poe, Edgar Allan, 227, 246
Pope, Alexander, 65 n, 186,
    193, 203
Pound, Ezra, 325; *quoted*, 100
Prévost, Marcel,
    Manon Lescaut, 264
Prior, Matthew, 30
Proust, Marcel, 243, 307, 321
Psalm, eightieth, 15
Psalms of David, 214
Pushkin, Alexander, 105, 138,
    144
    Boris Godunov, 159–61, 181

Quintilian, 69

Rabelais, François, 241
Racine, Jean Baptiste, 17, 24,
    26, 75, 107, 108, 138;
    neo-classic form and clas-
    sic myth in, 36, 37, 75–
    105, 188, 292, 330; "un-
    translatability" of, 45–50,
    101–5; compared to Cor-
    neille, 50, 53, 67, 71–3,
    76, 78, 81, 100; dislike of
    theatre, 76–7, 98, 101;
    and Euripides, 80, 81–3,
    85, 106, 331; audience of,
    82, 83, 115, 310; and the
    romantics, 153, 164, 174,
    187, 222, 232; verse of,
    279; *quoted*, 77

Racine (*continued*)
    Andromache, 105
    Athalie, 46, 77, 79, 80, 97–
    100, 193, 196, 214;
    quoted, 99
    Bérénice, 50, 71, 77, 78, 79,
    80, 102; *quoted*, 71, 79,
    104
    Britannicus, 48
    Esther, 77, 97–8
    Iphigénie, 48, 77, 80, 81–4,
    86, 105; *quoted*, 76, 82–3
    Phèdre, 3, 10, 46, 49, 50,
    77, 79, 80, 98, 117, 193,
    197; analysis of, 84–97;
    language of, 102–4, 105;
    quoted, 87, 88–9, 90, 91,
    92, 94, 95, 102–3
Radcliffe, Ann, 204
Rembrandt, 187
Richards, I. A., *quoted*, 129
Richardson, Samuel, 195
Richelieu, 53
Richter, Jean Paul, 282
Rilke, Rainer Maria, 47, 322
Rimbaud, Arthur, 241, 271
Rojas, Fernando de,
    Celestina, 248
Rostand, Edmond, 49, 165,
    310
Rousseau, Jean Jacques: effect
    on tragedy, 125, 127, 130,
    134, 135, 136; and roman-
    ticism, 142, 173, 176, 198
    Confessions, 48; *quoted*, 136
    Nouvelle Héloïse, La, 195
Rymer, Thomas, 34–8, 39, 40,
    41, 188; *quoted*, 36–7
    *Tragedies of the Last Age,
    The*, 35

St.-John Perse (Alexis Léger),
    47
Saint-Simon, Claude Henri de
    Rouvroy, Count de, 79
Saintsbury, George, *quoted*, 44

INDEX